Scratch

Scratch

HOME COOKING FOR EVERYONE MADE SIMPLE, FUN, AND TOTALLY DELICIOUS

MARIA RODALE

With Melanie Hansche

PHOTOGRAPHS BY CON POULOS AND STACEY CRAMP

RODALE

RODALE *wellness*

Live happy. Be healthy. Get inspired.

Sign up today to get exclusive access to our authors, exclusive bonuses, and the most authoritative, useful, and cutting-edge information on health, wellness, fitness, and living your life to the fullest.

Visit us online at RodaleWellness.com
Join us at RodaleWellness.com/Join

Rodale books may be purchased for business or promotional use or for special sales. For information, please write to:
Special Markets Department, Rodale Inc., 733 Third Avenue, New York, NY 10017.

Printed in China

Rodale Inc. makes every effort to use acid-free ⊗, recycled paper ♻.

Book design by Rae Ann Spitzenberger
Photographs by Con Poulos (recipes) and Stacey Cramp (lifestyle)
Food styling by Simon Andrews
Prop styling by Paige Hicks
Hand lettering by Veljko Zajc

Other images by B. Calkins/Shutterstock (pages 72, 250);
Flas100/Shutterstock (pages 28–29, 194); Peter Kotoff/Shutterstock (pages 2, 156);
and Tina Rupp (pages iii, 110, 282)

Library of Congress Cataloging-in-Publication Data is on file with the publisher

ISBN-13: 978–1–62336–643–8

Distributed to the trade by Macmillan

2   4   6   8   10   9   7   5   3   1   hardcover

We inspire health, healing, happiness, and love in the world.
Starting with you.

*To my family, immediate, extended,
and adopted, and anyone who has ever sat
at my table and appreciated my cooking,
but especially to my daughters:
Maya, Eve, and Lucia*

Asparagus,
Feta, and Herb
Salad (page 32)

contents

The delicious fresh taste of summer's tomatoes is reason enough to start gardening. Tomatoes come in more than 10,000 varieties!

Introduction

I believe anyone can cook. I believe that a home-cooked meal made from scratch—preferably with organic ingredients (and maybe even homegrown)—is one of the greatest pleasures in life. I believe that when you cut through all the confusion about food and cooking—the fears and insecurities, social pressures, false ideals, or just plain not knowing where to begin—this is where you can begin, right here. I will help you.

In this book, you will find what you need to get to the essence of good, delicious food in the simplest way. So whether you are just beginning and don't even know how to cook an egg, or you're old and jaded like me and have seen it all, I'll show you how to get to simple, from scratch.

Cooking from scratch isn't about impressing friends and neighbors (although you probably will); it's about *nourishing* our families and ourselves. And the truth is, when it comes to making delicious and easy food from scratch, it truly is freaking easy! You can do this— I know you can. And I know you can because I did. Let me tell you my story.

I grew up in one of the most interesting moments, in the most interesting home, with the most interesting food stories possible if you were born in 1962. I spent my childhood on the first official organic farm in America, but I didn't realize that as a kid. All I knew was that the barn was filled with fascinating things, and the fruits and vegetables straight from plants were delicious, and the chickens, pigs, cows, and sheep were both adorable and good to eat.

Even still, I remember being hungry a lot. As the fourth child of five kids in a family where both parents worked, I was constantly foraging for food in my own home and in the garden, and watching what was happening in my friends' homes like a hungry anthropologist. Their food was different. Not all of the time, but some of the time. And in some cases there was no rhyme nor reason to it. For instance, we ate tomato soup from a can just like everyone else. We were never allowed to eat at McDonald's though, and yet a bucket of Kentucky Fried Chicken was a huge treat for us.

Being in a family business that published books and magazines about healthy food, organic gardening and farming, and fitness (at a time when we were pretty much the *only* ones doing it) brought all sorts of people from all over the world to our farm—often with extreme ideas of what was right or wrong to eat. In the late 1960s, the hippies started to come. In the 1970s, Olympic cyclists from all over the world came to eat at our house on a regular basis. Almost every dinner was some sort of adventure.

My mother fed them all. Not quite happily, mind you, but on time and in abundance. She was a living embodiment of a woman trapped in a traditional wife and mother role, yet who found true satisfaction in her job, which she was not paid for. The feminist movement was unfolding around her, but with five kids and a family business, equality would have to wait. We all helped, but usually not as much as she wanted us to.

And in our kitchen, like most kitchens around the world, some kind of drama would play out—the drama between my mother and father. The drama between kids. The drama between visitors with different food philosophies. The drama between people at work with different business philosophies. At some point I realized that I much preferred

The door to my grandparents' chicken house

Savory Spiced
Pumpkin Soup
(page 131)

to eat food than to participate in drama. But I watched and paid attention and started to notice things.

I noticed that once people were well fed they were a lot less angry. I noticed that a good meal unites people. I noticed that drinking was fine and fun until someone drank too much and then it wasn't fun at all. I noticed that skinny people weren't always happy or nice. And just because your body might be shaped like an athlete's, it wasn't always healthy. And I noticed that while people were arguing about what was the right way to eat and the wrong way to eat, it seemed to me that the most important thing was that the food should come from nature and be real, not fake. For example, I was always suspicious of margarine. It didn't taste right and it was artificial. I refused to eat it.

It seemed to me that the most important thing was that the food should come from nature and be real, not fake.

Of course, I wanted all my food to be organic. But it was super hard back then. This was the time when food co-ops were just starting, and the produce looked horrible and the grain often had moth infestations. We briefly had an organic grocery store in town, but it went out of business. So I had to mostly shop at the health food store, where choices were limited and the smell of weird vitamins filled the air. But in order to live I went to the regular supermarket just like everyone else. I was used to compromising.

When I went out on my own, as a single mother aged 20, my only cooking specialty at the time was a zucchini, garlic, and tomato sauté to which my mother said: "I hope you find someone to marry who likes garlic." So there I was in my little apartment with my little baby and a box of Bisquick—because that was ubiquitous in my mother's house—and one day I happened to read the label, which listed a bunch of highly refined and processed ingredients. I had an existential crisis.

You see, despite my father being the leader in the organic farming movement, and passionate about eating healthy, my mother was

Pennsylvania Dutch, which means she was hardheaded and cooked a certain way—her way, Bisquick included. And who could blame her? My father was known to bring surprise guests home for dinner all the time, without notice. And he expected dinner on the table every night at 5:30 p.m. sharp.

From my perspective, the best thing was that no matter who came to dinner, we all sat down together. It didn't matter what the meal was, the conversation was almost always fascinating. But I could often feel my father's shame about the difference between what he preached and what his wife practiced at home. So I decided then and there, with that Bisquick box in my hand, that I would learn to make healthier organic meals that tasted like good home cooking.

I was interested in making healthier, organic choices not only because I was a parent, but because for lunch I could go to our company dining room—called "Fitness House," and it was right across the street from my home—and get incredible, delicious organic meals. The chef was a woman named Nancy Albright, and she wrote *The Rodale Cookbook*, which was a bible of healthy recipes for many people at the time. Fitness House wasn't open to the public; it was only for Rodale's employees. It was the place where we all sat at communal tables and talked about anything and everything—particularly heated discussions about whether the Mac or PC would win the computer race!

My cooking bible was (and still often is) the original *Joy of Cooking*. I've never wanted the fancy stuff, just the basics from scratch so I could make them with organic ingredients. So instead of using Bisquick with the long list of strange and fake ingredients, I made my own pancakes in a pinch. Who needs a box when the original not only tastes better, but is actually *easier* to make? Yes, easier. *And* organic. It made me start to feel that whole generations of Americans were the victims of a hoax by the processed food companies. And maybe we still are.

My brother David was probably the first "foodie" I ever met. He left for New York City and Provincetown and made a living as a waiter while being a writer. When he came home he was always trying new things and telling stories of the foods he ate. He was hysterically

Rainbow chard, lacinato kale, and heirloom tomatoes

This Is Not a Diet Book

This is not a book about counting calories, avoiding meat, eggs, or dairy, or reducing your salt, sugar, or fat intake. There is gluten in this book.

This is not a book about trying to change who you are or what you like or don't like. This is not a book about tricking you into eating better or differently.

This is not a "healthy cooking" book in the way you may have been trained to think about a "healthy diet." There are no sprouts. There are no soy or artificial protein products trying to mimic familiar foods. No fake cheese. No fake anything.

Yeah, I know my surname is Rodale and you might think you know what kind of food I eat. You might even judge me without knowing the truth. I'm used to it.

This is a book about real food. Real, organic food.

This is a book about food you don't need to detox from because there's nothing toxic in it to begin with. In fact, real organic food keeps the toxins out of nature and our environment, too.

This is a book about foods that are not fads. Well, except maybe kale. But kale is so yummy! Kids love kale when done right.

But you are a grown-up. You can be trusted to moderate your own salt, sugar, fat, meats, and indulgences based on your own health beliefs and needs.

I don't believe in imposing my beliefs on others.

I believe in freedom. In the freedom to eat what you want, when you want it, and how you want it. I believe in the freedom to create in the kitchen, to experiment and learn. You can eat all the toxic fake stuff you want and I won't judge you.

But I will ask you to try something new. Something fresh.

(Just one bite. You'll like it!)

This is a book about *nourishment*. About family. About feeding your body, your brain, your heart, and your soul with good things. Delicious things. Things that come from nature. Things that make you feel good and healthy. Things that people have eaten for centuries, and we will keep eating into the future.

So maybe it's a healthy diet book after all. In the original best sense—the kind of diet we can all live with. Maybe this is the kind of diet that can feed the world.

funny and totally believed the Mac would win the race. But then he died of AIDS in 1985 and a shadow fell over our family.

I had moved to Washington, DC, with my daughter Maya for a job and realized just how spoiled I had been to have Fitness House food every day. I started to cook more out of necessity—for both financial reasons and taste. And then, just when I was starting to gain confidence in the kitchen, along came Martha Stewart, who brought the beauty of perfection to every part of our lives. Of course, with that beauty comes judgment. Am I worthy? My stuff looks like crap, but if it tastes good is it okay to serve? For my generation, her influence was perhaps the strongest, making it almost impossible for us to entertain without shame. Because we would never, ever, ever, be as good and perfect as Martha. And so I took my cooking underground. I cooked for my immediate family only, which at times was up to 30 people. And their gratitude and appreciation was all I needed.

When I met Lou Cinquino, my now ex-husband, I also met his extended family, which was a food revelation. First, they are Italian, so of course they love garlic. Second, they came from a food tradition that was so different from my own. They didn't really give a hoot about organic, although they grew and foraged much of their own food. Sugar? Bring it on. Even breakfast was often followed by dessert. As the granddaughter of a man who wrote *Natural Health, Sugar and the Criminal Mind*, I was scandalized, but wasted no time jumping right in!

The Cinquinos all loved to cook because they loved to eat, and the truth is, even though they couldn't afford to eat out, their food was better than anything you could get in a restaurant. My mother-in-law Rita Cinquino's famous line was: "Our poor food is your *gourmet* food!" This was often said in an accusatory tone with an undertone of pride. But she was right.

What the Cinquinos taught me is that cookies and food stored in Cool Whip containers isn't the end of the world (Louie Cinquino lived to 94, and as of this moment, Rita is still going at 94). My mother passed away from breast cancer at 81, but I saw up close and personal that her health issues were probably the result of emotional pain and alcohol rather than the steak she would order whenever she ate out. What I've mostly learned is not to judge other people. Everyone is on their own journey. And everyone is accountable and responsible for their own healing.

The world could be falling apart around me, but a good meal at least makes it bearable and gives me the strength to carry on.

As I was starting to travel and making my way up the corporate ladder, I was eating out in nicer and nicer restaurants, and I learned to appreciate home cooking in a whole new way. The rise of the celebrity TV chef was great for bringing attention to food and how it's grown, but not so great when it came to making everyday people feel confident in their own kitchens. And for many younger people whose mothers had gone out into the workforce and relied on frozen, fast, and restaurant foods, the simple art of home cooking was fading.

When my father died in a car accident in 1990, my mother pretty much stopped cooking all together. Without him to cook for, she lost her reason for cooking. I'll never forget the day we learned he had died and everyone had gathered at my mother's house. For some reason I had a huge bag of chicken pieces in my fridge and I brought them to her house and cooked for everyone. My oldest sister looked at me and said: "How can you cook at a time like this?" She was genuinely curious because all she was able to do was sit in shock. And my response was: "How can I not cook? People are hungry."

It was probably the moment when I became a really passionate cook. First, because if I wanted the foods I loved, there was no one left to cook them for me. And second, cooking became my refuge, my solace—my thing to do when nothing else could be done. The world could be falling apart around me, but a good meal at least makes it bearable and gives me the strength to carry on.

So I learned to cook. But I didn't just learn to cook, I learned to feed and nourish my family. I learned to adapt when kids became picky or gluten intolerant. And because I'm intensely curious, I didn't just learn to cook what I was familiar with, I learned to make and explore other cultures' and other people's family favorites, starting with my former in-laws Italian recipes. I even cooked a recipe as far-flung as Aboriginal "damper and dip," traditionally made with kangaroo from Australia, but substituted with America's native meat, buffalo. Plus, with my own Pennsylvania Dutch heritage, I am lucky enough to live in a place where hunting, snout-to-tail eating, and local family butchering never went out of style.

I started my blog, *Maria's Farm Country Kitchen,* for business reasons, but it quickly became personal. Back in 2009 everyone was talking about blogging. But like most things, I needed to do it myself to learn about it and understand it. I named it *Farm Country Kitchen* because the kitchen is where all the good stuff happens. And at the time there was quite a wide social divide between how high-end chefs (even the farm-to-table ones) were talking about food and how real people really lived and ate. And I even wanted to redeem the idea of

Nothing is as delightful as bare feet in the dirt! The soil is alive with billions of life-giving organisms that store carbon.

My grandparents' garden

"country," because at the time it was typical for people to say they loved all sorts of music except for rap and country!

The beauty of blogging is that you get feedback and conversation. You also see data and make connections. Suddenly my mashed potatoes blog post became a regular hit, spiking at holidays. I'd get comments and emails about my food, and I loved it. My kids became my guinea pigs. I'd make things and write recipes down and take pictures at the dinner table and ask them if a dish was "blog-worthy." Many times the answer was no. But if it was yes, it became a blog post.

In fact, my kids are the ones who asked me to write this cookbook. Sure, you can find a lot of these recipes online, but they are scattered all over the place and not very organized. I blog about food because cooking makes my kids happy and me happy, nourishing us and giving us strength for what we do.

People often ask me how I do what I do. (Or more typically it's actually a statement: "I don't know how you do it.") I am the chairwoman and CEO of a media company that has gone through the greatest disruption of our time—the Great Digital Disruption, when digital content and advertising stripped readers and revenue from traditional print businesses during the 2008 recession. I'm also the co-chair of a nonprofit, the Rodale Institute, which conducts scientific research on organic farming and helps farmers transition to organic. I have three girls born in three different decades ('80s, '90s, and '00s) and more often than not, when I am home, I make dinner from scratch. I don't cook because I have to, I cook because I want to and because it's the most intimate, nourishing, and primal pleasure I can give to my family and myself (I do like to cook and eat alone, too).

No matter how hard things have gotten, or how much tension or disappointment there has been among family members, we still sit

I don't cook because I have to, I cook because I want to and because it's the most intimate, nourishing, and primal pleasure I can give to my family and myself.

down and eat a home-cooked meal together and somehow things get better. I believe cooking is what makes us human. I believe food heals the heart and soul, as well as the body. I believe we ingest the energy of our food in more than just calories, but in life force and freshness, the *aliveness* of our food, and even the environment and intention with which the food was grown and raised.

My life has afforded me incredible experiences—travels around the world, eating the most delicious things you can imagine in restaurants and homes and at festivals. But there is still nothing better than coming home and sitting down at the table with my family and eating the food we made ourselves, often with produce grown in our garden.

As the third generation of the first family of organics, I've seen it all. I've seen fads come and go. Health and diet issues rise and fall. And trends go around and come back again. I've seen organic go from a subject of complete ridicule to a status symbol. I've seen up close and personal that just being fit or thin doesn't protect people from cancer. I've seen that being a vegetarian or vegan doesn't necessarily make someone a better, healthier, or happier person. I've seen that fat-free diets or sugar-free diets lead to lots of fake substitutes that are even worse than the original fat or sugar. And I've seen people who are technically obese live long and happy, healthy lives.

I want everyone to feel safe in their kitchens. Safe to experiment and learn. Safe to express their differences and creativity. Safe to try new things. And most important, safe to make a big damned mess and laugh about it, and serve the food we've made even if it's not perfect or "blog-worthy." I realized early on that we are all afraid of new things, or things we don't understand, whether it's a plant we are unfamiliar with, or a type of food we've never tried. I've seen people recoil when I say something is organic, as if organic means tofu and sprouts and things without flavor. I know it means super delicious and safe and nontoxic, made from real food, not fake. So I always say, let's start with where you are, with the foods you love. I'll show you that it can be even more delicious if it's organic. That's what I try to do—make you feel safe in the kitchen.

I always fall back on those familiar, wonderful, real organic meals that define home, family, and love. These are the recipes that have come out of my kitchen in the spirit of acceptance, love, and laughter. These are the recipes that my daughters now make and workshop into their own styles. These are the recipes that nourish our soul, while celebrating the abundance and deliciousness of nature at its best.

You can make any recipe in this book without using organic ingredients and it will be just as yummy and good. But I can tell you: It won't be as *alive* and nourishing. But I'm not here to judge. I'm here to show you that anyone can cook, and anyone can make totally delicious things simply and easily from scratch.

Me and my two youngest daughters in my favorite spot where I grew up

Spinach, cheese,
scallions, ham,
mushrooms, and pie
crust . . . create your
own quiche (page 24).

My Position on Food Terms

ORGANIC food means food that has been grown without toxic chemicals and inhumane methods that harm your health and the environment. Period. If you want the full definition, see "What Does Organic Really Mean?" on page 335. But if you have any doubt, look for the USDA certified organic label in your supermarket. It's a label you can trust.

FAT feeds the brain. Seriously, we need fat to be healthy and happy and to think at maximum capacity. But fat tends to store toxins and chemicals, so it's important to eat organic fats and real fats, not fake or chemical ones. Also, rather than trying to examine the specific scientific benefits or problems with each type of fat, think of your fats as a local resource. Before olive oil came to America, people used butter and lard. That's okay. It's real food.

SALT in moderation is fine. We need salt to be healthy. And while I like to use natural sea salt, I also use plain table salt with iodine in it because we need iodine for a healthy thyroid and iodine is hard to get from food alone. So think about your salt, but don't be afraid to use it.

SUGAR is not evil. But it's not a free ticket either. Sugar is a powerful substance that we all crave; the important thing is to manage our consumption in moderation and not overdo it. However, try to eat it from natural sources like honey or maple syrup, or use certified organic sugar.

VEGETARIAN AND VEGANS are my friends and I support them in their beliefs and practices. There are quite a few vegetarian and vegan recipes in this book. But I myself am not a vegetarian. I believe in the freedom to express our own food philosophies and in respecting others' beliefs as well. And if you are practicing vegetarianism based on saving the planet, here is my view on climate change. Climate change is the result of putting too many toxic chemicals and carbon dioxide into the atmosphere without putting it back into the ground. Organic soil stores carbon, and organic farming can heal climate change (See the white paper *Regenerative Organic Agriculture and Climate Change: A Down-to-Earth Solution to Global Warming*, authored by the Rodale Institute). Chemical farming destroys the soil's capacity to store carbon. Animals are an integral part of a healthy soil system and are required to make a healthy agricultural system work. Yes, we need to eat less meat. But what we really need is to transition more land and animal farming to organic. The most important thing you can do to stop climate change is to grow, buy, and eat organic food.

GMOS are to be avoided at all costs, because genetically modified crops are more likely to be sprayed with chemical herbicides that poison our environment and our bodies. Those chemicals also destroy the soil's ability to absorb and store carbon.

ALCOHOL is fine in moderation, but you won't find it in my kitchen. I haven't had a drink since 1999, so I don't like having alcohol in the house. I don't mind if people enjoy it in my company, but I don't want to cook with it and have learned to adapt accordingly, such as with my Sober Mini Fruitcakes (page 312).

LOCAL FOOD is awesome, but just because something is local doesn't make it organic. That's why local and organic is *always* the best choice.

MODERATION and **DIVERSITY** in our diets is essential. It's not good to eat the exact same thing every day. And it's not good to eat too much of any one thing. And if you aren't used to trying lots of new things, now is a great time to start. I always said to my kids: "Try it, you'll like it." And if that didn't work: "Take just one bite. What's the worst that

Brussels sprouts

can happen? You can spit it out." Of course, don't encourage someone to try certain foods if they have serious allergies, please!

HUNGER comes in all shapes and sizes. There is real hunger. But there is also "hunger" for other things—emotional comfort, stress relief, even sexual frustration. Learn to identify what your true hunger is and feed it with what will truly satisfy that hunger, not just food. Hunger also leads to "hangry," so if you or anyone you are around is angry or crying for no good reason, please give them a snack as soon as possible!

FARMERS grow our food. Without them, we would be in big trouble. That's why we should help them and empower them on the path toward organic farming.

GLUTEN is a real issue. I have seen my daughter Maya go from many migraines a month to one a year just by eliminating gluten. There are many reasons we are becoming more gluten intolerant—everything from the wheat varieties that have been chosen for mass production, to the way it's milled and stored, to the way it's often sprayed with Roundup before harvest to make it easier for farmers to harvest. The only way to know for sure is to experiment and, again, eat organic whenever possible.

BACON is the best, especially if it's organic.

One last note: Cooking doesn't buy love. And it's not an exchange for something else. I think lots of women are taught that food is a way to ask for other things, and then we get depressed when we don't get what we really want, whatever that is, whether it's the truth, a night out, sex, or some sort of reciprocation. Food is the language of intimacy, but it's not a substitute for intimacy. However, the kitchen table is a great place to have a deep conversation about anything. Cooking is ultimately a gift that is given, and like all gifts, should be given without expecting anything in return—except maybe help with the dishes! Or a "thank you"—that would be nice and just good manners.

The Cast

Throughout this book I mention family members on all sides and of different generations. Here is a handy guide to who is who and what their food issues are or were.

MY FATHER'S SIDE

My grandfather, known as **PAPA** to me but as **JI RODALE** to the world, is considered the founding father of the organic movement in America. He believed that sugar, wheat, and fluoride were harmful. He was a Polish Jew who grew up on the Lower East Side of Manhattan. He did not cook himself, but married a great cook.

My grandmother, known as **NANA, MRS. JI,** or simply **ANNA RODALE,** was a total pistol, artist, and awesome cook when my grandfather was alive; but after he died she pretty much relied on takeout Chinese food. She could not tolerate cheese or eggs.

My father, **ROBERT RODALE,** actually cooked a lot for a man of his time. Although it was mostly to eat stuff my mother wouldn't make: onion sandwiches, corn pones, cornmeal "mush," and other things not in this book. He constantly brought people over to dinner without telling my mother in advance.

MY MOTHER'S SIDE

GRANDMA HARTER, or **ARDATH HARTER,** used to always say she came from a family of French Huguenots, but mostly she was Pennsylvania Dutch. By the time I came along, she didn't cook much anymore but her inspiration is throughout this book. She was widowed before I was born, so I never met my grandfather, **STANLEY HARTER,** also Pennsylvania Dutch.

My mother, **ARDIE RODALE,** had five kids and many unexpected guests so she had to cook for large groups, and not always happily. She was a great cook, but like her mother-in-law, she lost interest in cooking after her husband died. Which, actually, was one of the things that forced me to learn to cook more.

My grandfather JI Rodale

My grandmother Anna Rodale

My great-great grandfather Cyrus Lessig

My grandmother Ardath Harter

My parents, Robert and Ardie Rodale

THE SIBLINGS

The best thing my father ever said to me was that I was the worst cook in my family. **HEIDI** ranked first, **HEATHER** was second, and I was last. Notice, the boys didn't get mentioned (although my brother **DAVID** who was an excellent cook had already passed away). It was a tough message to hear, but it inspired me to get better. Now we are all great cooks. And my brother **ANTHONY?** He had the good sense to marry a great cook, **FLORENCE.**

THE IN-LAWS

RITA CINQUINO, my former mother-in-law, gave me some of my best recipes of all. As an Italian—or rather Sicilian—there is almost nothing she would rather talk about than food. And while I didn't agree with everything about her cooking (what daughter-in-law does?), I completely respect her approach, which often stemmed from frugality and limited access to good food.

   LOUIE CINQUINO, my father-in-law, taught me how to cook with love. He was always a steady companion to my mother-in-law in the kitchen, sitting in the kitchen chair chopping, cutting, and helping out with whatever he was asked to do. He was also the master of gardening and cooking foraged food, whether it was wild mustard greens or wild cardoon, known as "gardooni" (see recipe, page 191). Both Rita and Louie showed me that moderation is truly the best approach to food, and that nothing in and of itself is evil. Louie just passed away at age 94 and was never known to turn any food down, especially dessert. His family was from Vasto, Italy, in the Abruzzi region.

   LOU CINQUINO is my ex-husband. I am forever grateful to him for introducing me to his extended Italian family and raising our lovely children together. Now that we are divorced, he is learning to cook on his own.

THE KIDS

I had **MAYA RODALE** when I was only 20 years old, so we kind of learned to cook together. By far my pickiest eater (the list is too long to publish here), she is now officially gluten free and can't tolerate eggs. She is married to **TONY HAILE,** who is even pickier than her (and British). The fact that they both love many of the recipes in this book is testament to my stubborn perseverance and proof that my cooking must be good.

    EVE CINQUINO came along when I was 37. She eats almost everything and has been known to cook on her own accord, whenever she feels like it. She is especially good at baking and will often make cookies or brownies for friends. She is also really, really good at math, which is very helpful in the kitchen; I will often call or text her if I need help dividing a recipe or figuring out kitchen math.

    LUCIA CINQUINO took her time joining our family. She was born when I was 44. She is also a true gourmand. She will often smell a food before she eats it, is willing to try anything, and has been known to sing like an opera singer after a good meal. She does not like foie gras (nor do I) or raw oysters (I do), but has tried them both. We both love to eat salad with our fingers.

Maya

Eve

Lucia

If I only ever ate one breakfast food forever, it would be eggs. They are so versatile and perfect. Fortunately, though, I don't have to pick just one breakfast food and neither do you. The important thing, as studies have shown, is to eat a good breakfast to start your day off right—fueled and nourished. Breakfast is also the perfect place to start cooking if you're a novice and still learning the basics. I'm always surprised when I meet people who don't know the basics of cooking, which is why I am writing this book. There is no shame in not knowing. In fact, I believe that life should be shame-free, especially in the kitchen. It's one of the most intimate places in our homes, the place we can be our true selves, having just woken up with messy hair and not even brushed our teeth . . . it's the place where our day begins.

The truth is, almost every recipe in this cookbook could be breakfast. Given their druthers, my kids would have soup every morning. Often, they prefer leftovers to traditional breakfast foods, or for that matter repurposing their leftovers into a breakfast dish, such as hard-boiled eggs in leftover marinara sauce. Having said that, we do love the classic breakfast stuff, too.

silky buttered eggs

Ever since having really good buttered eggs at the Trapp Family Lodge in Stowe, Vermont, decades ago, I have sought to re-create their delicious silkiness. This recipe is from that memory. I once made these for my daughter's British future father-in-law and he assured me I was making them the proper British way, which made me feel rather good. But what makes me feel even better is that my whole family loves them. **SERVES 4**

2 to 3 tablespoons unsalted butter

4 to 6 large eggs, lightly beaten

Salt

Buttered toast, for serving

1 In a medium cast-iron skillet, melt the butter over low heat.

2 Pour the eggs into the skillet and let them set slightly, about 20 seconds. Use a spatula to gently and slowly lift and drag the egg across the skillet (no need to stir, just a gentle folding). Repeat until big, soft curds form.

3 Cook the eggs slowly and stop when they are cooked to your liking. Some people like their eggs runny (but not me!), though make sure they don't dry out. Season with salt to taste and serve with toast, if desired.

TIP: You can embellish your eggs any way you like. My former mother-in-law would sprinkle them with grated Romano cheese and chopped mint. You can sprinkle them with chopped chives or parsley and serve with smoked salmon, too.

my flat omelet

My brother made this omelet for me once and I've never looked back. Think of it as more of an egg crêpe than an omelet. It's how I make my eggs all the time. And it's how my kids ask me to make eggs all the time. My favorite way to eat this is to fold it between two slices of soft (and preferably squishy) untoasted bread. **MAKES 1 OMELET**

1 tablespoon butter

2 large eggs, lightly beaten

Salt

1 In a medium cast-iron skillet, melt the butter over medium heat.

2 Pour the eggs into the skillet, swirling and tilting it so the egg covers the bottom of the skillet in a thin layer. Cook for a few minutes until the egg has set and is cooked around the edges.

3 Flip the egg and cook a minute more. Season with salt to taste.

TIP: You can fill this with anything you please after you have flipped it. Simply line one side with cheese, ham, or whatever you fancy and fold in half.

What's the Deal with Eggs

Before you can truly understand my philosophy on food, you must understand how I feel about the five important things about eggs: their color, their health benefits, how the hens are raised, storage temperature, and cooking style. Eggs are like a microcosm of my whole approach to food.

1. **COLOR:** When I was a kid growing up on an organic farm, eggshells were brown and the yolks were orange. But any time I went to a friend's house, the eggshells were white and the yolks were pale yellow. So I developed an inferiority complex about my family's eggs. It wasn't until I was in my early 30s and I read Masanobu Fukuoka's *The One-Straw Revolution* that I realized a truly healthy egg has orange yolks.

2. **HEALTH BENEFITS:** Remember when people used to demonize eggs? Too high in cholesterol, they said. Too much fat! Salmonella! Only eat the whites because the yolks are bad for you! I never bought into that. My theory is that if nature makes a chicken and that chicken makes an egg, and the egg has both yolks and whites and it tastes really good when cooked, then it must be good for you. Plus, eggs are high in omega-3 fatty acids, which are good for you.

3. **HOW HENS ARE RAISED:** The only way to truly know if you are eating a healthy egg is to buy organic, raise your own, or buy from someone you know. Why pay more? Because you are paying for happiness—organic does no harm to people, chickens, or nature—it's worth it. USDA guidelines guarantee that eggs that are certified organic come from cage-free, pasture-raised hens that have outdoor access and are treated humanely.

4. **STORAGE TEMPERATURE:** This may come as a surprise, but many countries outside of the United States do not refrigerate their eggs! Turns out refrigeration came from fear of salmonella. But neither way of handling eggs is right or wrong, it's just different. An egg is laid with a protective coating, and as long as that egg isn't washed, it's safe to store at room temperature for about 20 days. If that egg is washed, the protective coating is removed and the egg must be refrigerated, where it will last up to 50 days.

5. **THE COOKING STYLE:** Here is where things get emotional. Everyone from chefs to home cooks have very strong feelings on how eggs should be cooked. Runny or well-done, over-easy or sunny-side-up. But it doesn't really matter, does it? It's what you like that matters. That's why this chapter covers even the most basic ways to cook an egg.

foolproof poached eggs

Poached eggs are one of my favorite breakfast memories from childhood. The eggs were poached in water with a dash of vinegar and the toast still had lumps of butter on it that hadn't melted yet. Plus, my mom would cut it up into little bite-size pieces. This is my re-creation of that memory. **SERVES 1**

1 tablespoon apple cider vinegar

2 large eggs

Buttered toast, for serving

Salt and freshly ground black pepper

Chopped chives, for serving (optional)

1 In a small saucepan, bring 4 cups of water to a boil over high heat. Reduce the heat to a gentle simmer and add the vinegar. (The vinegar will help the eggs set.)

2 Crack an egg into a small bowl. When the water is at a simmer, slip the egg into the water and gently stir the water (this will help create a nice round shape). Repeat with the second egg.

3 Cook the eggs for 2 minutes for cooked whites and runny yolks. Remove from the water with a slotted spoon and drain on paper towels. Serve the eggs on buttered toast and season with salt and pepper to taste. You can sprinkle some fresh chives on them, if you like.

huevos rancheros

*If for some reason I had to choose one breakfast dish to live on forever,
it would be huevos rancheros. I have a rule that when I travel, if I
see huevos rancheros on the menu, I must order it. Consequently,
I've eaten all styles and types, from a delicate diet version in one of
LA's boutique hotels (not my favorite) to the green salsa–slathered
mess at an awesome diner in Wilson, Wyoming (now we're talking!).*

SERVES 4

Extra virgin olive
oil, for the skillet

4 corn or flour
tortillas
(see page 339)

4 large eggs

Mexicali Beans
(page 256)

1 cup shredded
Monterey Jack
or Colby cheese

Fresh Salsa
(page 172)

Guacamole
(page 173)

Hot sauce and
sour cream, for
serving (optional)

1 Lightly oil a large cast-iron skillet and set it
over medium-high heat. Cook the tortillas on
both sides until warmed through. Transfer
to a plate and cover with a kitchen towel to
keep warm.

2 Lightly oil the skillet again, crack in the eggs
and fry to your liking.

3 Transfer the tortillas to serving plates. Divide
the heated beans among the tortillas, sprinkle
with the cheese, and top with an egg. Serve
with salsa, guacamole, and, if desired, hot
sauce and sour cream.

Lucia
collecting
eggs

Swiss chard

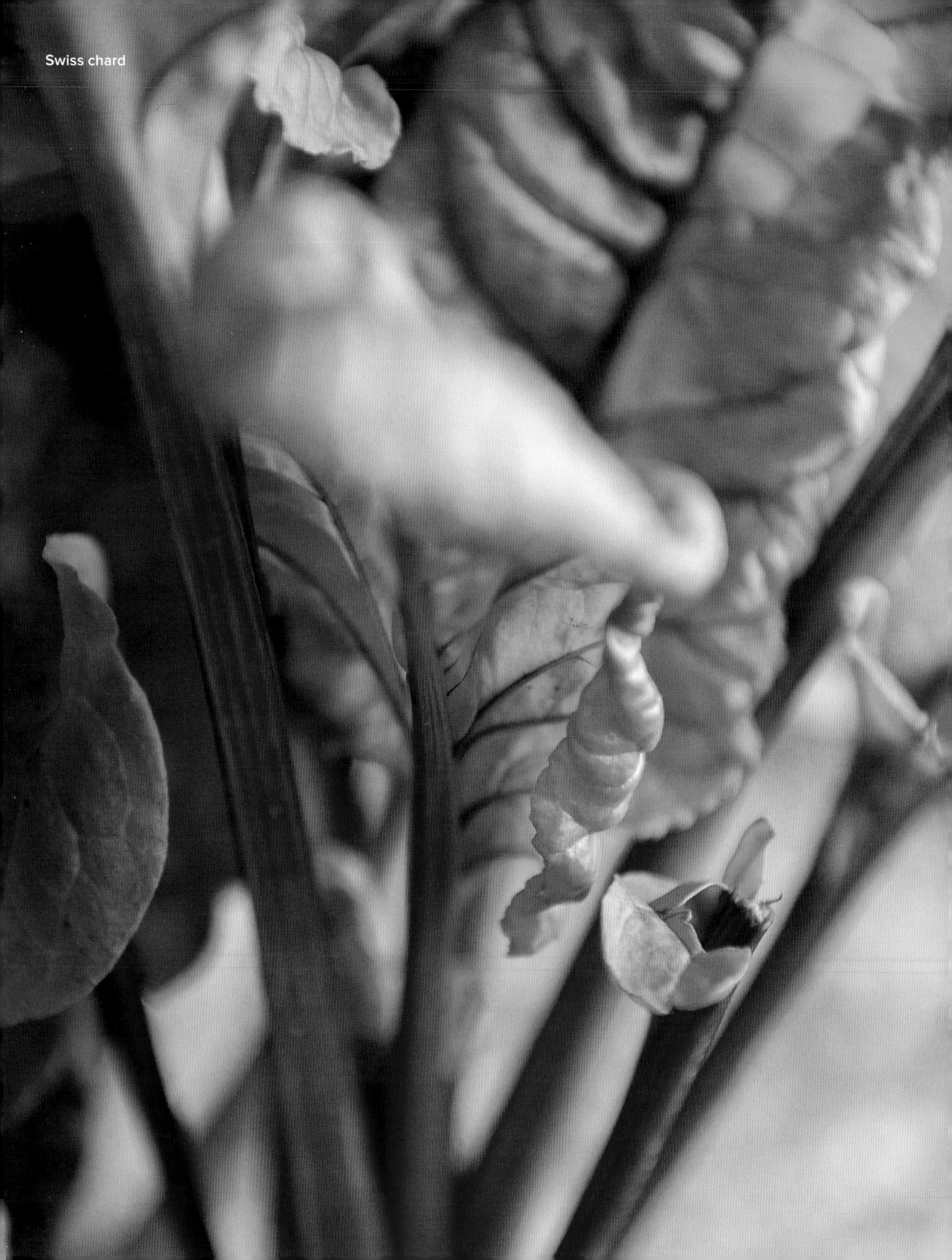

green eggs

This recipe is a simple and easy way to get more greens into your diet. It works with kale, chard, wild mustard greens, spinach, collards, or any other good dark, leafy green you can think of. To turn this into green eggs and ham, just add some chopped cooked ham to the egg mixture before you pour it on the greens, or serve with some slices of cooked smoked ham. **SERVES 2**

2 tablespoons extra virgin olive oil

1 cup firmly packed fresh greens, chopped

4 large eggs, lightly beaten

Salt and freshly ground black pepper

Buttered toast, for serving (optional)

Finely grated Romano cheese, for serving

1 In a medium cast-iron skillet, heat the oil over medium-high heat. Add the greens and cook, stirring, for 2 minutes, or until wilted.

2 Season the eggs with salt and pepper to taste and pour over the greens. Reduce the heat to low and cook for 8 minutes, or until the eggs have set.

3 Flip the eggs over and cook 1 to 2 minutes longer, until puffed. Serve with buttered toast, if desired. Pass Romano at the table.

classic french toast

When my youngest was 3 years old, she would always ask for French toast with "makeup syrup." That's maple syrup to the rest of us! The good thing about French toast is that it's just fine if the bread is a little stale, and whole grains get covered with so many other yummy things that kids never complain if you make it with hearty bread.

SERVES 2

2 large eggs

⅓ cup whole milk

2 tablespoons butter

4 slices whole-grain bread

Pure maple syrup and fresh berries, for serving (optional)

1 In a shallow bowl, whisk together the eggs and milk.

2 In a large cast-iron skillet, melt 1 tablespoon of the butter over medium-high heat.

3 Dip half of the bread slices into the egg mixture, shaking to remove the excess. (Don't let them soak too long, or they will be soggy!) Cook the bread 2 to 3 minutes per side, until golden. Repeat with the remaining butter and bread. If desired, serve drizzled with maple syrup and sprinkled with berries.

eve's crêpes

My daughter Eve loves crêpes. She loves them so much that she is the one who always makes them. She procured this recipe at school during International Week. Of course, you can fill them with anything you want, but these usually don't last past a sprinkle of sugar and a squeeze of lemon juice. **MAKES 15 TO 20 CRÊPES**

1 cup all-purpose flour

1 cup whole milk

4 large eggs

¼ cup water

2 tablespoons granulated sugar

1 tablespoon butter, melted, plus more for the skillet

Powdered sugar and lemon wedges, for serving

1 In a large bowl, whisk together the flour, milk, eggs, water, granulated sugar, and melted butter.

2 In a small cast-iron skillet, melt a little butter over medium heat. Ladle in enough of the batter to thinly coat the base of the skillet and cook until set, about 1 minute. Flip and cook for another minute.

3 Repeat with the remaining batter (you can keep the crêpes warm in a low oven). Dust with the powdered sugar and serve with the lemon.

breakfast sausage patties

My quest for a quick breakfast patty my teenager could heat up before school resulted in this recipe. I couldn't find delicious, organic breakfast patties in our supermarket, so I made them myself. Being the forward-thinking, slightly lazy mom that I am, I make them in big batches and freeze them. I haven't been able to perfect the flat, round shape of the commercial ones, but then these aren't made by a machine! **MAKES ABOUT 24 PATTIES**

4 pounds ground pork

1 tablespoon dried sage

2 teaspoons salt

1 teaspoon dried marjoram

1 teaspoon dried thyme

1 teaspoon freshly ground black pepper

Extra virgin olive oil, for cooking

1 In a large bowl, combine the pork, sage, salt, marjoram, thyme, and pepper and mix with your hands to combine.

2 Shape the mixture into ⅓-inch-thick patties 3 inches in diameter. In a large cast-iron skillet, heat a little oil over medium heat. Working in batches, add the patties and cook about 5 minutes per side, until browned and cooked through.

TIP: To freeze the cooked patties, let them cool to room temperature, freeze them on a baking sheet, and then and pop them in a freezer container.

FROM THE BLOG
"Since I am trying to 'watch it' with the cholesterol, and I don't eat pork anymore. I use turkey sausage meat already prepared, seasonings and all. All I have to do is bring it home, make the patties, and drop it in the pan. The source is from a sustainable farm in Maryland that treats its animals kindly and feeds them with organic feed." **—DONNA IN DELAWARE**

pancakes in a pinch

One morning after a sleepover, my daughter's friends asked for pancakes. I had run out of my usual organic mix and their parents were coming over in 25 minutes to pick them up. Shoot! So I pulled out The Joy of Cooking *and made pancakes from scratch and it reminded me just how easy they really are, no mix necessary. I have since adapted the recipe.* **SERVES 4**

2 cups all-purpose flour

2 tablespoons sugar

2 teaspoons baking powder

1 teaspoon salt

3 large eggs

1¾ cups whole milk

Butter, for cooking

Pure maple syrup and fresh berries, for serving (optional)

1 In a large bowl, combine the flour, sugar, baking powder, and salt. Add the eggs and milk and whisk until smooth and combined.

2 In a large cast-iron skillet, melt a little butter over medium heat.

3 Ladle the batter by ¼ cup into the skillet (I can usually fit 3 pancakes at one time) and cook for 3 minutes, or until bubbles appear on the surface. Flip and cook about 2 minutes longer, until the bottoms are golden. Transfer to a plate and repeat with the remaining batter (you can keep the pancakes warm in a low oven).

4 If desired, serve with maple syrup and berries.

FROM THE BLOG
"Served these over the weekend for my nieces and nephew—they were a huge hit! Thanks for sharing. I second the use of real organic maple syrup—we grew up with the commercial stuff and the real stuff is so much more amazing." —JEN

I always try to
serve plain
cut-up fruit with
every meal

TIP: For a Middle Eastern touch, add a splash of rose water to the sour cherries during cooking.

sour cherry breakfast parfait

Sour cherry season is so short, you need to make the most of it. If you see them, grab as many as you can, and plan to spend the afternoon pitting them and making the most beautiful magenta cherry sauce, which you can use for pies, dessert sauces, or my favorite, breakfast. Pitting them is messy work, so grab your kids, pull a stool up to the counter, and make it a family affair. **SERVES 1**

SOUR CHERRY SAUCE

1 quart sour cherries, pitted

½ cup sugar (or to taste)

PARFAIT

½ cup plain Greek yogurt

1 to 2 tablespoons slivered or sliced almonds, toasted

1 To make the sour cherry sauce: In a saucepan, combine the cherries and sugar and stir to combine. Bring to a simmer over medium heat and cook, uncovered, for 10 to 15 minutes, until the mixture has thickened. If the pan seems dry, add 1 to 2 tablespoons of water. Use immediately or freeze in small portions for future parfaits, or in a large portion for a pie.

2 To make the parfait: Spoon the yogurt into the bottom of a small bowl or jar. Top with ⅓ cup of the cherry sauce. Sprinkle with almonds to serve.

VARIATIONS

For a banana-maple parfait, layer 1 sliced banana over the yogurt, sprinkle with 3 tablespoons chopped walnuts, and drizzle with 2 tablespoons maple syrup.

For an almost-apple pie parfait, spoon ⅓ cup applesauce over the yogurt, sprinkle with 3 tablespoons chopped walnuts, and drizzle with 2 tablespoons maple syrup.

codfish cakes

When I was a kid, codfish cakes were one of my favorite winter breakfasts. When I grew up and started craving them, I figured out how to make them myself and now it's become a favorite family tradition to make them for Christmas breakfast. This recipe calls for salt cod, which you'll find in a lot of stores around the holidays because of its special place in Italian and Portuguese cuisines. **SERVES 4 TO 6**

1 pound salt cod or cooked firm white-fleshed fish

1 pound potatoes (3 to 4), peeled and cubed

1 tablespoon unsalted butter

¼ cup whole milk

Salt and freshly ground black pepper

1 large egg

2 tablespoons extra virgin olive oil or unsalted butter

Ketchup, for serving

1 If using salt cod, soak the fillet in 3 changes of cold water in the fridge for 24 hours to get rid of the excess salt. Drain.

2 Place the fish in a saucepan, and cover with 2 inches of water. Bring to a simmer (don't boil) over medium heat and cook 2 to 3 minutes, until flaky and tender. Drain and set aside to cool slightly.

3 In a medium saucepan of boiling water, cook the potatoes for 12 to 15 minutes, until just tender.

4 Drain the potatoes, return to the pan with the butter and milk, and mash with a hand masher until smooth. Set aside to cool slightly.

5 When cool, combine the fish and potatoes in a large bowl and season to taste with salt and pepper. Mix in the egg. Shape the mixture into ½-inch-thick patties 2½ inches in diameter.

6 In a large cast-iron skillet, heat the oil or butter over medium-high heat. Add the cod cakes and cook for 3 to 5 minutes per side, until golden, crispy, and heated through. Serve with ketchup.

FROM THE BLOG

"I saw your recipe and had a taste memory from my childhood 50 years ago in Connecticut. I remember eating fried codfish cakes with ketchup for lunch, and look forward to replicating the recipe for old times' sake. Thanks for evoking that memory!" —RONN

pennsylvania dutch–style creamed chipped beef

Around my part of Pennsylvania, go into any good diner worth its PA Dutch salt and you will see creamed chipped beef on the menu. It may sound strange, but it really isn't. I've decided that it's like the cousin of biscuits and sausage gravy. "Chipped" refers to the way the beef is cut: It's delicately, thinly sliced. Because it's salt-cured and then dried, it can be salty. You might need some help sourcing it through your butcher. **SERVES 4 TO 6**

2 tablespoons extra virgin olive oil

½ pound dried chipped beef, coarsely chopped

2 cups whole milk

¼ cup all-purpose flour

4 to 6 pieces buttered whole-grain bread, toasted

Freshly ground black pepper

1 In a medium cast-iron skillet, heat the oil over medium-high heat. Add the beef and cook, stirring, for a few minutes.

2 In a small bowl, whisk together the milk and flour until smooth. Add to the beef and stir to combine. Cook until thickened, a few minutes more.

3 To serve, spoon the beef mixture over the toast and season with pepper to taste.

FROM THE BLOG

"I'm a 63-year-old American who grew up in Iowa, is married to a Swede, and living in Sweden. When we visited the U.S. recently, my only request to my sister and Mom for food was English muffins and chipped beef!" —NIKKI

maya's farmers' market breakfast

This dish is so named because we pick up most of the ingredients at the farmers' market, especially in winter. It's our go-to weekend breakfast that keeps us full until dinnertime. It's also pretty easy to make and a great way to get a few servings of vegetables first thing in the morning. **SERVES 2**

2 large potatoes, peeled and halved

4 slices bacon, roughly chopped

½ onion, finely chopped

3 cloves garlic, finely chopped

6 mushrooms, sliced

Extra virgin olive oil, for cooking the eggs

2 large eggs

1 bunch leafy greens (kale, chard, or spinach), stems removed, leaves coarsely chopped

Grated Romano cheese and crushed red pepper flakes, for serving (optional)

1 In a medium saucepan of boiling water, cook the potatoes for 10 to 12 minutes, until just tender. Drain and set aside to cool slightly, then cut into slices.

2 In a large cast-iron skillet, cook the bacon over high heat, stirring, for a few minutes. Add the potatoes to the skillet and stir to coat evenly in the bacon drippings. Cook for about 3 minutes, or until the potatoes start to get golden.

3 Add the onion and garlic and cook, stirring, for 1 minute.

4 Add the mushrooms and cook, stirring, for 8 minutes, or until browned.

5 Lightly oil a separate skillet, crack in the eggs, and cook to your liking.

6 Add the greens to the potato mixture, stir, and cook for about 5 minutes, or until just wilted.

7 Divide the mixture between 2 plates and top each with an egg. If desired, sprinkle with Romano and pepper flakes.

breakfast quiche

I usually make quiche for dinner, but there's something very satisfying about a piece of quiche for Sunday breakfast. You can make the pie dough the night before and simply roll it out in the morning to speed up the process. Think of quiche as a blank canvas for any additions you want, from cheese to veggies. **SERVES 4 TO 6**

Incredibly Flaky Pie Dough (page 299), omitting the sugar

2 cups shredded cheese (such as Colby, cheddar, or Monterey Jack)

1½ cups whole milk

3 large eggs

2 tablespoons all-purpose flour

3 cups add-ins: chopped broccoli, mushrooms, baby spinach or kale leaves, cooked ham, onions, or artichoke

1 Preheat the oven to 375°F.

2 On a lightly floured surface, roll out the pie dough to a 13-inch round about ⅛ inch thick. Use to line the bottom and sides of a 9-inch pie dish. Trim any excess dough and press the edges with a fork.

3 In a large bowl, mix together the cheese, milk, eggs, and flour.

4 Mix in the add-ins of your choosing. Pour the mixture into the prepared pie shell and place the dish on a baking sheet.

5 Transfer to the oven and bake for 45 minutes, or until golden and the center feels firm to the touch. Remove from the oven and stand 10 minutes to cool and set.

Salad Days

If I had to live off one dish for the rest of my life, it would be salad (since gravy is too impractical). A good salad is sublime, deeply satisfying, and refreshingly nourishing. As an amateur restaurant critic, I always judge a restaurant by its house salad. Here are my criteria for ultimate salad happiness.

1. **THE LETTUCE SHOULD BE TOTALLY CLEAN, CRISP, AND WITHOUT ANY BROWN BITS.** It's astounding to me the lack of regard some restaurants (and people) pay to whether the lettuce is clean and fresh. One slightly rotting piece of lettuce can ruin the taste of the whole salad. Even if I buy prepackaged lettuce, I wash it at least twice in a salad spinner—many more times if it's home grown or from the farmers' market, since lettuce is notorious for hiding tiny pieces of dirt and bugs. And even if I'm making dinner for a huge crowd, I review each piece and pinch off the brown ends or discard the bad parts. Yes, this can be a bit tedious, but think of it as meditation.

2. THE DRESSING SHOULD BE HOMEMADE, PROPERLY BALANCED, AND EVENLY DISTRIBUTED. A salad dressing is meant to enhance the taste of the salad ingredients, not overwhelm them. And if you still taste it a few hours later, that's not a happy feeling (usually too much garlic). Plus, homemade dressing is so simple, inexpensive, and easy to make. The tiniest bit goes a long way if a salad is lovingly tossed. Having said that, I always keep a bottle of ranch dressing in the fridge, because the kids love to dip fresh veggies in it. What you won't find in this cookbook are recipes containing balsamic vinegar. Why? As an early adopter in the late 1980s, I think I reached my saturation point somewhere around 1995! Feel free to use it, but make sure it's the real thing.

3. THE SALAD SHOULD BE SEASONALLY APPROPRIATE. Salad ingredients are one of the most seasonally sensitive ingredients there are. Choosing the ingredients based on the season not only keeps salads interesting, but shows an awareness of, and connection to, nature that will be reflected in all other areas of your life.

kale salad with zesty lemon dressing

I never ate kale in a salad while growing up, but I remember tasting it for the first time at the restaurant ABC Kitchen in New York City in about 2010 and thinking that I simply had to replicate it at home. It's so good, even my kids love it. My youngest has been known to shout: "Yay, kale salad again!" I know, I have a weird family. **SERVES 4**

ZESTY LEMON DRESSING

1 tablespoon grated lemon zest

1 tablespoon fresh lemon juice

1 tablespoon white wine vinegar

¼ cup extra virgin olive oil

Salt

SALAD

1 large bunch lacinato (Tuscan) kale, stems removed

Salt

Leaves from 3 sprigs fresh mint, thinly sliced

1 jalapeño pepper, thinly sliced (optional)

1 To make the dressing: In a small bowl, combine the lemon zest, lemon juice, vinegar, and oil. Add salt to taste and whisk with a fork to combine.

2 For the salad: Soak the kale leaves in cold water for about 5 minutes. (I soak them right in the salad spinner.)

3 Add 2 tablespoons salt to the water and massage the kale to soften a little. Rinse the kale two or three times and dry in the salad spinner.

4 Roll the kale leaves up tightly and thinly slice. Transfer to a large bowl.

5 Pour the dressing over the kale, add the mint and jalapeño (if using), and toss well to combine.

watercress and walnut salad

*When I was a kid, restaurants used watercress as a garnish. My mother was obsessed with garnishes. She had a hard time eating anything that wasn't "garnished," but funnily enough she never used watercress. I'm fairly anti-garnish (except for wild violets), though somewhere along the way I developed a taste for watercress. And come spring, there is no better way to eat it than in a salad. **SERVES 4***

ORANGE DRESSING

1 tablespoon red wine vinegar

1 tablespoon fresh blood orange or orange juice

3 tablespoons extra virgin olive oil

Salt

SALAD

1 bunch watercress (about 4 ounces), tough stems trimmed

⅓ cup walnuts, toasted (see page 339)

Shaved Manchego or Romano cheese, for serving

Wild violets, for garnish (optional)

1 To make the dressing: In a small bowl, combine the vinegar, orange juice, oil, and salt to taste and whisk with a fork to combine.

2 For the salad: Place the watercress leaves and walnuts in large bowl. Pour over the dressing and toss to combine. Just before serving, sprinkle with the cheese and violets (if using).

TIP: If the taste of watercress is too peppery for you, you can mix this with some other milder salad leaves, such as butter lettuce. For a more substantial salad, you can also add citrus slices and crumbled goat cheese. Delicious.

asparagus, feta, and herb salad

In early spring, when the asparagus is coming in fast and it's young and tender, it's delicious to eat raw. And like many vegetables, it's the only way my kids will eat it. If you can't get tender asparagus, give it a quick blanch. Feel free to get creative with additions, too; this is just as tasty with toasted flaked almonds and crumbled goat cheese.

SERVES 4 TO 6

1 bunch (12 to 20 spears) asparagus

Leaves from 3 sprigs fresh mint, chopped

Leaves from 2 sprigs fresh basil, chopped

¼ cup pine nuts, toasted (see page 339)

¼ cup crumbled feta cheese

2 or 3 radishes, thinly sliced

LEMON DRESSING
1 tablespoon fresh lemon juice

1 tablespoon red wine vinegar

¼ cup extra virgin olive oil

Salt and freshly ground black pepper

1 Snap the woody ends off the asparagus spears and discard. Cut the spears into 2-inch pieces and slice each piece lengthwise into quarters. (I call this julienne without the fuss!)

2 In a saucepan of boiling water, blanch the asparagus for 1 minute. Scoop out and transfer to a bowl of ice water to stop the cooking process. Drain well.

3 In a large bowl, combine the asparagus, herbs, pine nuts, feta, and radishes.

4 To make the lemon dressing: In a small bowl, combine the lemon juice, vinegar, oil, and salt and pepper to taste and whisk with a fork to combine.

5 Just before serving, drizzle the dressing over the salad and toss to combine.

FROM THE BLOG
"One of the great really memorable experiences is finding, picking, and eating wild asparagus. Eating it raw from the garden or green market is the next best!" —CAROL

pea and mint salad

If there is any one thing worth growing in your garden, it's sweet, vibrant peas of all sorts. And about the same time the peas are popping, the mint is rising out of the earth and unfurling its sweet, tender tips. My favorite mint is apple mint, with soft, furry, sweet leaves. A salad is the perfect way to enjoy these two springtime beauties together. **SERVES 4**

SHERRY VINAIGRETTE

1 tablespoon sherry or red wine vinegar

3 tablespoons extra virgin olive oil

Salt

SALAD

2 cups shelled fresh peas, snow peas, or sugar snaps

1 head romaine lettuce, leaves torn

1 cup pea shoots (optional)

Leaves from 2 sprigs fresh mint, chopped

Shaved Parmesan or Romano cheese, for serving

1 To make the vinaigrette: In a small bowl, combine the vinegar, oil, and salt to taste and whisk with a fork to combine.

2 For the salad: In a large bowl, combine the shelled peas, lettuce, and pea shoots (if using). If using snow peas or sugar snaps, slice them first.

3 Drizzle the salad with the dressing, add the mint, and toss to combine. Before serving, sprinkle with the shaved cheese.

TIP: I pick my peas straight from the garden and like to use a mixture of shelled fresh peas and sugar snaps for this recipe.

pennsylvania dutch dandelion salad

Dandelion salad with hot bacon dressing is an old spring classic in my part of Pennsylvania; this recipe comes from my mother. It is traditionally quite a sweet salad to counter the bitterness of the greens, but you can adjust to taste. If you are going to harvest dandelion leaves wild from your lawn, make sure you pick them when they are very young, before the dandelion blooms. **SERVES 4**

4 cups young dandelion leaves*

5 slices bacon

2 tablespoons all-purpose flour

1½ cups water

3 tablespoons apple cider vinegar

3 to 5 tablespoons sugar (to taste)

1 tablespoon yellow mustard

Ground black pepper

1 large egg, hard-boiled (see page 338) and chopped

1 Wash the dandelion leaves well, dry in a salad spinner, and set aside.

2 In a large skillet, cook the bacon over medium-high heat until crispy. Transfer the bacon to paper towels to drain and set aside. Pour off all but half the pan drippings.

3 In a bowl, combine the flour, water, vinegar, sugar, mustard, and pepper and whisk to combine.

4 Add the mixture to the reserved drippings in the skillet and cook over medium heat, stirring, for 1 to 2 minutes, until thickened.

5 Transfer the dandelion leaves to a serving bowl, pour over the hot dressing, and toss to combine.

6 Crumble the bacon over the salad, top with the egg, and serve immediately.

* You can also buy cultivated dandelion greens, but the flavor won't be as intense as young wild dandelion leaves; as a result, you may need less sugar in the dressing.

my greek salad

On a hot summer's night, there's nothing better than a crunchy, cooling Greek salad. This is a favorite summer salad that you can turn into a full meal simply by adding some grilled chicken, shrimp, or lamb. The essential aroma in a Greek salad is the oregano. I like to add pine nuts. **SERVES 4**

GREEK DRESSING

1 tablespoon red wine vinegar

1 tablespoon fresh lemon juice

¼ cup extra virgin olive oil

¼ clove garlic, crushed in a press

¼ teaspoon dried oregano (or 5 fresh leaves, chopped)

Salt and freshly ground black pepper

SALAD

1 head romaine or iceberg lettuce, leaves torn

1 green bell pepper, thickly sliced

1 or 2 tomatoes, cut into wedges

1 cucumber, sliced

½ red onion, thinly sliced

½ cup kalamata olives

½ cup crumbled feta cheese

2 tablespoons pine nuts (optional), toasted (see page 339)

1 To make the dressing: In a small bowl, combine the vinegar, lemon juice, oil, garlic, oregano, and salt and black pepper to taste and whisk with a fork to combine.

2 For the salad: In a large bowl, combine the lettuce, bell pepper, tomatoes, cucumber, onion, and olives. Drizzle the dressing over the salad and toss to combine. Before serving, sprinkle with the feta and pine nuts (if using).

FROM THE BLOG

"Romaine lettuce is a good choice if you're growing it on your own. It holds up better in the summer heat than most other types. Plant in the shade of other plants, trees, bushes, or use shade cloth if your summers are very hot and/or humid. Pick in the morning, put in a plastic bag with damp paper towels, and store in the fridge until dinnertime to keep it crisp. If it still seems wilty, soak in ice water for about 20 minutes and it'll perk up." —CHRIS

lobster and avocado salad

One Mother's Day I had to make my own lunch, so I wanted something quick and easy yet indulgent without being unhealthy. For days, I had been craving the combination of lobster and avocado, so I whipped this up. A mandoline makes quick work of thinly slicing the vegetables. I happened to have some fresh lemon verbena in the garden and added that, but you could use your favorite herb. **Serves 4**

Lemon Vinaigrette

1 tablespoon finely grated lemon zest

1 tablespoon fresh lemon juice

1 tablespoon white wine vinegar

5 tablespoons extra virgin olive oil

Salt

Salad

1 head iceberg or romaine lettuce, leaves torn

1 cucumber, thinly sliced on a mandoline

5 radishes, thinly sliced on a mandoline

1 bulb fennel, trimmed, cored, and thinly sliced

2 avocados, sliced

1 pound cooked lobster meat, coarsely chopped

3 tablespoons pine nuts, toasted (see page 339)

Leaves from 2 sprigs basil, chopped

Leaves from 4 sprigs dill, chopped

Leaves from 2 sprigs lemon verbena, chopped (optional)

1 To make the vinaigrette: In a small bowl, combine the lemon zest and juice, vinegar, oil and salt in a small bowl and whisk with a fork to combine. Set aside.

2 For the salad: Arrange the lettuce leaves on a serving plate. Top with the cucumber, radishes, fennel, avocado, and lobster.

3 Drizzle the salad with the vinaigrette and sprinkle with the pine nuts and herbs.

Maya and Eve
shucking non-GMO
organic sweet corn

chopped summer salad

By July, it's usually too hot for lettuce to be happy in my garden. Fortunately, while the tomatoes might still be struggling to ripen, the other veggies are popping up all over. And the best way to enjoy these new vegetables is to chop them up and then toss with a simple dressing. In fancy restaurants they call this a chopped salad, and that's exactly what it is—no need to complicate it. **SERVES 4 TO 6**

1 cup chopped green things: green beans, snap peas, green bell pepper

1 cup chopped light-green things: celery, cucumber, fennel, zucchini

1 cup chopped colorful things: carrots, radishes, tomatoes, red bell pepper

½ cup fresh corn kernels

1 cup chopped protein (optional): ham, chicken, turkey, cheese, white beans

HERB VINAIGRETTE

2 tablespoons sherry vinegar

¼ cup extra virgin olive oil

½ cup chopped fresh herbs: parsley, dill, or basil

Salt and freshly ground black pepper

1 In a large bowl, combine all your chopped vegetables and protein (if using).

2 To make the vinaigrette: In a small bowl, combine the vinegar, oil, herbs, and salt and pepper to taste and whisk with a fork to combine.

3 Pour the dressing over the vegetables and toss to combine.

sweet-and-sour tomato and pepper salad

This quick and easy Pennsylvania Dutch recipe tastes just like my childhood summers. My mother used to make it and I always loved it—even after I learned how she made it, which seemed just plain weird. I mean, who's heard of sugar on a salad? But it works! Garden-fresh or heirloom tomatoes are best. **SERVES 4**

3 very ripe tomatoes, cut into rounds

2 green bell peppers, cut into rounds

1 tablespoon sugar

Pinch of salt

¼ cup apple cider vinegar

Freshly ground black pepper (optional)

1 Arrange the tomatoes and bell peppers in alternating layers on a serving dish.

2 Sprinkle with the sugar and salt and drizzle with the vinegar. If desired, season with pepper to taste.

TIP: I like to serve this salad with Ardie's Garlic Chicken (page 200) and fresh corn on the cob for a taste of pure summer happiness.

FROM THE BLOG
"Thank you so much for this recipe. My grandmother made this salad when I was a child in Pennsylvania (many, many years ago—I'm 85) and I have been searching frantically to find it." —B

american-style antipasto salad

Yes, you can make a fancy gourmet antipasto, but sometimes—especially if you were raised in America—you just want an all-American one, with deli ham and provolone. This is great for parties, or for a Friday night when you get takeout pizza and want a salad to go with it. Everything here is optional based on your preferences. **SERVES 6 TO 8**

1 head lettuce, leaves separated

8 ounces fresh mozzarella cheese, sliced

1 cup roasted red peppers, store-bought or homemade (see page 162)

1 jar (11 ounces) marinated artichokes, halved

½ cup green or black olives

1 tomato, sliced

6 pepperoncini peppers

1 cup pickled cauliflower

¼ cup chopped fresh Italian parsley leaves

4 round slices provolone cheese

4 slices deli ham

12 slices hard salami

ITALIAN DRESSING
2 tablespoons red wine vinegar

6 tablespoons extra virgin olive oil

½ teaspoon garlic powder

½ teaspoon onion powder

½ teaspoon dried oregano

¼ teaspoon dried thyme

2 tablespoons finely grated Romano cheese

Salt

) Arrange the lettuce leaves on a serving platter. Layer and decorate with the mozzarella, red peppers, artichokes, olives, tomato, pepperoncini peppers, pickled cauliflower, and chopped parsley.

2 Top each slice of provolone with a slice of ham and 3 slices of salami. Roll up into a cigar shape and cut into 3 or 4 pieces. Add to the platter.

3 To make the dressing: In a small bowl, combine the vinegar, oil, garlic powder, onion powder, oregano, thyme, Romano, and salt to taste and mix with a fork to combine. Drizzle the dressing over the salad to serve.

grilled faux caesar salad

Grilling lettuce doesn't sound that great until you've tried it: It's charry and delicious, plus it's a fun way to take advantage of an already hot grill in the summer. I don't like to use raw egg yolk or anchovies in my salad, which is why I call it a faux Caesar. **Serves 4**

CROUTONS

3 tablespoons unsalted butter

2 tablespoons extra virgin olive oil

1 clove garlic, finely chopped

2 cups cubed stale bread, oven-dried (see page 338)

Faux Caesar Dressing

1 tablespoon red wine vinegar

2 tablespoons fresh lemon juice

6 tablespoons extra virgin olive oil

1 clove garlic, smashed

Salt

Salad

3 heads romaine lettuce, halved lengthwise

Leaves from a few sprigs fresh basil or Italian parsley, chopped

⅓ cup finely grated Romano cheese

1 To make the croutons: In a large cast-iron skillet, melt the butter and oil over medium heat. Add the garlic and bread and cook, turning, until the croutons are golden and crunchy.

2 To make the dressing: In a small bowl, combine the vinegar, lemon juice, oil, garlic, and salt and whisk with a fork to combine.

3 For the salad: Prepare a grill to medium-high heat. Oil the grill grates and cook the lettuce heads, turning, until wilted and charred.

4 Transfer the lettuces to a platter, drizzle with the dressing (discarding the garlic), and top with the herbs, Romano, and croutons.

syrian salad

I have a favorite local Middle Eastern restaurant, Aladdin, which I've been going to for more than 20 years, even after it changed locations. And I've always loved this salad, despite the fact that it's certainly not organic, the lettuce is iceberg, and it's nothing fancy. The family who owns the restaurant is Syrian and they make everything from scratch. This recipe is straight from the chef's mouth. **SERVES 4**

SYRIAN DRESSING

1 tablespoon fresh lemon juice

3 tablespoons extra virgin olive oil

½ teaspoon garlic powder

Pinch of salt

SALAD

1 head iceberg lettuce, leaves torn

1 cucumber, sliced

1 tomato, cut into wedges

1 green bell pepper, thickly sliced

¼ cup kalamata olives

¼ cup coarsely chopped fresh flat-leaf or curly parsley leaves

½ cup crumbled feta cheese

1 To make the dressing: In a small bowl, combine the lemon juice, oil, garlic powder, and salt and whisk with a fork to combine.

2 For the salad: In a large bowl, combine the lettuce, cucumber, tomato, bell pepper, and olives. Drizzle the dressing over the salad and toss to combine. Before serving, sprinkle the salad with the parsley and feta.

my grandmother's potato salad

Grandma Harter only ever made three dishes that I remember: a grilled cheese sandwich; Pennsylvania Dutch ham, green bean, and potato soup (page 114); and this potato salad. You should make the salad a day in advance so the potatoes can absorb the dressing and flavors overnight in the fridge. You can adjust the sugar to taste—the PA Dutch liked it sweet! **SERVES 10 TO 12**

4 pounds waxy potatoes, unpeeled

½ cup chopped onion

2 cups chopped celery

4 large eggs, hard-boiled (see page 338) and chopped

Leaves from 3 sprigs fresh dill, chopped

DRESSING
¾ cup apple cider vinegar

1¼ cups whole milk

1 egg yolk

2 tablespoons brown mustard

¼ to ½ cup sugar (to taste)

2 tablespoons cornstarch, dissolved in a little water

Salt

1 In a saucepan of boiling water, cook the potatoes for 15 minutes, or until tender. Drain and set aside until cool enough to handle.

2 Slice the potatoes into bite-size pieces and place them in a large bowl with the onion, celery, and three-fourths of the hard-boiled eggs.

3 To make the dressing: In a small saucepan, combine the vinegar, milk, egg yolk, mustard, sugar, cornstarch mixture, and salt and bring to a boil over high heat. Reduce the heat to medium and stir until thickened.

4 Add the warm dressing to the potatoes and toss to combine. Refrigerate the salad overnight. Before serving, sprinkle with the reserved hard-boiled egg and dill.

Lacinato kale

roasted squash, kale, and seed salad

If you are looking for a delicious salad packed with nutrition and flavor that is a meal in itself, this is it. You can use leftover squash if you have it and feel free to experiment with the seeds. I like to roast my own pumpkin seeds (page 178). You can use any type of squash, but butternut is always good. **SERVES 4**

RED WINE VINAIGRETTE

1 tablespoon red wine vinegar

3 tablespoons extra virgin olive oil

Salt

SALAD

2 cups cubed (½-inch) butternut squash

2 tablespoons extra virgin olive oil

Salt

1 head lettuce (such as butter lettuce), leaves torn

1 bunch lacinato (Tuscan) kale, stems removed, leaves thinly sliced

3 radishes, thinly sliced

2 tablespoons unsalted roasted pumpkin seeds

2 tablespoons roasted sunflower seeds

1 To make the vinaigrette: In a small bowl, combine the vinegar, oil, and salt to taste and whisk with a fork to combine.

2 For the salad: Preheat the oven to 400°F.

3 Place the squash in a baking dish, add the oil and salt to taste, and toss to coat. Roast for 30 minutes, or until deep golden and caramelized. Set aside to cool slightly.

4 Place the lettuce, kale, radishes, and seeds in a salad bowl and toss to combine. Add the squash and the dressing and toss gently to coat.

tomato, mozzarella, and avocado salad

We often think of tomatoes as a summer pleasure, but in reality they are a late-summer pleasure. And just as they are ripening, so are avocados. I've taken these seasonal partners and combined them for my version of the ubiquitous tomato and mozzarella salad. To me it's like the last tastes and textures of summer—sweet, savory, and soft.

SERVES 4

8 ounces fresh mozzarella cheese, cut into 8 slices

2 large tomatoes, cut into 8 slices

1 avocado, sliced

¼ cup good-quality extra virgin olive oil

Salt and freshly ground black pepper

1 Arrange the mozzarella slices in a single layer on a serving plate.

2 Layer the tomato slices over the cheese and top with the avocado slices.

3 Drizzle with the olive oil and season generously with salt and pepper.

TIP: I often like to top this salad with chopped fresh herbs (such as basil), thinly sliced red onion, and micro greens.

broccoli and bacon salad

Every once in a while I get a hankering for that broccoli and bacon salad that is popular in certain supermarkets and cafés and at picnics. But it's usually a bit too heavy, rich, and sweet, and filled with unexpected surprises, like raisins. This is my lighter version, which probably means it's lower in calories, but I'm not one to count those—for me, it's all about flavor. **SERVES 4**

CREAMY DRESSING
1 tablespoon red wine vinegar

½ cup mayonnaise

1½ tablespoons sugar, or to taste

Pinch of salt

SALAD
1 head broccoli, cut into florets

8 slices bacon

1 small red onion, finely chopped

1 red bell pepper, finely chopped

1 To make the dressing: In a small bowl, combine the vinegar, mayonnaise, sugar, and salt and whisk with a fork to combine.

2 For the salad: In a saucepan of boiling water, blanch the broccoli for 1 minute. Drain and refresh under cold water. Drain well and set aside.

3 In a large cast-iron skillet, cook the bacon over medium-high heat until crispy. Drain on paper towels, then coarsely chop.

4 In a large bowl, combine the broccoli, bacon, onion, and bell pepper. Pour on the dressing and toss well to combine.

TIP: I like to leave the salad in the fridge for a day or two so the flavors can really develop.

pickled pepper and cabbage salad

This sweet and tangy salad used to be easy to buy premade in Pennsylvania Dutch country, but now, not so much. When I asked my knowledgeable PA Dutch source about it, she said: "Nobody makes it good anymore." Then I met another "Dutchy" named Craig Koller. He sent me his mother's recipe, which originated at the St. John's Lutheran Church in Kutztown. It's traditionally a very sweet salad; I cut a lot of sugar from the original recipe. **SERVES 14 TO 16**

2 heads cabbage, cored

2 tablespoons salt

1 large onion, finely chopped

1 head celery, finely chopped

2 green bell peppers, finely chopped

1 red bell pepper, finely chopped

TIP: This salad is best when you make it the day before serving, which lets all the flavors develop. It will keep refrigerated for several days.

1 Finely slice the cabbage on a mandoline, then finely chop by hand. Rinse and drain in a colander. Transfer the colander to a large bowl, add the salt, and let stand for 2 hours.

2 Drain any excess liquid from the bowl and transfer the cabbage to the bowl. Massage the cabbage for 1 to 2 minutes to tenderize. Add the onion, celery, and bell peppers and toss to combine.

FROM THE BLOG
"My grandmother made this for every fall/winter holiday, but just called it cabbage salad. Her recipe is essentially the same as yours, but she did not salt the cabbage—just grated it." **—BETTY**

DRESSING

3 cups distilled white vinegar

1½ cups water

3 cups sugar, or to taste

1 teaspoon celery seeds

1 teaspoon mustard powder

1 teaspoon freshly ground black pepper

3 To make the dressing: In a saucepan, combine the vinegar, water, and sugar and bring to a boil over medium heat. Stir until all the sugar is dissolved. Remove from the heat and set aside to cool completely.

4 Add the celery seeds, mustard, and pepper to the dressing and whisk to combine. Pour the dressing over the salad and toss well to combine.

The original experimental test gardens at my grandparents' farm

blt salad

I have a confession to make. This recipe is adapted from a salad I ate at a restaurant in Manhattan called Aretsky's Patroon. It's one of those swanky steakhouses generally full of men in suits and a few ladies (like me), and it has a solid menu and great service. When I tested the salad on my family, I knew it was a hit when my daughter exclaimed with utter joy: "It's a BLT!" There were no leftovers.

SERVES 4

8 slices bacon

4 slices stale bread, cut into cubes

Pinch of salt

2 tomatoes

1 head iceberg lettuce, leaves separated and coarsely torn

BLT DRESSING
1 tablespoon red wine vinegar

1 tablespoon mayonnaise

3 tablespoons extra virgin olive oil

1 In a large cast-iron skillet, cook the bacon over medium-high heat until crispy. Drain on paper towels and set aside. Pour off all but 2 tablespoons of bacon drippings from the pan.

2 In the same skillet, cook the bread cubes in the bacon drippings over medium heat, turning, until golden and crunchy. Sprinkle with the salt and set aside.

3 Chop 1½ of the tomatoes. Squeeze the seeds and juice from the remaining tomato half into a bowl and reserve for the dressing (discard the tomato flesh).

4 Divide the lettuce leaves and chopped tomatoes among 4 bowls. Crumble the bacon and divide among the bowls.

5 To make the dressing: To the bowl with the reserved tomato pulp, add the vinegar, mayonnaise, and oil and whisk to combine.

6 To serve, drizzle the dressing over the salads and top with the croutons.

salmon niçoise salad

This is a recipe I love to make in the summer when I'm entertaining because it looks fabulous on a big platter. I prefer to make it with salmon rather than the classic tuna, simply because I think salmon tastes better and wild-caught salmon is more sustainable than tuna (although I do love a good tuna sandwich now and then). **SERVES 4**

DIJON VINAIGRETTE
1 tablespoon white wine vinegar

3 tablespoons extra virgin olive oil

¼ teaspoon Dijon mustard

1 shallot, finely chopped

1 teaspoon finely grated lemon zest (optional)

Salt and freshly ground black pepper

SALAD
1 pound skin-on wild-caught salmon fillet, cut into 4 pieces

2 cups lettuce leaves

2 large potatoes, boiled and sliced

2 cups chopped green beans, blanched (see page 337)

2 large tomatoes, cut into wedges

4 large eggs, hard-boiled (see page 338) and quartered

½ cup niçoise olives

Leaves from 2 sprigs fresh thyme

1 To make the vinaigrette: In a small bowl, combine the vinegar, oil, mustard, shallot, lemon zest (if using), and salt and pepper to taste and whisk with a fork to combine.

2 For the salad: In a large skillet, cook the salmon, skin-side down, over high heat for 4 to 5 minutes, or until the skin is crispy. Turn and cook for another 1 minute or until browned and cooked to your liking.

3 While the salmon is cooking, arrange the lettuce leaves on a serving platter and layer with the potatoes, green beans, tomatoes, eggs, and olives.

4 Top the salad with the salmon, drizzle with the vinaigrette, and sprinkle with the thyme leaves.

quinoa, kale, and sunflower seed salad

I first discovered this recipe in Laurie David's book The Family Cooks, *which is a great cookbook. To me, this recipe is the epitome of "clean food" in that you just feel really healthy and light after eating it. As with most recipes, I tweaked it slightly to suit my family's tastes: I cut down the quantities, and omitted the dried fruit, which I just don't care for in a salad. Though feel free to personalize it, too.* **SERVES 4**

LEMON DRESSING

1 teaspoon finely grated lemon zest

3 tablespoons fresh lemon juice

3 tablespoons extra virgin olive oil

½ teaspoon salt

SALAD

½ cup red or white quinoa, rinsed

1 rib celery, chopped

1 carrot, chopped

3 lacinato (Tuscan) kale leaves, stems removed, leaves thinly sliced

¼ cup unsalted roasted sunflower seeds

¼ cup chopped fresh parsley leaves, Italian or curly

1 To make the dressing: In a small bowl, combine the lemon zest, lemon juice, oil, and salt and whisk with a fork to combine.

2 For the salad: Cook the quinoa according to package directions, making sure all the water is absorbed. Spread out on a baking sheet to cool.

3 In a bowl, combine the cooled quinoa, celery, carrot, kale, sunflower seeds, and parsley. Pour in the dressing and toss to coat.

TIP: Quinoa, which is a seed rather than a grain, comes in three colors: white, red, and black. The white variety has the mildest flavor and cooks quickest; red is slightly more chewy and needs a few minutes more cooking time, while black has the most robust flavor and texture and will need 5 minutes more cooking time.

no-mayo coleslaw

When it's party time and there's barbecue and grilled meats on the menu, then a slaw is a must. But I prefer one without mayonnaise; something about the vinegar in this recipe cuts through the smoky grease of any good barbecue. You can use regular, red, savoy, or napa cabbage, or for fun, a mixture thereof. **SERVES 10 TO 12**

DRESSING

½ cup apple cider vinegar

6 tablespoons sugar, or to taste

6 tablespoons vegetable oil

½ teaspoon celery seeds

½ teaspoon salt

SALAD

1 large head cabbage, cored and thinly sliced on a mandoline

1 red onion, thinly sliced on a mandoline

1 green bell pepper, thinly sliced on a mandoline

1 To make the dressing: In a small saucepan, combine the vinegar and sugar over medium heat and stir until the sugar has dissolved. Transfer to a bowl and mix in the oil, celery seeds, and salt. Set aside to cool.

2 In a large bowl, combine the cabbage, onion, and bell pepper. Pour the dressing over the cabbage mixture and toss to coat.

three-bean salad

Every once in a while I get a hankering for that old-fashioned three-bean salad that people always served at picnics when I was growing up. It's basically a quick-pickled bean salad, which only takes about 10 minutes to make. Although, like many things, it gets better with age—it tastes best when left in the fridge for a few hours or overnight to let the flavors develop. **SERVES 4**

½ pound fresh or frozen green beans

1 can (14 to 19 ounces) kidney beans, drained and rinsed

1 can (14 to 19 ounces) chickpeas, drained and rinsed

1 red onion, thinly sliced

1 red bell pepper, thinly sliced

SWEET-SOUR DRESSING

½ cup apple cider vinegar

⅓ cup extra virgin olive oil

⅓ cup sugar, or to taste

1 teaspoon salt

1 teaspoon freshly ground black pepper

1 In a medium saucepan of boiling water, cook the green beans for 3 to 4 minutes, until tender. Drain, refresh under cold water, drain well, and place in a bowl.

2 Add the kidney beans, chickpeas, onion, and bell pepper.

3 To make the dressing: In a small bowl, combine the vinegar, oil, sugar, salt, and black pepper and whisk with a fork until the sugar has dissolved. Pour over the salad and toss to combine.

TIP: You can also use other beans, like black beans, butter beans, or cannellini beans.

classic orange and fennel salad

This salad, a very traditional Italian dish, is easy, refreshing, and delicious. It takes about 5 minutes to prepare and is the perfect complement to a rich, wintry comfort meal. I make it with Cara Cara navel oranges, which have a beautiful jewel-like salmon color and fragrant flavor. They are in season during January and February, but you could use any type of orange. **SERVES 4**

2 oranges

1 large bulb fennel or 2 bulbs baby fennel, halved lengthwise

¼ cup extra virgin olive oil

Salt and freshly ground black pepper

Micro greens, for garnish (optional)

1 Using a sharp knife, cut away the rind from the oranges and slice crosswise into rounds. Arrange in a circle on individual salad plates or on one big serving plate.

2 Trim the tops and bottoms from the fennel, reserving the fronds. Cut out the woody end of the core and thinly slice crosswise on a mandoline.

3 Arrange the fennel slices over the orange, ensuring there are no seeds. Drizzle with the oil, season with salt and pepper, and top with the fennel fronds and, if you want to be fancy, some micro greens!

quinoa tabbouleh

The world has embraced hummus, but its traditional partner tabbouleh often gets overlooked. I love Middle Eastern food and a good tabbouleh is divine. However, I wanted to experiment by substituting the typical bulgur wheat with quinoa to make a gluten-free version. It worked! I made this with flat-leaf Italian parsley, but curly works just as well and is more classic. **SERVES 4 TO 6**

LEMON DRESSING

¼ cup fresh lemon juice

¼ cup extra virgin olive oil

¼ teaspoon garlic powder

SALAD

½ cup white quinoa, rinsed

1 cup diced tomatoes

4 cups chopped fresh Italian parsley leaves

5 scallions, chopped

2 tablespoons chopped fresh mint leaves

1 To make the dressing: In a small bowl, combine the lemon juice, oil, and garlic powder and whisk with a fork to combine.

2 For the salad: Cook the quinoa according to package directions, making sure all the water is absorbed. Set aside to cool.

3 In a large bowl, combine the quinoa, tomatoes, parsley, scallions, and mint. Pour in the dressing and toss well to combine.

heidi's salad

My older sister Heidi was the first one of us to go to California and come back with a new way of cooking and eating in the early '70s. This salad dressing, along with her signature salad, has become a family tradition, and it is so colorful that it reminds me of her paintings. I especially crave it with a good crispy, gooey serving of homemade mac and cheese (page 83). **SERVES 6 TO 8**

SOY DRESSING

2 teaspoons soy sauce or tamari

1 tablespoon fresh lemon juice

3 tablespoons extra virgin olive oil

1 small clove garlic, smashed

SALAD

4 cups torn romaine lettuce leaves

1 cup chopped green beans

½ cup sliced carrots

½ cup fresh or thawed frozen peas

1 cup finely sliced red cabbage

¼ cup chopped fresh dill leaves

1 To make the dressing: In a small bowl, combine the soy sauce, lemon juice, oil, and garlic and whisk with a fork to combine.

2 For the salad: In a large bowl, combine the lettuce, beans, carrots, peas, cabbage, and dill. Remove the garlic from the dressing and discard. Pour the dressing over the salad and toss to combine.

alice waters's salad dressing

It's not every day that Alice Waters comes to dinner. Oh, the pressure! One thing I do to relieve the pressure is get guests involved in the kitchen. And honestly, I was dying to see how Alice makes salad dressing, because salads are one of her specialties. I had some lovely freshly picked salad greens from my local farmer friend George DeVault, and I asked her if she could please make the dressing and we could all watch and learn. Here is her recipe. **SERVES 4**

DRESSING
Coarse sea salt

1 clove garlic

1 tablespoon red wine vinegar

3 tablespoons extra virgin olive oil

Freshly ground black pepper

1 large bowl salad greens

1 To make the dressing: Place a little salt in the bottom of a mortar, add the garlic and grind it with the pestle until creamy.

2 Add the vinegar and mix with a spoon. Add the oil and mix with a fork to combine.

3 Taste the dressing for balance—it shouldn't be too vinegary, salty, or oily. Add black pepper.

4 Drizzle the dressing one spoonful at a time over the greens and toss gently with your hands. Repeat this process until all the greens are lightly dressed and everything is perfectly delicious.

carrot and radish salad with blood orange vinaigrette

Around late December and early January, blood oranges start to come into season. They are delicious, nutritious, and a rare treat that make a salad sweet—but not too sweet. Sometimes I also add raw sliced rutabaga or turnips to this salad and perhaps some thinly shaved Manchego or P'tit Basque cheese. **SERVES 4 TO 6**

BLOOD ORANGE VINAIGRETTE

1 tablespoon fresh blood orange or orange juice

1 tablespoon red wine vinegar

¼ cup extra virgin olive oil

Salt

SALAD

1 head lettuce, leaves torn

2 carrots, thinly sliced on a mandoline

3 radishes, thinly sliced on a mandoline

½ blood orange, peeled and sliced

3 tablespoons slivered almonds, toasted

1 To make the blood orange vinaigrette: In a small bowl, combine the juice, vinegar, oil, and salt to taste and whisk with a fork to combine.

2 For the salad: In a large bowl, combine the lettuce, carrots, radishes, orange slices, and almonds. Pour over the vinaigrette and toss gently to combine.

carrot, feta, and almond salad

You know those times when your fridge is either empty or pathetically filled with shriveled produce? (Yes, even my fridge can look like that!) Usually, all that's left standing at that point are the carrots. Especially in the dead of winter. That's exactly when you should make carrot salad. **SERVES 4**

HERB DRESSING

1 tablespoon apple cider vinegar

3 tablespoons extra virgin olive oil

1 tablespoon chopped fresh Italian or curly parsley leaves

1 tablespoon chopped fresh mint leaves

1 tablespoon chopped fresh dill leaves

Salt and freshly ground black pepper

SALAD

6 to 8 large carrots, shredded or grated

¼ cup crumbled feta cheese

⅓ cup sliced almonds, toasted

1 To make the dressing: In a small bowl, combine the vinegar, oil, herbs, and salt and pepper to taste and mix with a fork to combine.

2 For the salad: Place the carrots in a large bowl, pour over the dressing, and toss to combine. Before serving, sprinkle the salad with the feta and almonds.

TIP: If I make this in the warmer months, I like using a mixture of fresh herbs straight from the garden, but you can use all mint or all cilantro—whatever is your favorite and in season. It's also fun to use purple heirloom carrots for color, as you can see in the photo we did on set!

pomegranate salad

My nephew had a Spanish girlfriend once, and she made a salad similar to this one for Christmas. November and December are the perfect time of year for pomegranates, when they are ripe and juicy. This lovely girlfriend made the salad with escarole, a mildly bitter variety of endive lettuce, but I've prepared it with a mixture of iceberg lettuce and homegrown micro greens because organic escarole can be hard to find. The colors make it a lovely festive salad. **SERVES 4**

SHERRY GARLIC VINAIGRETTE

1 tablespoon sherry vinegar

¼ cup extra virgin olive oil

1 small clove garlic, smashed

Salt

SALAD

1 pomegranate

1 head escarole, butter, or iceberg lettuce, leaves torn

2 cups micro greens or baby salad greens

1 To make the dressing: In a small bowl, combine the vinegar, oil, garlic, and salt to taste and whisk with a fork to combine. Discard the garlic before serving.

2 For the salad: Roll the pomegranate on your kitchen counter to help loosen the seeds inside. Cut into quarters and gently pull the seeds from the fruit, discarding any white membrane. (I do this over a bowl as it can get a little messy with the vibrant juice!)

3 Place the lettuce leaves and greens in a bowl, top with the pomegranate seeds, drizzle with the dressing, and toss to combine.

TIP: I've been known to roast some confit duck legs and shred the meat into this salad. It's super good.

chilled italian seafood salad

When I was married to an Italian, there was no getting around the Christmas Eve feast of the seven fishes dinner. It was always a struggle to get to seven fishes, but one way to do it was to make a seafood salad. Let's just say the marriage didn't stick, but the salad did. It's still a highly requested holiday treat in our house and is utterly simple, but therein lies its deliciousness. **SERVES 6 TO 8**

LEMON-PARSLEY VINAIGRETTE

1 tablespoon sherry vinegar

¼ cup extra virgin olive oil

½ tablespoon grated lemon zest

2 tablespoons fresh lemon juice

Leaves from a few sprigs fresh Italian parsley, finely chopped

SALAD

½ pound squid, with tentacles, cleaned

1 pound raw wild-caught shrimp, peeled and deveined

½ pound frozen cooked lobster meat, thawed and coarsely chopped

Lemon slices, for serving

1 To make the vinaigrette: In a small bowl, combine the vinegar, oil, lemon zest, lemon juice, and parsley and whisk with a fork to combine.

2 For the salad: In a saucepan of boiling water, cook the squid and shrimp for 3 to 5 minutes, until just cooked. Drain and put on a bed of ice immediately to stop the cooking process.

3 Place the seafood in a bowl, pour over the dressing, and toss to combine. Refrigerate for 3 to 4 hours to chill. Serve with lemon slices.

TIP: You can buy cleaned squid and shrimp from your fishmonger, if you prefer.

beet, citrus, and crispy goat cheese salad

Beets seem to be one of those polarizing vegetables that people either love or hate. I love them. My kids hate them. So this is a salad I make when I don't quite care what they think or when I'm entertaining. You can also make this with raw beets thinly sliced on a mandoline. **SERVES 4**

RED WINE VINAIGRETTE

1 tablespoon red wine vinegar

3 tablespoons extra virgin olive oil

1 small shallot, finely chopped

Salt

SALAD

3 red or golden beets

1 orange, peeled and thinly sliced into rounds

¼ cup walnuts, toasted (see page 339)

1 log (4 ounces) goat cheese, chilled

½ cup coarse dried breadcrumbs (see page 338)

1 cup micro greens or baby salad greens

1. To make the vinaigrette: In a small bowl, combine the vinegar, oil, shallot, and salt in a small bowl and whisk with a fork to combine.

2. For the salad: Preheat the oven to 375°F. Wrap the beets in foil and roast for 1 hour or until tender. Remove from the oven and cool slightly.

3. Peel the beets (the outer layers should slip straight off) and slice into rounds.

4. Layer the orange and beet slices onto a serving platter. Sprinkle with the walnuts and set aside.

5. Preheat the broiler to high. Slice the goat cheese into 4 rounds, and gently press into the breadcrumbs. Place in a lightly oiled baking dish. Broil for 5 minutes, or until golden and slightly molten.

6. To serve, pour the dressing over the salad, sprinkle with the micro greens, and top with the warm goat cheese.

Noodle
Love

Oh gluten, it's been a rough few years, hasn't it? You're the poster child for the inherent problem we have with food—we love to demonize something. Fat. Sugar. Salt. Gluten. But wait, isn't pasta an essential part of the Mediterranean diet? And don't people who eat the Mediterranean diet live a longer life than the rest of us? So it can't be that bad for us, in moderation. This chapter embraces the noodle (or pasta, if you prefer) in full glory. Skip it if you want to. Substitute if you must. But always, always eat organic.

Why is organic so important when it comes to wheat, which is what most pasta is made from? There is growing evidence that it's not the wheat itself that people are becoming sensitive to, but the combination of overhybridization and overuse of chemicals in its production. Because wheat is such an important part of the diet in many cultures, a lot of effort has been put into increasing productivity by creating "super wheat," which may be less digestible than our native originals. It is also common practice to spray wheat with glyphosate right before harvest in order to increase yield and make the wheat easier for the farmer to harvest. Unfortunately, easier for the farmer doesn't necessarily mean easier for your body to digest.

But enough about the yucky stuff, noodles are all about the yummy stuff. Just make sure they are organic, eat them in moderation, live like a Mediterranean (which also means walking a lot and enjoying life), and you'll be fine! You can use plain or whole wheat pasta in these recipes. If you must, you can substitute gluten-free pasta, but make sure you adjust the cooking time as it tends to cook faster than conventional pasta.

spätzle

Spätzle are a type of German pasta. Meaning "little sparrows," they're small egg-based noodles or dumplings that are served to soak up gravy, butter, or sauce. Spätzle, like most comfort foods, aren't hard to make at all. I cook mine using a spätzle maker, but according to my blog readers, you can also use a colander or a cheese grater to form the nuggety shapes. **SERVES 4**

4 large eggs

¾ cup whole milk

2 tablespoons extra virgin olive oil

2 cups all-purpose flour

½ teaspoon salt

1 tablespoon butter

Chopped fresh Italian parsley leaves, for serving

1 In a large bowl, combine the eggs, milk, oil, flour, and salt and whisk to combine. Allow the mixture to rest for 30 minutes (this will make for a smoother dough).

2 Bring a large saucepan of water to a boil over high heat. Working in batches, ladle a little of the dough into the spätzle maker, "grate" it into the water and cook for a few minutes or until the noodles rise to the top.

3 Remove the spätzle from the pan with a slotted spoon and drain in a colander. Repeat with the remaining dough.

4 Toss the spätzle with the butter and serve immediately with any dish or stew that has a good amount of gravy. Alternatively, melt the butter in a large cast-iron skillet over medium-high heat, add the spätzle, and cook for 2 to 3 minutes, until the edges start to brown and go crispy. Serve sprinkled with the parsley.

homemade pasta

Making pasta from scratch may seem hard, but it's not. Here's a great story to show you why. My kids and I were sitting on the couch wondering what to eat. We decided on soup. "I wish we had some plain pasta to put in it," I said. "I'll make some," said my daughter Eve, age 17. "I'll help!" said Lucia, age 8. Fifteen minutes later, we had homemade pasta. And fifteen minutes after that, my wish came true. Here is Eve's recipe, which she learned in Italy. **SERVES 2**

¾ cup all-purpose flour

1 large egg

1 Pour the flour onto a clean work surface and create a well in the center.

2 Add the egg to the well and using a fork, slowly and gradually combine the flour with the egg, starting at the inner edge of the well.

3 When the mixture is dry enough to knead, use your hands to bring it together and start kneading. Knead for about 5 minutes—the dough should feel a little elastic.

4 Flatten the dough and feed through a pasta machine at the thickest setting. Repeat 7 times, using a thinner setting each time.

5 Cut or slice the shapes you prefer from the pasta, using a knife or the setting on your pasta machine.

6 Cook in a large saucepan of boiling water for 1 to 2 minutes, until al dente. Drain and serve.

TIP: To increase the quantity of pasta, simply multiply the flour and egg. If using whole wheat flour, only use ½ cup of whole wheat flour to 1 egg.

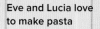

Eve and Lucia love
to make pasta

A manual pasta
roller is helpful

Cook fresh or
cook dry later

Choose your own shapes!
The recipe is the same.

basic tomato sauce

If there is one thing to make from scratch and have on hand all winter long, it's homemade tomato sauce. Over the years I've tried everything and this is my final verdict: Taking off the skins and removing the seeds makes the sauce too sweet and it's not worth the effort. Putting in the whole tomato makes the sauce too watery. Using the whole tomato, but squeezing out some of the juice, makes it just right.

MAKES 1 QUART

5 pounds tomatoes

1 clove garlic, peeled

1 teaspoon salt

Leaves from 1 sprig fresh basil

1 tablespoon extra virgin olive oil

TIPS: This basic recipe can be used as a base to make other sauces. I like to add a little butter and serve with pasta and Romano cheese. The best way to maximize your efforts is to quadruple this recipe and make a big batch. If you don't grow your own organic tomatoes, head to the farmers' market in late August and buy a big basketful. You won't regret it.

1 Cut out any brown spots from the tomatoes, core, halve through the equator, and gently squeeze the juice from the tomatoes. (Don't squeeze too hard; you still want a bit of juice in there.)

2 Working in batches, place the tomatoes in a food processor or blender with the garlic, salt, and basil and process to combine. If you prefer a chunky tomato sauce, simply cut the tomatoes into quarters and roughly mash with a potato masher.

3 In a large saucepan, heat the oil over medium heat. Add the tomato pulp, stir, and reduce the heat to low. Simmer, stirring occasionally, for 2 hours, until the sauce has reached your desired consistency.

4 Pour the hot sauce into wide-mouthed glass jars, leaving 1 inch of space at the top for the sauce to expand. Let the jars cool before you put them in the freezer to freeze for up to 10 months (be sure to label and date them!).

marinara sauce

This is a fresher and quicker pasta sauce than the basic sauce on page 77, but it still freezes well. It's best made with fresh, not canned, tomatoes. If you're serving it with pasta, add the pasta to the marinara sauce in the pan, toss to combine, and let it sit for a few minutes to maximize the flavor. If you like your sauce a little spicy, feel free to add a pinch of cayenne pepper. **MAKES 1 QUART**

¼ cup extra virgin olive oil

8 cloves garlic, finely chopped

5 pounds tomatoes, chopped

¼ cup chopped fresh basil leaves

1 teaspoon salt

1 In a large soup pot heat the oil over medium-low heat. Add the garlic and sauté gently for 2 minutes until soft.

2 Add the tomatoes, bring to a simmer, then reduce the heat to low and cook for 30 to 45 minutes.

3 Add the basil and salt and stir to combine. Use immediately or pour the hot sauce into wide-mouthed glass jars, leaving 1 inch of space at the top for the sauce to expand, and refrigerate or freeze.

TIP: This is quite a juicy sauce. You can simmer it for longer to thicken, if desired, about another 30 minutes.

baked ziti

No good Italian event would be complete without a big vat of ziti. The Italians are experts at making delicious, easy food that doesn't break the bank, and ziti is at the top of that list. Serve with a simple salad with Italian dressing, and you've got a delicious and affordable meal your whole family will love. **SERVES 6**

1 pound ziti pasta

3 cups tomato sauce, store-bought or homemade (page 77)

8 ounces low-moisture mozzarella cheese, shredded

8 ounces fresh mozzarella cheese, sliced

⅓ cup grated Romano cheese

1 Preheat the oven to 375°F.

2 Cook the pasta according to package directions. Drain and transfer to a 12 × 8-inch baking dish.

3 Add the tomato sauce and two-thirds of the grated mozzarella to the pasta and mix to combine. Top with the remaining grated mozzarella as well as the slices of fresh mozzarella and sprinkle with the Romano. Bake for 30 minutes, or until golden and bubbling.

TIP: You can sneak in some vegetables if you want, such as chopped spinach, peas, or mushrooms. You can also add ricotta cheese. You can even add cooked ground beef or sausage, which makes it taste like lasagna, but a heck of a lot easier to make! Double this for a party.

manicotti from heaven

On one of the first trips to visit my future in-laws, Rita Cinquino served manicotti. I had never, ever tasted anything so good before. And as much as I loved Lou back then, I have to say the manicotti might have sealed the deal. It's a bit of an effort to make, but so worth it. The secret is that the manicotti shell is made like a crêpe. This is my godson Geoffrey's favorite meal. **SERVES 4 TO 6**

CRÊPES

1 cup water

4 large eggs

1 cup all-purpose flour

Pinch of salt

Extra virgin olive oil, for the skillet

FILLING

1 pound ricotta cheese

⅓ cup grated Romano cheese

1 large egg

Leaves from 2 sprigs fresh Italian parsley, chopped

Salt and freshly ground black pepper

Basic Tomato Sauce (page 77)

1 Preheat the oven to 350°F.

2 To make the crêpes: In a bowl, whisk together the water and eggs. Add the flour and salt and whisk to combine.

3 Lightly oil an 8-inch skillet and heat over medium heat. Ladle in just enough batter to lightly cover the bottom of the pan. Cook for 1 minute each side or until golden. Repeat; you should get about 10 crêpes. Stack them on a plate and set aside (they won't stick together).

4 To make the filling: In a bowl, mix together the cheeses, egg, parsley, and salt and pepper to taste.

5 To assemble the manicotti, spread 3 tablespoons of the filling into the center of each crêpe and roll up to enclose (like a cigar).

6 Spoon half the tomato sauce into the bottom of a 13 × 9-inch baking dish. Top with the filled manicotti and spoon over the remaining sauce. Bake for 30 minutes, or until bubbling.

slow 'n' crispy mac 'n' cheese

This is how my mom made mac 'n' cheese. It works really well as a big party dish as well as a weeknight dinner. My favorite part is the crispy topping. You can leave out the pine nuts if you prefer. **SERVES 6**

1 pound elbow or rotini pasta

8 ounces cheddar cheese, shredded

4 ounces Colby cheese, shredded

1 cup whole milk

3 tablespoons butter

Salt

CRISPY TOPPING
½ cup coarse dried breadcrumbs (see page 338)

3 tablespoons extra virgin olive oil or melted butter

¼ cup pine nuts (optional)

1 Preheat the oven to 350°F.

2 Cook the pasta according to package directions. Drain and return to the pot.

3 Add the cheeses, milk, butter, and salt to taste to the pasta and stir until the cheese is melted and everything is combined. Spread the mixture in a 12 × 8-inch baking dish.

4 To make the crispy topping: In a small bowl, mix to combine the breadcrumbs, oil, and pine nuts (if using). Sprinkle the breadcrumb mixture over the pasta. Transfer to the oven, and bake for 40 minutes, or until golden and bubbling.

quick 'n' gooey mac 'n' cheese

For years I made the longer, baked version of mac 'n' cheese (page 83). But, finally, half my family confessed that they liked this speedy version better. The other half, including me, still prefer the longer, crispier version, so I am giving you both recipes so that you can decide. This is great for weeknight dinners when you need something fast, filling, and delicious. **SERVES 6**

1 pound elbow or rotini pasta

8 ounces cheddar cheese, shredded

4 ounces Colby cheese, shredded

1 cup whole milk

3 tablespoons butter

Salt

1 Cook the pasta according to package directions. Drain and return to the pot.

2 Add the cheeses, milk, butter, and salt to taste and mix until the cheese and butter have melted.

TIP: You can stir in some peas, chopped baby spinach leaves or kale, sautéed mushrooms, or chopped cooked ham if desired.

spaghetti with eggs

This is a classic Cinquino family recipe that I would never have believed tasted good until I tried it. Now we fight over the eggs, so I've added more than usual to this recipe so there are plenty. Adding a whole onion to the cooking sauce is a technique I pinched from famous Italian cookery writer, Marcella Hazan. It adds so much flavor, but you remove the onion before you serve the sauce. **SERVES 4**

3 cups tomato sauce, store-bought or homemade (page 77)

4 tablespoons (½ stick) butter

1 medium onion, peeled but left whole

6 large eggs, hard-boiled (see page 338), peeled

1 pound spaghetti

Grated Romano cheese, for serving

1 In a deep, medium saucepan, heat the sauce over low heat until warmed through. Add the butter and the whole onion and stir to melt and combine the butter.

2 Add the eggs and continue to cook gently over low heat while you cook the pasta.

3 Cook the pasta according to package directions. Drain and divide among 4 serving bowls.

4 Discard the onion and divide the sauce among the bowls, adding eggs to each. Pass grated Romano at the table.

abruzzi fish stew

When I first met Louie Cinquino, whose parents were from Abruzzi, Italy, all he could talk about was the region's famous fish stew. (Although he had never eaten it himself—it was a matter of legend.) So when we went to Abruzzi to visit relatives, we had to have the fish stew. It was incredible. What I now know, many years later, is that I will never be able to exactly replicate the taste—the fish were fresh from the Adriatic and the olive oil was freshly pressed—but I could come close. Use whatever fish is readily available to you. **SERVES 8**

2 pounds assorted fish and shellfish (such as snapper, cod, red mullet, clams, mussels, and shrimp)

4 large tomatoes, chopped

4 cloves garlic, chopped

⅓ cup extra virgin olive oil

⅓ cup chopped fresh Italian parsley leaves, plus extra for serving

Salt and freshly ground black pepper

1 pound spaghetti

1 Preheat the oven to 375°F.

2 To prepare the seafood, cut the fish into 2- to 3-inch pieces, scrub the clams and mussels, and peel and devein the shrimp.

3 In a heavy-bottomed 12-inch ovenproof skillet or Dutch oven (Italians traditionally use an earthenware dish), combine the tomatoes, garlic, oil, parsley, and salt and pepper to taste. Cover with a lid and bake the mixture for 10 minutes.

4 Season the fish with a little salt and pepper and gently place in the tomatoes. Cover and bake for another 10 minutes, or until the fish is opaque.

5 Scatter the shellfish over the top, cover, and continue to bake for 10 minutes, or until all the shells have opened and the shrimp is opaque.

6 While the seafood is baking, cook the spaghetti according to package directions. Drain.

7 Add the pasta to the pan with the seafood and mix gently to combine. Sprinkle with parsley and serve family style.

A Note about Italian Seafood and Cheese

Apparently there is a hot, never-ending debate about whether or not you are allowed to put cheese (such as Romano or Parmesan) on seafood dishes in Italy. After being married to an Italian for 20 years, I realized that for the Italians, the debate is the fun part. As a born-and-bred American mutt, I say break the rules and do whatever you want! I like cheese— Romano cheese.

no-cook summer tomato and mozzarella pasta

I call this my no-cook pasta because you don't have to cook the sauce. I made this up when my family and I were all starving and it was hot. I happened to have some fresh organic rigatoni pasta from my local farmers' market on hand and tried a fresher take on a conventional tomato-based sauce. Everyone loved it and it was so easy; it makes an excellent summer pasta dish. **SERVES 4 TO 6**

1 pound pasta, such as rigatoni

5 tablespoons extra virgin olive oil

1 or 2 cloves garlic, finely chopped

5 or 6 small tomatoes, chopped

8 ounces fresh mozzarella cheese, torn into small pieces

¼ cup chopped fresh basil leaves

¼ cup chopped fresh Italian parsley leaves

Freshly ground black pepper

Grated pecorino cheese, for serving

1 Cook the pasta according to package directions.

2 Meanwhile, in a large bowl, combine the oil, garlic, tomatoes, mozzarella, basil, and parsley and toss to combine.

3 Drain the pasta, add to the bowl, and toss to coat, adding more oil if necessary. Season with pepper to taste and pass grated pecorino at the table.

FROM THE BLOG
"Make the pasta out of zucchini or yellow squash spirals and it really could be a no-cook 'pasta.' Plan on trying it soon :)" —JOYCE

my dad's spaghetti sauce

My dad didn't make dinner very often, but when he did, this was his specialty. It's a Bolognese sauce, but we didn't call it that. His secret ingredient was maple syrup. He also used a bit of red wine, but since we're now an alcohol-free household we just skip that part; but feel free to add about ⅓ cup. You can also use sausage instead of beef.

SERVES 4

¼ cup extra virgin olive oil

1 white onion, chopped

1 green bell pepper, chopped (optional)

4 cloves garlic, chopped

1 pound ground beef

3 cups tomato sauce, store-bought or homemade (page 77)

1 can (6 ounces) tomato paste

1 tablespoon Italian seasoning

1 tablespoon maple syrup

Salt

1 pound spaghetti

Grated Romano cheese, for serving

1　In a large saucepan, heat the oil over medium-high heat. Add the onion and bell pepper (if using) and cook, stirring, for 5 to 6 minutes, until starting to brown and soften. Add the garlic and cook, stirring, for 1 minute, or until golden.

2　Add the ground beef and cook for 5 minutes, stirring, or until browned.

3　Add the tomato sauce and paste, Italian seasoning, maple syrup, and salt to taste and bring to a simmer. Cook for 20 minutes, or until thickened slightly.

4　While the sauce is simmering, cook the spaghetti according to package directions.

5　Drain the pasta and divide among 4 bowls. Spoon the sauce over the pasta and pass grated Romano at the table.

my garden pasta

This dish is more Greek-inspired than Italian. I invented it after getting home from a trip and finding nothing in the fridge, but everything in the garden. And it only took about 20 minutes to make—10 of those minutes just waiting for the water for the pasta to boil! If I'm making a grown-up version, I like to add red pepper flakes; you could add olives and capers, too. **SERVES 4**

1 pound fettuccine

2 tablespoons butter or extra virgin olive oil

10 small tomatoes, chopped

1 handful green beans, halved

Leaves from 2 sprigs fresh basil, chopped

¼ cup pine nuts, toasted (see page 339)

Salt and freshly ground black pepper

Grated Romano cheese, for serving

1 Cook the fettuccine according to package directions.

2 Meanwhile, in a large skillet, heat the butter or oil over medium heat. Add the tomatoes, beans, and basil and cook for 10 minutes, or until the beans are tender.

3 Add the pine nuts and salt and pepper to taste and stir to combine.

4 Drain the pasta, divide among 4 plates, and top with the sauce. Pass grated Romano at the table.

TIP: I used Rattlesnake pole beans and heirloom Romano beans.

lasagna

When I was younger, making lasagna felt like a rite of passage. I would make it for boyfriends to prove that I was suitable or worthy. Sad, right? Now I just make it because it tastes good. It's a bit of a process, but worth the work—especially for a large group because you can put it together in advance and cook it later, or even freeze it.

SERVES 6 TO 8

1 box (12 ounces) dried lasagna sheets

2 tablespoons extra virgin olive oil

3 cloves garlic, chopped

1 pound ground beef (or sausage or both)

6 cups tomato sauce, store-bought or homemade (page 77)

1 can (6 ounces) tomato paste

¼ cup chopped fresh basil leaves

¼ cup chopped fresh Italian parsley leaves

½ teaspoon dried oregano

15 ounces ricotta cheese

1 Preheat the oven to 350°F.

2 Cook the lasagna sheets according to package instructions, but just shy of al dente. Drain and set aside in a single layer on parchment paper.

3 In a large saucepan, heat the oil over medium-high heat. Add the garlic and cook, stirring, for 1 minute, or until golden. Add the meat and cook for 5 minutes, stirring, or until browned.

4 Add the tomato sauce, tomato paste, and herbs and stir to combine. Reduce the heat to low and simmer the sauce for 15 minutes to thicken.

5 Spoon one-quarter of the sauce into the bottom of a 13 × 9-inch baking dish or lasagna pan. Top with a single layer of pasta sheets, followed by one-third of the remaining sauce, ensuring the sheets are well covered. Layer with one-third each of the ricotta and shredded mozzarella.

8 ounces low-moisture part-skim mozzarella cheese, shredded

8 ounces fresh mozzarella cheese, sliced

½ cup grated Romano cheese

6 Top with another single layer of pasta sheets, half of the remaining sauce, and half each of the remaining ricotta and shredded mozzarella. Repeat for a final layer of pasta, sauce, and cheese (you will have 3 layers in total).

7 Top with the sliced fresh mozzarella and grated Romano. Bake for 45 minutes, or until golden and bubbling. Let rest in the pan for 15 minutes before serving.

yvon chouinard's pasta

A long time ago, I went to the home of Yvon Chouinard to write an article. He is the founder of the outdoor brand, Patagonia. He made me dinner—actually, we made it together, but it was his recipe and I just helped shell the edamame. This is a recipe from memory, but I've made it a few times since and it's yummy. **SERVES 6 TO 8**

1 pound thin spaghetti or angel hair pasta

4 medium tomatoes, chopped

½ small white onion, finely chopped

1 pound shelled edamame, steamed

⅓ cup extra virgin olive oil

Salt and freshly ground black pepper

1 Cook the pasta according to package directions.

2 Meanwhile, place the tomato, onion, and edamame in a large bowl.

3 Drain the pasta and add to the bowl with the oil and salt and pepper to taste and toss to combine. Divide among plates to serve.

asparagus and lemon cream pasta

This is a fresh and delicious pasta dish to make in the springtime when asparagus is in peak season. It's nice for entertaining or for a quick, luxurious, and easy vegetarian dinner. **SERVES 4**

1 pound linguine

2 tablespoons extra virgin olive oil

2 tablespoons butter

1 red onion, chopped

1 clove garlic, chopped

1 bunch asparagus, trimmed and cut into thirds

1 cup heavy (whipping) cream

1 lemon

Salt

Chopped fresh mint and Italian parsley leaves, for serving

Grated Romano cheese, for serving

1 Cook the linguine according to package directions.

2 Meanwhile, in a large skillet, heat the oil and butter over medium-low heat. Add the onion and garlic and cook for 4 to 5 minutes, until soft. Add the asparagus and stir to combine.

3 Add the cream, increase the heat to medium, and bring to a simmer, stirring occasionally.

4 Finely grate the lemon zest into the sauce, reserving the lemon. Drain the pasta and add to the skillet. Toss to combine and cook until just heated through. Remove from the heat.

5 Halve the lemon and squeeze the juice over the pasta. Serve sprinkled with salt, mint, and parsley. Pass grated Romano at the table.

clam linguine

There are two types of clam sauces: creamy and noncreamy (not counting the tomato-based sauce that I don't really care for). This one is creamy. This is a quick, delicious, and comforting clam sauce that just makes you feel good. **SERVES 4 TO 6**

1 pound linguine

2 tablespoons extra virgin olive oil

2 tablespoons butter

2 cloves garlic, chopped

1 pound chopped fresh clams

1 cup heavy (whipping) cream

½ cup grated Romano cheese

¼ cup chopped fresh Italian parsley leaves

Salt and freshly ground black pepper

1 Cook the linguine according to package directions.

2 Meanwhile, in a large skillet, heat the oil and butter over medium-high heat. Add the garlic and cook, stirring, for 1 minute, or until golden. Add the clams and cook, stirring, for 5 minutes.

3 Add the cream and ¼ cup of the Romano and heat until it just comes to a boil.

4 Drain the pasta and add to the skillet with the parsley and salt and pepper to taste and toss to combine. Divide among plates and pass the remaining grated Romano at the table.

TIP: If you like it spicy, simply add a little cayenne pepper to the sauce. If you've got kids who don't like things too spicy, just bring the cayenne pepper to the table and let everyone spice things up as much as they want.

my really green pesto pasta

I had been making pesto for 20 years and it was totally delicious. However, I was mystified why it often turned brown. I was determined to figure out how to make it stay vivid bright green on the plate. The answer astounded me, but it works every time—blanching the basil leaves. Yes, blanching! A quick dip in boiling water is all the leaves need. Who knew? **SERVES 6**

2 cups fresh basil leaves

1 pound pasta of your choice

3 tablespoons pine nuts, toasted (see page 339)

1 clove garlic, peeled

½ cup grated Romano cheese

½ cup extra virgin olive oil

1 tablespoon fresh lemon juice

½ teaspoon salt

1 Bring a large saucepan of water to a boil over high heat.

2 Place the basil leaves in a colander and submerge in the boiling water, stirring constantly, for 10 seconds.

3 Transfer the colander to a large bowl of iced water and stir to refresh the basil. Drain the basil on paper towels or a kitchen towel.

4 Cook the pasta according to package directions.

5 Meanwhile, in a blender or small food processor, combine the basil, pine nuts, garlic, Romano, oil, lemon juice, and salt and blend until smooth. If you don't have a blender, you can make this in a mortar and pestle, too.

6 Drain the pasta, return to the pan, and toss with the pesto.

TIP: For a creamy version, just add a little cream when tossing the pesto through the pasta.

spicy broccoli rabe and sausage pasta

If you're looking for a quick, totally satisfying meal, this is it. It's pretty versatile—I'll often serve it as a weeknight meal because it's easy, but it's also great for a casual dinner party. If you have diners who can't tolerate spice, serve the red pepper flakes separately.

SERVES 6

1 pound pasta of your choice

4 tablespoons extra virgin olive oil

1 pound sausages, cut into 1-inch pieces

2 cloves garlic, chopped

2 cups chopped broccoli rabe or regular broccoli florets

¼ cup chopped fresh Italian parsley leaves

Crushed red pepper flakes or hot chili oil

Salt and freshly ground black pepper

Grated Romano cheese, for serving

1 Cook the pasta according to package directions.

2 Meanwhile, in a large skillet, heat 2 tablespoons of the oil over medium-high heat. Add the sausage and cook, stirring, for 6 minutes, or until browned.

3 Add the garlic and broccoli rabe and cook, stirring, for 1 to 2 minutes.

4 Drain the pasta and add to the skillet with the remaining 2 tablespoons oil, the parsley, and pepper flakes, salt, and black pepper to taste. Toss to combine. Divide among serving plates. Pass grated Romano at the table.

TIP: Instead of slicing the sausage, you could also simply remove the casings and crumble the meat into the skillet.

haluski

Where I live in Pennsylvania, there is a large contingent of Eastern European immigrants, and one thing you see at almost every church festival is haluski—cabbage and noodles (not to be confused with its cousin halupki, which are stuffed cabbage rolls). This is totally delicious, even if you're not a cabbage fan. You can use regular, savoy, or napa cabbage—the latter two will require less cooking time.

SERVES 4 TO 6

1 stick (4 ounces) butter

1 large onion, chopped

1 head cabbage, cored and chopped

1 pound wide egg noodles (I use Kluski egg noodles)

Salt and freshly ground black pepper

1 In a large heavy-bottomed saucepan, melt the butter over medium-low heat. Add the onion and cook, stirring, for 10 minutes, or until softened but not browned.

2 Add the cabbage, cover, and cook, stirring occasionally, for 30 minutes, or until softened.

3 Meanwhile, cook the noodles according to package directions.

4 Drain the noodles, add to the pan along with salt and pepper to taste and toss to combine. Divide among plates to serve.

TIP: You can serve this as a simple main dish (it's very easy to upsize for a potluck party) or as a side dish with meats.

squid ink and seafood pasta

Squid ink pasta is black pasta that looks scary, but unless you've tried it, you won't appreciate its subtle deliciousness. It's perfect for pairing with seafood, given that its inky color comes from the sea itself. It has a lovely depth of flavor. If you like, you could add a few roughly chopped fresh tomatoes during the last few minutes of cooking time. **SERVES 4**

1 pound squid ink pasta

3 tablespoons butter

2 cloves garlic, finely chopped

½ pound squid, with tentacles, cleaned and chopped

½ pound shrimp, peeled and deveined

½ pound cooked lobster meat, coarsely chopped

3 tablespoons extra virgin olive oil, for serving

¼ cup chopped fresh Italian parsley leaves

Salt and freshly ground black pepper

⅓ cup grated Romano cheese

1 Cook the pasta according to package directions.

2 Meanwhile, in a large skillet, melt the butter over medium-high heat and cook until golden. Add the garlic and cook, stirring, for 1 minute, or until golden.

3 Add the squid, shrimp, and lobster all at once and cook, stirring, for 2 to 3 minutes, until just cooked.

4 Drain the pasta and add to the skillet. Drizzle with the oil, sprinkle with the parsley and salt and pepper to taste, and toss to combine. Divide among serving plates and pass grated Romano at the table.

TIP: You can buy cleaned fresh or frozen squid from your fishmonger. Fresh will always taste best.

brown butter and egg noodles

This is more of a side dish, but a classic one that my mother made and often served with pork chops. The browned butter adds a whole different, richer flavor to the noodles. You can cook this dish with any type of pasta, but I like the flavor of egg noodles. **SERVES 6 AS A SIDE**

12 ounces wide egg noodles

5 tablespoons butter

Salt

1 Cook the noodles according to package directions.

2 Meanwhile, in a small skillet, melt the butter over medium-high heat and cook for about 2 minutes, or until golden and browned.

3 Drain the noodles and return to the saucepan. Pour the browned butter over the noodles, sprinkle with salt to taste, and toss to combine.

sausage, pepper, and gravy pasta

Where do recipes come from? From necessity, distant memories, and problem solving, mostly. This one came from the fact that my littlest one won't eat hamburger, but loves sausage. And I had some fresh pasta and a green pepper from my late-summer garden. It tasted remarkably similar to a dish I order from my local Chinese restaurant's secret menu—without the spice! **SERVES 4 TO 6**

1 pound pappardelle or tagliatelle pasta

1 pound sweet or hot Italian sausage, loose or casings removed

1 green bell pepper, chopped

⅓ cup all-purpose flour

2 cups water

Salt and freshly ground black pepper

Grated Romano cheese, for serving

1 Cook the pasta according to package directions.

2 Meanwhile, in a medium cast-iron skillet, fry the sausage meat over medium-high heat, breaking up the meat with a spoon, for about 4 minutes, or until just browned and cooked through.

3 Add the bell pepper and cook, stirring, for 4 minutes, or until slightly browned and softened.

4 In a small bowl, whisk together the flour and water. Add the mixture to the skillet and cook for 2 minutes, or until thickened. Sprinkle with salt and pepper to taste and mix to combine.

5 Drain the pasta and divide among serving plates. Top with the sausage and gravy and pass grated Romano at the table.

chilled peanut noodles

I'm not a huge fan of peanut butter. But every once in a while I get a craving. And in the summer, it's nice to eat a cold, savory, and satisfying dish. I think this recipe originally came from the Moosewood Cookbook. I have an old Xerox of the recipe in my recipe notebook, covered in sticky stuff. But I've made a few alterations. For example, I don't include the sprouts from the original recipe. **SERVES 6**

1 pound soba noodles or whole wheat spaghetti

⅓ cup smooth peanut butter

2 tablespoons hot water

3 tablespoons soy sauce

2 tablespoons rice vinegar

1 tablespoon toasted sesame oil

1 tablespoon hot chili oil (optional)

1 cucumber, halved lengthwise and sliced into half-moons

Black or white sesame seeds, for garnish

Chopped fresh cilantro leaves and scallions, for garnish

Lime wedges, for serving

1 Cook the noodles according to package directions. Drain, rinse under cold water, and transfer to a large bowl. Set aside.

2 In a bowl, whisk together the peanut butter, hot water, soy sauce, vinegar, sesame oil, and chili oil (if using).

3 Add the sauce to the noodles and toss to coat. Add the cucumber and toss to combine.

4 Refrigerate the noodles for 2 hours to chill. Toss before serving, adding more peanut butter thinned with warm water if the noodles seem dry. Garnish with sesame seeds, cilantro, and scallions. Serve with lime wedges.

Super
Soups &
S'wiches

If there is one lesson I've learned from making soups, it's that simple is almost always better. In fact, soup is one of the easiest and quickest things you can make to fill a hungry tummy. It's also one of those things that you can make in bulk and freeze, especially the stock, the foundation of any good soup.

I have a pretty firm opinion on homemade stock. When I was younger, I wanted to make chicken soup just like my grandmother's. I read the best cookbooks at the time and they would list 15 or 20 ingredients just for the stock alone, including herbs, carrots, celery, onions, and spices. But it never tasted right. It would be too sweet or just not brothy enough. And then I figured it out: meat and bones, water and salt. That's all you need. And it's the same whether it's chicken, goose, beef, or lamb. Meat and bones, water and salt. Oh, and it's good if there is a bit of fat on the meat. Fat gives flavor. (Fat also feeds the brain, says my doctor.)

Now among the trendsetters, this is called bone broth, but the truth is, this is the way it's been done forever. That doesn't mean you can't put other stuff in it. Just wait and put it in at the end. That's how it goes from stock to soup!

We are a soup-loving family. Every one of my kids could eat soup for every meal including breakfast, lunch, dinner, and snacks. The recipes in this chapter aren't fancy or glamorous, but they are the soups that have fed the hungry growing hearts and souls of my family forever. These soups keep us healthy, nourished, loved, and deeply connected to our heritage.

At the end of this chapter, you will find the soup's natural partner, the sandwich. You don't have to eat them together. There's no denying that a good sandwich is practical, quick, and easy. And always hits the spot. You know that spot—the one that's starving and needs something fast and tasty before you get hangry. I only eat these in moderation, but they are the collection of ones that hit the spot.

homemade chicken stock

Homemade stock embodies my whole food philosophy, which is that the absolute best things are totally simple and real. I have a freezer stash of stock so that I can always make a healing soup for anyone who's not feeling well, flavor recipes that call for stock, or just make tasty soup for dinner. This recipe works for other birds, as well as beef and ham bones. Your chicken can be raw, or the carcass of a previously roasted chicken, including rotisserie chicken from the store. **MAKES ABOUT 3 QUARTS**

1 whole chicken

Salt

1 Place the chicken in a large soup pot. Fill the pot with cold water until the chicken is completely covered.

2 Bring to a boil over high heat, reduce the heat to low, and skim any foam from the surface and discard. Simmer for at least 2 hours, until the meat is falling off the bones, or up to 4 hours for a richer stock. Remove from the heat and let cool slightly.

3 Strain the stock into another large pot and add salt to taste. Pick the meat from the bones, discarding the bones and skin. At this stage, you can use the meat in a soup or refrigerate for sandwiches and salads.

4 To freeze, ladle the stock into freezer containers or jars, leaving an inch or two at the top for the stock to expand. Stock will hold for up to 3 months. (Don't forget to label it!).

mom's chicken noodle soup

This is my mother's traditional recipe, which is simple and delicious. If I'm feeling particularly lazy, I just have the plain stock with a little shredded chicken and egg noodles in it. **SERVES 4**

1 tablespoon extra virgin olive oil

1 cup chopped onion

½ cup chopped celery

½ cup chopped carrot

Salt

6 cups chicken stock, store-bought or homemade (page 111)

1½ cups egg noodles

1½ cups shredded cooked chicken

¼ cup chopped fresh Italian parsley leaves

Freshly ground black pepper

1 In a large soup pot, heat the oil over medium heat. Add the onion, celery, carrot, and a pinch of salt. Cook, stirring, for 8 minutes, until the vegetables are softened.

2 Add the stock and bring to a boil. Reduce to a simmer, partially cover, and cook for about 20 minutes.

3 Meanwhile, cook the noodles according to package directions. Drain.

4 Add the chicken and noodles to the soup and cook for 5 minutes to warm through. Stir in the parsley and season with salt and pepper to taste. Ladle into bowls to serve.

healing chicken broth

If someone in my family isn't feeling well or coming down with a head cold, I make this simple healing broth for them to drink straight from a mug. This is precisely why it's handy to keep some homemade stock on hand in the freezer. **SERVES 4**

4 cups chicken stock, store-bought or homemade (page 111)

2 tablespoons grated fresh ginger

2 cloves garlic, finely chopped

1 dried or fresh cayenne pepper (optional)

Extra virgin olive oil, for frying (optional)

1 In a medium saucepan, bring the stock to a boil over high heat.

2 Add the ginger and garlic, reduce the heat to medium, and simmer for a few minutes.

3 If using the cayenne pepper, fry it in a little oil in a small skillet over high heat until golden and blistered. Add it to the broth and allow the pepper to infuse until the desired spiciness is reached. Ladle the broth into mugs to serve.

ham, green bean, and potato soup

When I'd visit Grandma Harter as a kid, she only ever served two things. For lunch, it was a grilled cheese with a pickle on the side and tea in a golden teacup, which always made me feel very special. For dinner, it was Pennsylvania Dutch ham, green bean, and potato soup. This is what I cooked for Alice Waters when she came to dinner. She drank the broth straight from the bowl! If you want a meatier soup, you can use two ham hocks. The hocks can be salty, so you may not need to add extra salt. Serve with crusty bread and butter. **SERVES 4**

1 smoked ham hock or shank, about 2 pounds

6 potatoes, cut into small cubes

3 cups chopped green beans

Salt and freshly ground pepper

1 Place the hock in a large soup pot and fill with enough water to fully submerge the hock. Bring to a boil, reduce the heat to low, and simmer for at least 2 hours, until the meat is falling off the bone, or up to 6 hours. Add more water during the cooking time, if necessary.

2 Remove the hock from the broth and set aside to cool slightly. Shred the meat, discarding any fat and the bone.

3 Return the meat to the broth with the potatoes and beans and simmer for 20 minutes, or until the vegetables are tender. Season with salt and pepper to taste.

FROM THE BLOG
"This is also a favorite childhood recipe of mine. Guess my mom was a rebel—she used yellow wax beans!" **—PAT**

Lucia picking purple potatoes

sausage, potato, and cabbage soup

This is a very simple, easy, healthy, and wholesome soup that's great for lunch, dinner, or even breakfast! (My kids are big on eating soup for breakfast.) The soup takes about 30 minutes to make and won't last long. **SERVES 4**

1 tablespoon extra virgin olive oil

1 pound sausages, casings removed

6 large potatoes, cut into cubes

1 head savoy or napa cabbage, cored and sliced

Salt

8 cups water or chicken stock, store-bought or homemade (page 111)

Grated Romano cheese, for serving

1 In a large soup pot, heat the oil over medium-high heat. Crumble the sausage meat into the pot and cook, stirring, for 5 minutes, until well browned.

2 Add the potatoes and cook, stirring, for 2 to 3 minutes. Add the cabbage and a pinch of salt and stir to combine.

3 Add the water or stock and simmer for 20 minutes, or until the potatoes are tender and cooked through. Season with salt to taste, ladle into bowls, and pass grated Romano at the table.

vegetable and elk soup

I am lucky to have a few hunter friends who sometimes bring me elk. Elk doesn't taste gamey at all and actually has quite a mild flavor. It's delicious in this soup. If you can't get elk, you can substitute other ground meat such as beef or bison. **SERVES 4 TO 6**

⅓ cup extra virgin olive oil

1 pound ground elk

1 onion, chopped

4 carrots, chopped

4 ribs celery, chopped

Kernels from 2 ears corn

⅓ cup fresh or frozen peas

2 tomatoes, chopped

6 medium Yukon Gold potatoes, chopped

2 tablespoons unsalted butter

8 cups water

Salt and freshly ground black pepper

Leaves from a few sprigs fresh herbs, for serving

1 In a large soup pot, heat the oil over medium-high heat. Add the meat and cook, stirring, until well browned, about 5 minutes.

2 Add the onion, carrots, celery, corn, peas, tomatoes, and potatoes and stir to combine. Add the butter and cook for 3 to 4 minutes.

3 Add the water or stock and salt and pepper to taste. Reduce the heat to low and simmer for 30 minutes, or until the vegetables are tender. Ladle into bowls and serve sprinkled with the herbs.

clean-out-the-fridge minestrone soup

It's amazing how you can pull a tasty soup together from stuff you might otherwise throw out. Any vegetable, root, or leafy thing that's on the verge can go in. You don't need meat. You don't need bouillon cubes. All you need is an assortment of food, some stock, and a pot.

SERVES 8

2 tablespoons extra virgin olive oil

1 large onion or leek, chopped

1 cup chopped carrot

1 cup chopped celery

3 cloves garlic, finely chopped

½ cup chopped turnip (optional)

½ cup chopped celeriac (optional)

1 cup chopped tomatoes

6 cups chicken stock, store-bought or homemade (page 111)

2 cups Basic Tomato Sauce (page 77)

8 ounces small pasta such as ditalini

1 can (14 to 19 ounces) white beans, drained and rinsed

Salt and freshly ground black pepper

Chopped fresh basil and/or Italian parsley leaves, for serving

Grated Romano cheese, for serving

1 In a large soup pot, heat the oil over medium-high heat. Add the onion, carrot, and celery and cook, stirring, for 5 minutes, or until softened. Add the garlic and cook, stirring, for 1 minute.

2 Add the turnip and celeriac, if using. Add the tomatoes, stock, and tomato sauce and stir to combine. Cover and simmer for 25 minutes, until the vegetables are tender.

3 Meanwhile, in a separate saucepan, cook the pasta according to package directions.

4 Drain the pasta and add to the soup along with the beans and salt and pepper to taste. Cook for 1 to 2 minutes to warm through. Ladle into bowls, sprinkle with the herbs, and pass grated Romano at the table.

tomato, chickpea, and rice soup

My yoga teacher, Holly, taught me how to make this soup, and it's delicious. She based it on a Marcella Hazan recipe she found online, but of course we modified and simplified it a bit. We made it on a cold winter's day, and it was the most heartwarming, soul-satisfying soup you can imagine. Don't worry about the amount of oil, it gives the soup a lovely richness. Feel free to add more stock if you prefer a thinner soup. **SERVES 4 TO 6**

½ cup extra virgin olive oil

4 cloves garlic, peeled

1 can (14 ounces) whole peeled tomatoes

Leaves from a few sprigs fresh rosemary, chopped

2 cans (14 ounces each) chickpeas, drained and rinsed

4 cups vegetable stock or chicken stock, store-bought or homemade (page 111)

Crushed red pepper flakes (optional)

Salt and freshly ground black pepper

1 cup Arborio rice

Grated Romano cheese, for serving

1 In a soup pot, heat the oil over medium heat. Add the whole cloves of garlic and cook, stirring, for 2 minutes, or until golden.

2 Carefully add the tomatoes and lightly mash them with a potato masher to break them down a little. Reduce the heat to low and simmer for 20 to 25 minutes.

3 Add the rosemary and chickpeas, increase the heat to medium, and cook for 1 to 2 minutes. Add 1 cup of the stock, the pepper flakes (if using), and salt and black pepper to taste. Cover and simmer for 15 minutes.

FROM THE BLOG
"This soup was awesome! I thought the olive oil might have been too much, but as there's no other fat in the recipe, it needed it for mouthfeel and richness. It was very flavorful because of the rosemary and garlic." **—JANICE**

4 Ladle two-thirds of the soup, including the garlic, into a blender and process until smooth.*

5 Return the puree to the pan with the remaining 3 cups stock and bring to a boil. Add the rice, reduce the heat to medium, and simmer for 20 to 25 minutes, until the rice is cooked. Divide among bowls and pass grated Romano at the table.

* This step is totally optional, but results in a lovely thick, smooth soup.

venison chili

I know some people have mixed feelings about hunting. But if you are going to eat meat, you might like to think about supporting your local hunters, given the smaller ecological footprint of wild game. I am fortunate to know some very kind hunters who share their meat with me. You can also make my chili with ground beef or bison. **SERVES 6 TO 8**

¼ cup extra virgin olive oil

2 pounds ground venison

1 teaspoon chili powder

1 teaspoon ground cumin

1 tablespoon salt

1 green bell pepper, chopped

1 onion, chopped

3 ribs celery, chopped

3 cloves garlic, finely chopped

1 can (28 ounces) crushed tomatoes

3 fresh tomatoes, chopped

2 cans (14 to 19 ounces each) kidney beans, drained and rinsed

1 can (14 to 19 ounces) pinto or black beans, drained and rinsed

Fresh green onions (optional)

Cheesy Cowgirl Cornbread (page 264), for serving

1 In a large heavy-bottomed pot, heat the oil over medium-high heat. Add the meat and cook, stirring, for 5 minutes, or until well browned.

2 Add the chili powder, cumin, and salt and stir to combine.

3 Add the bell pepper, onion, celery, and garlic and cook for 10 minutes, or until softened.

4 Add the crushed tomatoes, fresh tomatoes, and beans and simmer for 15 minutes, or until slightly thickened. Ladle into bowls, garnish with green onions, if you like, and serve with the cornbread.

goose, barley, and white bean soup

One of my earliest memories of my grandmother involve this soup. One day she sat me down at her little round kitchen table and served it in a formal white china bowl with good silver and a linen napkin. I never got the recipe, but I have re-created it by taste. You could use chicken stock, but there is something very rich and wonderful about goose stock. You can use the bones from a roast goose you've eaten for an autumn or winter feast. **SERVES 4**

1 cup pearl barley

4 to 6 cups goose or chicken stock, store-bought or homemade (page 111)

1 can (14 to 19 ounces) white beans, drained and rinsed

Salt and freshly ground black pepper

1 Cook the barley according to package directions.

2 Meanwhile, in a large saucepan, heat the stock over medium-high heat.

3 Drain the barley and add it to the stock along with the beans and salt and pepper to taste. Cook for 2 minutes to warm through. Ladle into bowls to serve.

FROM THE BLOG
"A nice simple, warming soup! I made it without the beans and added bits of goose, onion, and a little bit of chopped kale or parsley. Served with a crispy baguette and fresh, creamy butter." —**DONNA**

"I make the same soup with turkey necks. Brown them with some onions, celery root, and carrots, cover with water, add a bay leaf, some salt, and 1 tablespoon vinegar and simmer. Thanks for posting your rendition of your grandmother's soup." —**SADHVI**

escarole, farro, and chicken soup

There's just something about escarole in a soup that is so clean and nourishing. When I serve this soup at dinner along with some garlic bread (see recipe page 164), it's always accompanied by a long silence and the sounds of slurping and the scraping of spoons on bowls.

SERVES 4 TO 6

1 cup farro

3 cups water

8 cups chicken stock, store-bought or homemade (page 111)

1 head escarole, trimmed and chopped

Salt

Grated Romano cheese, for serving

1 In a medium saucepan, combine the farro and water and bring to a boil over high heat. Reduce the heat to low, cover, and cook for 15 to 20 minutes, until tender.

2 Meanwhile, in a large soup pot, heat the stock over medium heat.

3 Drain the farro and add it to the stock along with the escarole and salt to taste. Ladle the soup into bowls and pass grated Romano at the table.

vegetarian borscht

I am the only person in my house who eats beets. When I really crave them, I make borscht. I first ate borscht when my sister Heidi made it when I was younger. She cooked it from some hippie paperback cookbook that's long since been lost. I've tried meat-based borscht in restaurants—and even made it once—but there is a cleanness and purity to vegetarian borscht that feeds my slightly Eastern European soul. **SERVES 4**

3 tablespoons extra virgin olive oil

3 small onions, chopped

3 cloves garlic, chopped

1 small head savoy or napa cabbage, cored and thinly sliced

3 red beets, peeled and shredded

3 carrots, peeled and shredded

3 potatoes, unpeeled, cut into small cubes

3 fresh tomatoes, chopped, or 1 can (14.5 ounces) chopped tomatoes

8 cups water

1 tablespoon vegetable bouillon paste

1 tablespoon fresh lemon juice

A few sprigs fresh Italian parsley or dill

3 whole cloves

2 dried or fresh bay leaves

Salt

Plain yogurt and fresh dill sprigs, for garnish

1 In a large soup pot, heat the oil over medium-high heat. Add the onions and garlic and cook, stirring, for 2 minutes. Add the cabbage, beets, carrots, potatoes, and tomatoes and stir to combine. Cook for 5 minutes.

2 Add the water, vegetable bouillon, lemon juice, herbs, cloves, bay leaves, and salt to taste and stir to combine. Bring to a boil, then reduce the heat to low and simmer for 1 hour. Remove and discard the cloves and bay leaves.

3 Ladle the soup into bowls. Serve topped with a spoonful of yogurt and sprinkled with the dill.

FROM THE BLOG

"I added tomato paste, grated ginger, and vinegar, and topped with a bit of feta! Thanks for the inspiration." —EMILY

turkey and vegetable noodle soup

This soup has a special place in my family's heart. It's the soup Rita Cinquino made whenever we came to visit. Rita's soup was always made with ring noodles, carrots, and a sprinkling of Romano cheese. Peas were optional, as her daughter didn't like peas. This soup is also really good with some tiny meatballs (page 213). **SERVES 8**

1 turkey carcass

2 cups chopped carrots

16 ounces ring noodle pasta

2 cups frozen peas

2 cups Mini Meatballs (optional; page 213)

Salt

Grated Romano cheese, for serving

TIP: You can make this soup with any stock. In fact, Rita often made it with a combination of turkey and beef stock.

1 In a large soup pot, combine the turkey carcass and enough water to cover and bring to a boil over high heat. Reduce the heat to low, cover, and simmer for 2 to 3 hours.

2 Strain the stock and place 10 cups in a large soup pot over medium heat. (At this point, freeze any leftover stock you are not going to use.) Add the carrots and cook for 20 minutes, or until tender.

3 Meanwhile, in a separate saucepan, cook the noodles according to package directions.

4 Drain the noodles and add to the soup along with the peas, meatballs (if using), and salt to taste and stir to combine. Cook for 2 minutes, or until the peas are tender and the meatballs are warmed through. Ladle into bowls and pass grated Romano at the table.

pasta fagioli

Italians have as many versions of pasta fagioli as they have spaghetti. Although I am not Italian, the fact that I was married to an Italian, have given birth to half-Italians, and also have the name Maria qualifies me, I think, as an honorary Italian. This is my version.

SERVES 4

1 tablespoon extra virgin olive oil

2 small cloves garlic, chopped

6 cups chicken stock, store-bought or homemade (page 111)

2 cans (14 to 19 ounces each) white beans, drained and rinsed

1 teaspoon dried rosemary, or leaves from a sprig or two of fresh, chopped

1 cup small pasta, such as orzo or ditalini

Salt and freshly ground black pepper

Grated Romano cheese, for serving

1 In a large soup pot, heat the oil over medium-low heat. Add the garlic and cook, stirring, for 1 minute. Add the stock, beans, and rosemary and simmer for 15 minutes.

2 Meanwhile, in a separate saucepan, cook the pasta according to package directions.

3 Drain the pasta and add to the soup. Season with salt and pepper to taste and stir to combine. Ladle into bowls and pass grated Romano at the table.

savory spiced pumpkin soup

A long time ago on the Caribbean island of St. John, in a little shack of a restaurant surrounded by goats and lapping waves, we had pumpkin soup that tasted like heaven. I've had many pumpkin soups since, but none as good as that one. It was slightly spicy and creamy, with a hint of curry. Much better than most pumpkin soups that are too sweet and taste like pie. This is my re-creation of that soup. **SERVES 4**

4 tablespoons (½ stick) butter

1 white onion, chopped

2 cloves garlic, finely chopped

1 teaspoon ground turmeric

1 teaspoon ground ginger

1 teaspoon curry powder

1 tablespoon chopped fresh Italian parsley leaves

2 pounds pumpkin, peeled, seeded, and chopped

2 cups vegetable or chicken stock, store-bought or homemade (page 111)

2 tablespoons fresh lime juice

½ cup heavy cream or coconut milk, plus extra for serving

Salt and freshly ground black pepper

1 In a large soup pot, melt the butter over medium-high heat. Add the onion and cook, stirring, for 5 minutes, or until translucent. Add the garlic, turmeric, ginger, curry powder, and parsley and cook, stirring, for 1 minute.

2 Add the pumpkin and stock, bring to a simmer, and cook for 30 minutes, or until the pumpkin has softened completely.

3 In batches, transfer the soup to a blender and process until smooth. Return the soup to the pot and add the lime juice, cream, and salt and pepper to taste. Stir to combine and cook until warmed through. Ladle into bowls and drizzle with a little cream to serve.

beef vegetable soup

This is a soup I remember my mom making often, and it brings back happy memories of her kitchen. You can change the vegetables depending on the season or what you have available, but the essential ones are listed below. The broth will taste better if you brown the beef and bones a bit first. I pick cheap cuts, such as pieces of shank, that still have a bit of fat and meat on them as this helps give the soup a richer flavor. **SERVES 8**

¼ cup extra virgin olive oil

2 pounds beef with bones

Salt

2 onions, chopped

1 cup chopped carrots

2 cups chopped celery

6 medium potatoes, cut into cubes

2 cups chopped tomatoes

2 cups chopped vegetables: kale, cabbage, turnips, peas, green beans

⅓ cup chopped fresh Italian parsley leaves

Freshly ground black pepper

1 In a large heavy-bottomed pot, heat the oil over high heat. Add the meat and bones and cook for a few minutes, turning, until nicely browned.

2 Add enough cold water to the pot to completely cover the bones and bring to a boil. Skim any foam from the surface and discard. Reduce the heat to medium and simmer for 2 hours. Add salt to taste.

3 Strain the stock into a large soup pot. Add all the vegetables and cook for 30 minutes, or until the potatoes have softened.

4 Add the parsley and pepper to taste and ladle into bowls to serve.

TIP: Feel free to experiment. You can add different herbs or different beans or vegetables. Make it yours! Some of you may want to sauté the vegetables before you add the broth, which will intensify the flavor.

lamb and barley soup

This is a one-pot-wonder soup that tastes like a historical novel set in the British Isles. You know the kind, where the characters come in from a long day of riding on the moors on some sort of an adventure to a little hidden cottage with a warm fire and someone has cooked a warm pot of lamb and barley soup, which makes everything good in the world. Serve with good crusty bread, if desired. **SERVES 8 TO 10**

2 tablespoons extra virgin olive oil

1½ to 2 pounds lamb shanks (about 2)

12 cups water

1 onion, peeled and halved

2 cups hulled or pearl barley

1 onion, chopped

1 cup chopped carrots

Salt and freshly ground black pepper

¼ cup chopped fresh Italian parsley leaves

1 In a large heavy-bottomed pot, heat the oil over high heat. Add the shanks and cook, turning, for 3 to 5 minutes, until browned.

2 Add the water and the onion halves to the pot and bring to a boil. Skim any foam from the surface and discard. Reduce the heat to medium, cover, and simmer for 1 hour.

3 Add the barley, chopped onion, and carrots. Cover and simmer for 1 hour more, or until the meat is falling from the bones.

4 Shred the meat from the shanks and return to the soup, discarding the bones. Discard the onion halves. Add salt and pepper to taste and stir to combine. Ladle into bowls and sprinkle with parsley.

new england clam chowder

I went to boarding school in Massachusetts and have very happy memories of getting a big bowl of New England clam chowder at the Boston airport. Over the years, it's become one of my favorite soups, one I almost always order whenever I see it on a menu. But when I tried to make it at home, I couldn't get that thick creamy texture or the clean, simple taste. Finally I discovered that the secret is a lot of butter, a short cooking time, and a very simple list of ingredients.

SERVES 4 TO 6

1 stick plus
4 tablespoons
(6 ounces) butter,
cubed

2 heaping
tablespoons all-
purpose flour

1 pound fresh
or frozen clams,
chopped

2 large potatoes,
cut into small dice

6 cups whole milk

Salt

1 In a large soup pot, melt 2 tablespoons of the butter over medium-high heat. Add 1 heaping tablespoon of the flour and cook, stirring with a wooden spoon, until all the flour is incorporated and the mixture is golden.

2 Add the 1 stick of butter and heat, whisking, until melted and incorporated.

3 Add the clams and cook for 5 to 6 minutes. Add the potatoes and stir to combine.

4 Meanwhile, in a small skillet, melt the remaining 2 tablespoons butter over medium-high heat. Add the remaining heaping tablespoon of flour and cook, stirring, until incorporated and golden.

5 Slowly whisk in the milk, then add the mixture to the clams, stirring until thickened. Cook for 5 to 10 minutes, until the potatoes are tender. Season to taste with salt.

15-minute oyster stew

I have loved oyster stew since I was a small girl. For some reason I remember it as a Christmas food. Fresh oysters are essential to give the stew its ocean-y goodness. The other essential ingredient is oyster crackers (page 169). The crackers give the soup its thickness and satisfying fullness. **SERVES 4**

1 stick (4 ounces) butter

1 pound shucked raw oysters, with their liquid

4 cups whole milk

Salt and freshly ground black pepper

Oyster Crackers (page 169)

1 In a large saucepan, melt the butter over medium-high heat until slightly browned.

2 Add the oysters and cook for 5 to 10 minutes, until their sides are ruffled.

3 Add the milk and salt and pepper to taste and cook for 2 to 4 minutes, until warmed through. Be careful to never let the soup boil. Serve with the oyster crackers.

TIP: I buy my oysters freshly shucked from a fishmonger or the seafood counter of a grocery store.

holly's almost-indian lentil soup

One night, instead of doing handstands, my wonderful yoga teacher, Holly, made soup for my girls and me, and it was divine. As she stirred the soup, she chanted the invocation to Ganesha and we all sat transfixed, feeling like we were all good witches watching a magical potion come to life. We all ate every last drop. **SERVES 6**

3 tablespoons extra virgin olive oil

1 onion, diced

Salt and freshly ground black pepper

1 cup bulgur

1 cup red lentils

1 cup chopped fresh dill leaves

1 cup chopped fresh cilantro leaves, plus extra for serving

2 tablespoons butter

8 cups water

1 tablespoon vegan chicken bouillon paste (see Tip)

1 can (14 to 19 ounces) chickpeas, drained and rinsed

2 cups chopped fresh spinach leaves

½ cup plain yogurt, plus extra for serving

1 In heavy-bottomed pot, heat the oil over medium heat. Add the onion, season with salt and pepper, and cook, stirring, for 10 minutes, or until golden and caramelized.

2 Add the bulgur, lentils, dill, cilantro, and butter and cook for 1 to 2 minutes, until the mixture is combined and the butter has melted.

3 Add the water and vegan chicken bouillon, bring to a simmer, and cook for 30 minutes.

4 Add the chickpeas and spinach, stir to combine, and cook until warmed through.

5 Place the yogurt in a small bowl, add a little of the broth from the pot, and whisk to combine. Gradually add the yogurt mixture to the pot, stirring, until combined. Divide the soup among bowls. Serve topped with a dollop of yogurt and sprinkled with cilantro.

TIP: If you're not vegetarian, you could use 8 cups Homemade Chicken Stock (page 111) in place of the water and vegan bouillon.

nana's lentil soup

Rita Cinquino always had a pot of soup on the stove when we came to visit. One of my favorites was this lentil soup, and it's so easy to make. She would serve it with kluski *noodles (soft egg noodles) or rice. If using, cook the noodles separately and add them to the soup at the end of the cooking time. With simple ingredients, this soup never fails to fill the house with an incredible aroma.* **SERVES 6 TO 8**

1 pound brown or French green lentils

1 onion, chopped

½ cup chopped carrots

½ cup chopped celery

3 cloves garlic, chopped

Leaves from a few sprigs fresh Italian parsley

1 bulb fennel, trimmed, cored, and chopped (optional)

8 cups water or chicken stock, low-sodium store-bought or homemade (page 111)

1 cup chopped fresh tomatoes or canned crushed tomatoes

Salt and freshly ground black pepper

Grated Romano cheese, for serving (optional)

1 In a large soup pot, combine the lentils, onion, carrots, celery, garlic, parsley, fennel (if using), and water or stock. Bring to a boil over high heat. Reduce the heat to low, cover, and simmer for 45 minutes.

2 Add the tomatoes and simmer for another 15 minutes.

3 Season with salt and pepper to taste and stir to combine. Ladle into bowls. If desired, pass grated Romano at the table.

the simplest tomato soup

I grew up in the Andy Warhol generation of tomato soup—it came from a can. The best tomato soup I have ever eaten was made with four ingredients: tomatoes, butter, salt, and a little olive oil. It was from a place called The Kitchen in Boulder, Colorado. I re-create it all the time. This is a basic soup to which you can add any number of things. Cream if you want it creamy. Fresh herbs such as basil and parsley. Think of Andy Warhol. The soup is the canvas, and you are the artist. Serve with crusty bread or a grilled cheese. **SERVES 2**

4 tomatoes, chopped

4 tablespoons (½ stick) butter

Salt

Extra virgin olive oil, for serving

) If you prefer a smooth soup, puree the tomatoes in a blender until smooth.

2 In a medium saucepan, melt the butter over medium heat. Add the tomatoes and salt to taste and simmer for 10 minutes. Divide between bowls and drizzle with a little oil.

summer gazpacho

I originally made this soup as an experiment and served it to my daughter and a friend. The next week, I saw her friend's mom and she asked me for the recipe; she said her daughter loved it! That to me is the best compliment. And when I showed her the recipe (written in pencil in my little notebook) she was shocked at how easy it is. That made me even happier because one of my goals in life is to make cooking simple and easy for everyone. **Serves 4**

5 large very ripe tomatoes, halved

¼ red onion, chopped

1 small green or red bell pepper, chopped

1 teaspoon salt

Extra virgin olive oil, freshly ground black pepper, and basil leaves, for serving

1 Grate the tomato halves over a bowl using the large holes on a box grater, leaving the skin behind to discard.

2 Puree the tomato in a blender or food processer until smooth. Add the onion, bell pepper, and salt and blend until foamy and smooth. Ladle into bowls and serve drizzled with some oil.

From the Blog
"I put everything in my food processor (skin and all) instead of grating the tomatoes and yum! I love the simple recipes the best. My girls are 9 and 10 and I will make this again with them!" —MARFA

summer vegetable soup

There's always that moment in late summer when you look in the fridge and discover you have more vegetables than it's possible to eat. And that's where this soup comes in. I also call this freedom soup, because you're free to put in any vegetable you like. The recipe doesn't include onion and garlic, but if you can't imagine a soup without them, put them in. Isn't freedom fantastic? **SERVES 6 TO 8**

2 tablespoons butter

2 cups chopped carrots

2 cups chopped celery

2 cups sliced savoy or napa cabbage

2 cups chopped zucchini

1 cup fresh corn kernels

2 cups chopped tomatoes

Water or chicken stock, store-bought or homemade (page 111)

Salt and freshly ground black pepper

Leaves from a few sprigs fresh basil and Italian parsley, chopped

Grated Romano cheese, for serving (optional)

1 In a large soup pot, melt the butter over medium-high heat. Add the carrots, celery, and cabbage and cook, stirring, for 5 minutes, or until slightly softened.

2 Add the zucchini, corn, and tomatoes and cook for 5 minutes, or until softened. Add enough water or stock to cover and simmer for 10 to 15 minutes, until the vegetables are tender.

3 Add salt and pepper to taste, add the herbs, and stir to combine. Ladle into bowls and pass grated Romano at the table.

TIP: My secret trick to add a burst of flavor to this soup is to garnish it with a spoonful of pesto. See my recipe on page 98.

italian wedding soup

My kids love Italian wedding soup, so I was determined to figure out a homemade recipe that was easy, relatively quick, and as satisfying to them as the store-bought stuff. The trick is to have a stash of homemade tiny meatballs (page 213) on hand in the freezer, as well as some homemade chicken stock. **SERVES 4 TO 6**

8 cups chicken stock, store-bought or homemade (page 111)

2 cups Mini Meatballs (page 213)

10 ounces frozen chopped spinach, drained, or 2 cups chopped fresh spinach

Salt and freshly ground black pepper

2 cups acini di pepe or other small soup pasta

¼ cup grated Romano cheese, for serving

1 In a large saucepan, bring the stock to a boil over medium-high heat. Add the meatballs, spinach, and salt and pepper to taste and simmer for 15 minutes.

2 Meanwhile, in a separate saucepan, cook the pasta according to package directions.

3 Drain the pasta and add to the soup. Cook for 2 minutes to warm through. Divide the soup among bowls and pass grated Romano at the table.

roast pork, cabbage, and garlic butter sandwich

A very long time ago, I was in Puerto Rico with my brother-in-law, who lived there for a time. He took us to lunch at a casual restaurant on a side street in Old San Juan and we ate the most delicious sandwiches. Years later I was back in Puerto Rico but couldn't for the life of me find the restaurant. So I had to re-create the sandwich at home! **MAKES 2 SANDWICHES**

4 tablespoons (½ stick) butter

1 clove garlic, finely chopped

1 crusty baguette, halved crosswise and split lengthwise

4 slices mild cheese, such as provolone

4 ounces leftover roast pork (see recipe, page 227), thinly sliced

2 cups finely shredded green cabbage

Salt and freshly ground black pepper

1 In a small saucepan, melt the butter over low heat. Add the garlic and cook, stirring, for 3 minutes, or until fragrant.

2 Toast the cut sides of the baguette under the broiler or on a grill pan over high heat.

3 Brush the garlic butter over the insides of the baguette. Divide the cheese, pork, and cabbage between the bottoms of the baguette pieces. Season with salt and pepper. Sandwich with the tops and serve.

a healthy hoagie

There are more than 15 names for this style of sandwich found across the country—subs, grinders, heros—but the hoagie is a Pennsylvania specialty. I love them. I'm not a fan of the squishy white bread and mystery meats that many conventional types are made with though, so I make this healthier, organic version at home. **MAKES 2 HOAGIES**

4 slices ham

6 slices hard salami

2 soft whole wheat or whole-grain hoagie rolls

4 slices provolone cheese

1 tomato, thinly sliced

½ small red onion, thinly sliced

1 cup finely sliced iceberg lettuce

6 pepperoncini peppers (optional)

HOAGIE DRESSING

1 tablespoon red wine vinegar

3 tablespoons extra virgin olive oil

Salt and freshly ground black pepper

Pinch of dried oregano

1 Assemble the sandwiches by layering the ham and salami on the bottoms of the buns. Top with the provolone, tomato, onion, lettuce, and peppers (if using). Set aside.

2 To make the dressing: In a small bowl, combine the vinegar, oil, salt, pepper, and oregano and whisk with a fork to combine.

3 Drizzle the sandwiches with the dressing, sandwich with the tops of the buns, and serve.

my philly cheesesteak

The original cheesesteak, as served in the City of Brotherly Love, does not have tomato sauce on it. But I grew up about an hour outside of Philly, where you could find the best cheesesteak at a family restaurant called the Brass Rail, which uses sauce. While the sauce is a notoriously secret recipe, I have re-created it from taste.

MAKES 4 CHEESESTEAKS

"SECRET" SAUCE

3 cups tomato sauce, store-bought or homemade (page 77)

1 whole onion, peeled

CHEESESTEAK

Extra virgin olive oil, for cooking

1 pound chipped beef or bison steak*

Salt

4 slices American cheese

4 steak rolls

Sliced sour dill pickles

Pickled hot peppers (optional)

1 To make the sauce: In a small saucepan, combine the tomato sauce and whole onion and cook over medium-high heat for 15 minutes, or until the sauce has absorbed some of the onion's flavor. Set aside, discarding the onion.

2 For the cheesesteak: In a large cast-iron skillet, heat a little oil over medium-high heat, add the meat, and cook, stirring, for 10 minutes, or until browned and cooked through. Season with salt to taste.

3 Place a slice of cheese inside each bun. Divide the meat evenly among the buns and top with 3 or 4 rounds of sliced dill pickles and hot peppers (if using). Spoon over some of the secret sauce to serve.

*Chipped refers to the cut of the beef: it's delicately, thinly sliced. Source it from your local butcher.

TIP: You will probably have leftover sauce, which you can put on pasta or pizza.

due-for-a-comeback club sandwich

The club sandwich is at least 100 years old and, I think, due for a comeback. Much as Southern food has had a resurgence in the past few years, so should the club sandwich. You can make it using the leftover turkey from Thanksgiving, or you can buy organic deli turkey or chicken at the supermarket. **MAKES 2 SANDWICHES**

4 slices whole-grain bread, toasted

Mayonnaise, for spreading

3 ounces cooked turkey or chicken meat

3 ounces sliced ham

4 slices bacon, crisp-cooked

1 tomato, sliced

1 cup shredded iceberg lettuce

Pickles and potato chips, for serving (optional)

1 Spread one side of all the bread slices with mayonnaise. Layer 2 slices with the turkey or chicken followed by the ham, bacon, tomato, and lettuce.

2 Sandwich with the remaining bread slices and cut the sandwiches in half. Fix the pieces with a toothpick to hold them together.

3 Serve with pickles and chips, if desired.

tunafish salad sandwiches

I know, you're thinking do you really need a recipe for basic tunafish salad? I didn't think so until my daughter asked me how to make it. So here is a recipe for the novices out there. I only use wild-caught tuna from sustainable sources, and I also prefer the kind marinated in oil in glass jars. **MAKES 2 SANDWICHES**

1 jar (4.5 ounces) wild-caught tuna in oil, drained

1 tablespoon mayonnaise

2 ribs celery, finely chopped

Salt and freshly ground black pepper

4 thick slices whole wheat bread

1 Place the tuna in a small bowl and mash with a fork. Add the mayonnaise, celery, and salt and pepper to taste and mix well to combine.

2 Spread the mixture on two of the bread slices and sandwich with the remaining slices.

lobster rolls at home

I've been visiting Maine for 20 years to drop the kids off at camp, and have become an expert consumer of the lobster roll. The two constant winners when it comes to any sort of lobster roll contest are the Clam Shack in Kennebunkport, and Red's Eats in Wiscasset. Both are amazing. I think the secret is in the simplicity of their approach. Simple means lobster, bun, and melted butter. If you can't make it to Maine for the real thing, here is the recipe. **MAKES 2 SANDWICHES**

7 ounces fresh or frozen (thawed) cooked lobster meat, coarsely chopped

Salt

2 hot dog buns or burger rolls

6 tablespoons salted butter

Chopped celery leaves, for garnish (optional)

1 Make sure that the lobster meat is only slightly cooler than room temperature. You don't want it too chilled or the lovely sweet flavor of the lobster meat won't come through. Sprinkle the lobster with salt.

2 Toast both sides of the buns on a hot grill pan over high heat. Transfer to 2 plates and divide the lobster between the buns.

3 In a small saucepan, melt the butter over medium-high heat and cook until just golden. Spoon the butter liberally over the buns. If desired, sprinkle with celery leaves.

simple grilled cheese

Everyone should learn how to make a grilled cheese sandwich. The variations are endless, but the basic is always loved and welcome. You can use any type of bread and any type of melting cheese, but the key is cooking the sandwich in butter in a skillet. This goes great with my simple tomato soup (page 139). **MAKES 1 SANDWICH**

1 tablespoon butter

2 slices American cheese

2 slices bread

1 In a large cast-iron skillet, melt the butter over medium-low heat.

2 Sandwich the cheese between the bread slices and cook the sandwich for 4 minutes per side, until golden and the cheese has melted. Be careful not to burn the outside of the sandwich before the cheese has melted.

classic sloppy joe

This was regular summer party food when I was a kid. It's my mother's recipe, straight from her sticky recipe card.

MAKES 4 TO 6 SANDWICHES

2 tablespoons olive oil

2 pounds ground beef

1 cup chopped onion

1 cup ketchup

½ cup water

2 tablespoons mustard

2 tablespoons vinegar

2 tablespoons Worcestershire sauce

2 tablespoons sugar

1 teaspoon salt

½ teaspoon freshly ground black pepper

4 to 6 hamburger buns

1 In a large cast-iron skillet, heat the oil over medium heat. Add the beef and onion and cook for 6 to 8 minutes, until the beef is well browned and the onion is softened.

2 Add the ketchup, water, mustard, vinegar, Worcestershire sauce, sugar, salt, and pepper and stir to combine. Cook for 15 minutes, or until thickened slightly.

3 To serve, divide the mixture among the bottoms of the buns and sandwich with the tops.

chicken and gravy on toast

I often have leftover roasted chicken and gravy on toast. It's one of my cravings. But once I didn't have any leftovers, so I made a cheat's version using some chicken breast and stock from the freezer to make gravy. My kids ask for this dish all the time. **SERVES 4**

2 tablespoons
unsalted butter

2 tablespoons
extra virgin
olive oil

3 or 4 small
boneless, skinless
chicken breasts
(about 1 pound
total)

4 cups chicken
stock, store-bought
or homemade
(page 111)

½ cup all-purpose
flour

Salt

4 slices whole
wheat bread,
toasted

1 In a large cast-iron skillet, heat the butter and oil over medium-high heat.

2 Cut each breast into 3 even pieces and cook for 8 minutes, or until browned on both sides.

3 Add the chicken stock to the skillet and cook for 5 minutes, or until hot. Transfer 1 cup of the stock to a small bowl and mix with the flour until well combined.

4 Bring the chicken and stock to a boil, add the flour mixture, and stir until thickened. Season with salt to taste. To serve, top the toasts with the chicken and a little gravy.

open-faced tomato, bacon, and cheese sandwiches

When I was a kid, this is what my mom would make us for lunch on a good day. It was my favorite sandwich. I remember that I usually ate three of them if I was allowed to. It contains bacon, which is the mascot of all foods in my family—a true uniting force!

MAKES 4 SANDWICHES

8 slices bacon

2 English muffins, split and toasted

1 tablespoon mayonnaise

1 tomato, sliced

4 slices American cheese

1 In a large cast-iron skillet, cook the bacon over medium-high heat until crispy. Drain on paper towels and set aside.

2 Preheat the broiler to high.

3 Spread the cut sides of all 4 toasted muffin halves with mayonnaise. Divide the tomato, bacon, and cheese among the muffins. Arrange on a baking sheet and broil until melted and golden.

Whether it's an after-school snack, something to tide you over until dinner, or a prelude to a dinner party, all the recipes in this chapter started with a question: What's something quick and easy I can serve that's organic? This collection of snacks and appetizers is the answer. Most are quite simple and can be eaten with your hands. And although casual, all are worthy of being served to even the most illustrious dinner guests. One of my favorite snacks is the crispy fried chickpeas at the restaurant Prune in Manhattan's East Village. Many people make the pilgrimage to chef Gabrielle Hamilton's delicious restaurant. We now make a version of that dish at home (page 170) for a quick snack whenever we are hungry—the simpler, the better.

The primary influences in this chapter are Mediterranean, Mexican, and American cuisines, though feel free to mix and match any of these dishes as part of a spread.

rustic catalan tomato bread

*This recipe is called pa amb tomàquet (literally, "bread with tomato")
in Catalan; I discovered it on a trip to Barcelona. It's basically raw
tomato pulp and salt on bread. It's a signature Catalan dish and it's so
freaking easy. According to my Spanish friend Alberto, you just cut a
tomato in half and rub it on toasted or untoasted bread with salt and
olive oil. Use the best bread, tomatoes, and oil you can.* **SERVES 2**

**2 very ripe
tomatoes**

Sea salt

**2 slices crusty
bread, such as
ciabatta**

**1 clove garlic,
halved (optional)**

**Good-quality
extra virgin olive
oil, for drizzling**

1 Cut the tomatoes in half and grate the cut
sides over a bowl using the large holes on a
box grater. Add salt to taste and stir to
combine.

2 Toast the bread on a hot grill or on a grill pan
until golden and the edges are charred. (If you
have really crusty fresh bread, you don't have
to toast it if you don't want to.) If you like, rub
the cut garlic clove over both sides of the bread.

3 Spread the bread with the tomato pulp and
drizzle with the oil to serve.

TIP: If you are entertaining, make a big bowl of pulp
and let people spoon it on to the bread themselves.
Decorate the pulp with a generous swirl of olive oil.

olive tapenade

Most store-bought tapenade is too salty for me, so I've borrowed this recipe from a woman I know, a lovely painter named Sandy Corpora, whose tapenade is amazing. But the fact that she made it for me once over 15 years ago and I've made it ever since with my own variations means, I hope, that the statute of limitations on stealing a good recipe is up! **SERVES 4**

1 cup niçoise olives

1 clove garlic, finely chopped

Leaves from 1 sprig fresh rosemary, chopped

1 teaspoon finely grated lemon or orange zest (optional)

Sea salt and freshly ground black pepper

¼ cup extra virgin olive oil

Sliced crusty baguette, for serving

1 Pit the olives with a small knife and coarsely chop the flesh (this is a chunky tapenade).

2 Transfer the olives to a small bowl, add the garlic, rosemary, and citrus zest (if using), and mix to combine. Season with salt and pepper to taste.

3 Add the oil and stir to combine. Serve with the bread.

TIP: You can also use your favorite brined olive in this recipe.

broccoli cheese bites

I woke one Super Bowl Sunday with an abundance of leftover broccoli and thought it would be fun to start the day with some canapés. Actually, if you know me, you know I don't give a hoot about American football, but there was snow on the ground, the bills were paid, and we had no social obligations, so it felt like a day for a party. These are so easy and tasty; they'll be gone in flash. **MAKES 24**

1 tablespoon extra virgin olive oil

2 cups finely chopped cooked broccoli

1 cup shredded Gruyère or cheddar cheese

2 large eggs

2 tablespoons all-purpose flour

2 tablespoons unsalted butter, melted

2 tablespoons whole milk

Salt and freshly ground black pepper

) Preheat the oven to 350°F. Grease 24 cups of a mini muffin tin with the oil.

2 In a bowl, combine the broccoli, cheese, eggs, flour, melted butter, milk, and salt and pepper to taste and mix well to combine.

3 Spoon some of the mixture into each muffin cup and bake for 10 to 15 minutes, until golden.

FROM THE BLOG
"Maria, you are a genius! Not just a great way to get kids to eat their veggies, but husbands, too! Delicious!" —LACY

roasted peppers

This recipe is not only delicious but is also a great way to preserve a bounty of peppers at the end of summer. The peppers are dressed at the end Cinquino-style (a nod to my Italian family), with olive oil, parsley, and garlic for a burst of vibrant flavor. Serve as part of an antipasto platter or salad (page 41), on a sandwich, or even on a pizza.

SERVES 4 TO 6

6 green or red
bell peppers

½ cup extra virgin
olive oil

Leaves from 4
sprigs fresh Italian
parsley, chopped

1 or 2 cloves garlic
(to taste), chopped

Salt and freshly
ground black
pepper

1 Char the whole peppers on a hot grill, over an open flame on the stove, or under the broiler, turning, for 10 minutes, or until evenly blackened and blistered. Transfer to a bowl covered with a plate and let cool. (The steam will make it easier to peel the peppers.)

2 Peel the skin from the cooled peppers. Core and seed the peppers. Place the peppers in a clean, shallow dish. Pour the oil over the peppers and add the parsley, garlic, and salt and black pepper to taste. Serve immediately or store in the fridge for up to 2 weeks.

TIP: If you have plenty of summer peppers to preserve, simply place them in sterilized mason jars, cover with oil, and freeze.

You can use any color pepper for roasting. You can also roast hot peppers. Just be sure to keep track of which is which.

garlic bread three ways

Garlic bread is my nemesis. For some people, it's chocolate. For me, it's garlic bread. It's the reason I could never completely give up carbs. So here are the three classic ways I make it—golden and crispy, soft and squishy, and grilled and rubbed. My mother made it the first way, my former mother-in-law the second way (causing me to put on 5 pounds in one weekend!), and the third way is just a little more modern. **SERVES 6**

1 loaf Italian bread

1 stick (4 ounces) butter, at room temperature

4 cloves garlic

Grated Romano cheese (optional)

¼ cup finely chopped fresh Italian parsley leaves (optional)

FOR GOLDEN AND CRISPY BREAD

1 Preheat the broiler.

2 Thickly slice the bread and arrange the slices in a single layer on a baking sheet (you might need to do this in batches).

3 In a small saucepan, melt the butter over medium heat. Crush the garlic, add to the butter, and cook gently for 1 minute. Spoon the butter over the bread, sprinkle with a little cheese (if using) and broil for 3 minutes, or until golden. If desired, sprinkle with parsley.

FOR SOFT AND SQUISHY BREAD

1 Preheat the oven to 350°F.

2 Slice the loaf of bread without cutting all the way through so the slices are still attached. Place the loaf on a big piece of foil.

3 Chop the garlic, mix with the butter and parsley (if using), and spread the mixture on both sides of each slice. Wrap tightly in the foil and bake for 15 to 20 minutes.

FOR GRILLED AND RUBBED BREAD

1 Omit the butter and use halved garlic cloves.

2 Preheat the grill to high.

3 Slice the bread and grill on both sides until golden and charry. Rub one side of each slice with a cut clove of garlic and drizzle with a little olive oil.

eve's hummus

I know I've done something right as a mom when my teenager tries multiple times to make her own version of hummus just the way she likes it, and keeps on trying until she gets it just right. Once she did, she wrote it down in my recipe notebook. Eve prefers a chunkier hummus and makes this with a mortar and pestle, so no power tools are necessary. She's a smart one, my Eve. **SERVES 6**

1 can (14 to 19 ounces) chickpeas

1 tablespoon tahini

1 to 2 tablespoons fresh lemon juice (to taste)

1 tablespoon extra virgin olive oil

1 large clove garlic, crushed in a press

½ teaspoon salt

Extra virgin olive oil and paprika, for garnish

Pita, chips, or Homemade Crackers (page 168), for serving

1 Reserving ¼ cup of the liquid, drain the chickpeas and rinse.

2 Place the chickpeas and the reserved liquid in a mortar and grind with a pestle until you have a paste. You may need to do this in batches depending on the size of your mortar.

3 Transfer the ground chickpeas to a bowl, add the tahini, lemon juice, oil, garlic, and salt and mix with a wooden spoon until well combined. If it's too thick, you can thin it out with a little water.

4 Garnish with a little drizzle of oil and sprinkling of paprika. Serve the hummus with pita, chips, or crackers.

homemade crackers

It started with a picture I saw in the local paper about making crackers from scratch. I saved it, but then never found it again. So I decided to experiment. A quick search online and I was disturbed by the complexity of the recipes I found. I wanted the quickest, easiest, no-fuss option, so I pulled the essence out of the recipes I saw and came up with these simple crackers. My kids now ask for them constantly; a batch never lasts more than 24 hours. **SERVES 6 TO 8**

2 cups whole wheat pastry flour

⅔ cup warm water

⅓ cup extra virgin olive oil, plus extra for the pan

Salt

TIP: The potential variations for this recipe are endless: You can use different flours, add dried herbs, or sprinkle with spices, such as za'atar, or seeds, such as sesame.

1 Preheat the oven to 375°F. Grease a 17 × 11-inch rimmed baking sheet with oil.

2 In a bowl, combine the flour, water, oil, and 1 teaspoon salt and stir until combined and a dough forms. Place the dough in the center of the prepared baking sheet and roll out roughly with a rolling pin or use your hands, and press it into the corners. No need to be fussy here, rustic is great!

3 Use a knife or pizza cutter to cut even squares, rectangles, or whatever shape takes your fancy. Sprinkle with salt and bake for 15 minutes, or until golden. Set aside to cool (the crackers will harden as they cool). Store in an airtight container for up to 5 days.

FROM THE BLOG
"Dear Recipe: Where you been all my life?! I'm serious. Dear Author: You are a true genius in the way you organized this recipe. Thank you, you saved me two or more hours of unnecessary kneading and waiting. Thanks." —KATINKA

oyster crackers

One of the reasons I learned to cook was so I could eat food that's guaranteed organic. And since I've never been able to find organic oyster crackers in the store, I taught myself to make these on a snow day. I will never have to buy a box ever again—they are so easy and delicious. **MAKES 30 CRACKERS**

1 cup all-purpose flour

1 teaspoon salt

1 teaspoon baking powder

3 tablespoons butter, cut into small cubes

⅓ cup warm water

1 Preheat the oven to 375°F.

2 In a bowl, mix together the flour, salt, and baking powder. Add the butter and incorporate with your fingertips until it resembles wet sand. Add the water and mix just until a dough comes together.

3 Pinch off grape-size pieces of dough and roll each into a small ball. Place on a baking sheet and bake for 15 to 20 minutes, until golden. Allow to cool on the baking sheet.

crispy fried chickpeas

I first tasted these delicious tidbits at a Lower East Side Manhattan restaurant called Prune. When I tried making them at home, my kids ate them like candy and my Italian in-laws begged for the recipe. It's a great snack or a very delicious appetizer for entertaining. **SERVES 4**

1 can (14 to 19 ounces) chickpeas, drained and rinsed

1 cup olive oil

Salt

1 Drain the chickpeas on paper towels to remove any excess moisture.

2 In a small pot, heat the oil over medium-high heat until a chickpea thrown into it starts to sizzle.

3 Fry the chickpeas, gently shaking the pot, for 8 to 9 minutes, until deep golden brown. Remove from the oil with a slotted spoon and drain briefly on paper towels, where they'll crisp as they cool. Season with salt, then transfer to a bowl.

TIPS: If you'd rather not fry them, coat the chickpeas in oil, spread them on a baking sheet, and bake in a 375°F oven for 30 minutes, until crispy. You can add a pinch each paprika and cayenne or your favorite spice blend after the chickpeas cool.

fresh salsa

When I have an abundance of ripe tomatoes, I love to make salsa, and there's no better salsa than fresh salsa. It's so easy to make. According to my nephew Nicholas Cinquino, who spent time with a family in Mexico, this is really as simple and authentic as it gets. **SERVES 4**

2 large tomatoes, chopped

1 small red or white onion, finely chopped

1 to 2 tablespoons chopped fresh cilantro (to taste)

1 to 2 teaspoons fresh lime juice (to taste)

1 teaspoon extra virgin olive oil

Salt

1 In a small bowl, mix together the tomatoes and onion.

2 Add the cilantro, lime juice, oil, and salt to taste and mix to combine.

TIP: Serve with tortilla chips as a snack, or with Nachos (page 174) or My Tacos (page 215).

guacamole

Guacamole is super easy to make and it happens to be pretty nutritious, too. Choose ripe avocadoes that are soft around the top near the stem. I think the smaller Hass variety is the best for guacamole. Optional extras are finely diced red onion, jalapeños, and cilantro, but I prefer a simple guac. **SERVES 4**

2 avocados

2 tablespoons fresh lemon or lime juice

Salt

1 Halve the avocadoes, remove the pit, and scoop the flesh into a bowl. Mash coarsely with a fork.

2 Add the lemon or lime juice and mash to combine.

TIP: Serve with corn tortilla chips as a snack, with Huevos Rancheros (page 8), or with Nachos (page 174).

nachos

Nachos are one of those things I make as a snack, but also as a quick lunch or dinner for one. My first job after college was working in Washington, D.C., and the office was right above a tiny Mexican restaurant called the Lauriol Plaza. I would get nachos almost every day for lunch—they were damned tasty! That tiny restaurant now takes up a whole block! This recipe is based on my memory of those nachos. **SERVES 2**

½ bag (about 6 ounces) tortilla chips

½ pound Monterey Jack cheese, shredded

½ cup Mexicali Beans (page 256)

Fresh Salsa (page 172)

Guacamole (page 173)

Sour cream, for serving

Pickled jalapeños, for serving (optional)

1 Preheat the oven to 350°F.

2 Place the chips in a small baking dish, top with the cheese, and bake until the cheese has melted, about 10 minutes. (Or broil for 5 minutes.)

3 Top with the beans, salsa, guacamole, sour cream, and jalapeños (if using).

classic deviled eggs

You know deviled eggs have made a comeback when they're on almost every hipster menu in America. I love that something like a deviled egg can be a hipster favorite while also being the most coveted item brought to a potluck, usually by an older woman who dishes out advice as good as her food. For some reason, organic eggs seem much harder to peel than others. If you use my steaming technique (page 338), you will never have a problem peeling an egg again! **MAKES 12**

6 large eggs, hard-boiled (see page 338)

1 heaping tablespoon mayonnaise

2 teaspoons yellow mustard

TIP: These eggs are a blank canvas; you can get as creative as you want with add-ins and toppings, such as spices, herbs, cheese, bacon, and so forth.

1 Gently peel the cooled eggs and halve them lengthwise. Scoop out the yolks and place them in a small bowl. Rinse the whites and gently pat dry if necessary.

2 Add the mayonnaise and mustard to the yolks and mix until smooth.

3 Transfer the yolk mixture to a small zip-top bag and cut a tip off one corner of the bag. (You can also use a piping bag if you have one.) Gently pipe the yolk mixture into the whites.

FROM THE BLOG
"I add paprika to the mayonnaise along with a little mustard and some crispy crumbled bacon. Outstanding!" —SUE

pickled red beet eggs

*On a lark, I once made these pickled red beet eggs. As most Dutchies
know, they're a real Pennsylvania Dutch delicacy, and beautiful to
boot, but almost impossible to find organic. Of course, I've pickled the
beets from scratch rather than using canned ones, which most recipes
call for. The cinnamon and cloves make them "real darn goot." Now I
make them all the time. They are beautiful on salads.* **MAKES 6 EGGS**

**6 large red beets,
trimmed**

6 cups water

**1 cup apple cider
vinegar**

½ cup sugar

1 stick cinnamon

6 whole cloves

½ teaspoon salt

**6 large eggs, hard-
boiled (see page
338) and peeled**

**1 shallot, finely
chopped (optional)**

1 In a saucepan, combine the beets and water
and bring to a boil over high heat. Cook for 20
minutes, or until tender. Remove the beets and
set aside to cool, reserving the cooking liquid.

2 Strain the cooking liquid (about 4 cups) into a
separate saucepan. Add the vinegar, sugar,
cinnamon stick, cloves, and salt and bring to a
boil. Cook for a few minutes, stirring, until the
sugar has dissolved.

3 Place the eggs and shallot (if using) into a
large glass jar and pour the hot liquid over the
top.

4 When cool enough to handle, slip the skins off
the cooked beets, slice or quarter, and add to
the jar. Cover with a lid and refrigerate for
1 week. Cut the eggs in half and serve with the
beets as a snack, or slice the eggs and toss both
in a salad. The eggs will keep refrigerated for
about 1 month.

roasted pumpkin seeds

Carving pumpkins is fun. But even more fun is eating freshly roasted pumpkin seeds left over from a Halloween pumpkin.

MAKES ABOUT 1 CUP

Seeds of 1 carving pumpkin (or other variety)

Extra virgin olive oil, for roasting

Sea salt

Soy sauce, for roasting (optional)

1 Preheat the oven to 375°F.

2 After you've scooped the seeds from the pumpkin, separate them from all the pumpkin fibers but don't wash them; the juices are full of flavor.

3 Spread the seeds on a baking sheet, add a liberal dash of oil, and toss to coat.

4 Add a little salt (or a dash of soy, if desired, which caramelizes nicely on the seeds). Roast for 20 minutes, or until golden and crispy.

TIP: These are great as a snack, tossed into salads, or used to garnish my Savory Spiced Pumpkin Soup (page 131).

cheese crisps

I've always wanted to make cheese straws, but they seem fussy and hard. So this is my attempt to make them super simple. I adapted this from a recipe in my favorite magazine, Garden & Gun. *I didn't roll them into straws because I am such an unfussy cook; making little coins is easier. Or you could simply roll out the dough and use a pizza cutter to cut it into squares.* **MAKES ABOUT 50 COINS**

1 cup whole wheat pastry flour

½ cup finely shredded extra-sharp cheddar cheese

2 tablespoons finely grated Romano cheese

4 tablespoons (½ stick) butter, at room temperature

1 egg yolk

1 tablespoon extra virgin olive oil

Salt

TIP: You can doctor these crisps any way you want by using different cheeses or by adding herbs or a pinch of cayenne pepper for spice.

1 In a bowl, combine the flour, cheeses, butter, egg yolk, oil, and ½ teaspoon salt and mix until a dough forms.

2 In the bowl, or on a lightly floured surface, knead several times to create a soft, cohesive, and slightly greasy dough ball. Form the dough into a log and roll gently until it holds its shape and is about 1 inch thick. Wrap in plastic wrap and refrigerate until firm, about 30 minutes, or until ready to use.

3 Preheat the oven to 350°F. Line a baking sheet with parchment paper.

4 Remove the log from the refrigerator, unwrap, and slice into ⅛-inch-thick coins. Place on the prepared baking sheet, sprinkle with a little salt, and bake for 15 to 17 minutes (keep an eye on them), until browned around the edges and firm to the touch.

5 Transfer to a wire rack to cool completely.

pickled vegetables

I crave vegetable pickles and it's really hard to source organic ones. So when I happened to find an old Cinquino family cookbook, I was happy to discover this recipe. These vegetables were topped with good olive oil and oregano, but I love to eat them straight from the jar. They are not sweet at all. Feel free to mix and match your favorite veggies.

MAKES 2 QUARTS

1 small head cauliflower, cut into florets (about 2 cups)

1 rib celery, thickly sliced

1 cucumber, sliced

1 carrot, sliced

1 red bell pepper, cut into strips

1 small eggplant, sliced

2½ cups distilled white vinegar

2 cups water

1 Divide the cut vegetables evenly between two cleaned and sterilized 1-quart glass jars.

2 In a bowl, mix together the vinegar and water. Pour over the vegetables to cover. Seal with lids and refrigerate for at least 1 day before using. Store in the fridge for 1 to 2 weeks.

You can pickle almost any vegetable. It's a great way to preserve summer's bounty.

popcorn from scratch

I never quite took to the whole microwave popcorn thing. Sure, it's easy, but making popcorn from scratch is easy, too—and it tastes so freaking delicious! Even better with real butter. Anyhow, I make homemade popcorn all the time, and my kids have requested I put it in writing because it's an essential snack in our house. This is a recipe that involves listening. **SERVES 4**

¼ cup extra virgin olive oil or coconut oil

½ cup popcorn

4 tablespoons (½ stick) unsalted butter, melted

Salt

1 In a large heavy-bottomed pan with a tight-fitting lid, combine the oil and popcorn. Place the pan over high heat and cover with the lid. After 1 to 2 minutes you will start to hear popping. This will quickly escalate into a crescendo of popping (like the grand finale at a fireworks show). At that point, reduce the heat to medium-low.

2 Allow the corn to keep popping, shaking the pan occasionally, until the noise starts to slow down and you don't hear any popping for 5 consecutive seconds. Remove the pan from the heat.

3 Transfer the popped corn to a bowl and drizzle with the melted butter. Toss to combine and season with salt to taste.

cheese ball

If you ever wonder what I think about when I'm not in a million business meetings or taking care of things at home or planning my kids' schedules, well it's this: How do I make an organic cheese ball? I get a craving for one every Christmas and the store-bought ones always taste a bit weird. So this is my attempt at something more natural. By the way, you can make this into a log if you prefer that look. **SERVES 8 TO 10**

8 ounces cream cheese, at room temperature

½ cup shredded cheddar cheese

½ cup shredded Monterey Jack cheese

1 cup coarsely chopped toasted pecans (page 339)

Thinly sliced baguette or Homemade Crackers (page 168), for serving

) In a bowl, combine the cream cheese and shredded cheeses and mix with your hands as if you are kneading dough—let your warm hands soften up the cheeses and mix them together.

2 Scatter the nuts on a large plate. Roll the cheese into a ball shape and roll evenly in the nuts. Set on a plate and serve with the bread or crackers.

VARIATIONS

Things you can add to the cheese: Crumbled cooked bacon, chopped chives or parsley, freshly ground black pepper, paprika, a pinch of cayenne pepper, finely chopped pickled hot peppers. Smoked cheeses are also nice.

Things you can add to the coating: Other nuts such as walnuts or hazelnuts, finely chopped parsley, spices such as paprika.

stuffed mussels

For some strange reason, my kids love mussels. Plain steamed mussels are fine, but these are awesome. This is based on an Italian antipasto recipe I saw in a magazine—but it's been fairly significantly modified, and I've added a Spanish twist. Let's just say these are good enough to serve at a fancy dinner party, either as an appetizer or hors d'oeuvre. Or you can just make them and sit and eat them all up, no party required. **SERVES 4**

2 pounds mussels (about 50), cleaned

TOPPING
½ cup fresh breadcrumbs

½ cup finely grated Romano cheese

2 tablespoons finely chopped fresh Italian parsley leaves

3 tablespoons unsalted butter, melted

2 tablespoons good-quality extra virgin olive oil

Salt and freshly ground black pepper

2 tomatoes

Lemon wedges, for serving (optional)

1 Place the mussels in a large pot. Cover, set over high heat, and cook, shaking the pot, until the mussels open, about 3 minutes. Discard any unopened shells.

2 Remove the top shell and place the mussels in the half shell on a baking sheet.

3 Preheat the broiler to high.

4 To make the topping: In a small bowl, mix together the breadcrumbs, Romano, parsley, melted butter, oil, and salt and pepper to taste.

5 Halve the tomatoes and use your fingers to scoop out and discard the seeds. Grate the cut sides of the tomatoes on the large holes of a box grater into a bowl. Discard the remaining skins.

6 Spoon a dollop of the breadcrumb mixture onto each mussel. Broil for 3 minutes, or until golden. Spoon a little of the tomato pulp over the mussels and serve with lemon wedges, if you wish.

smoked trout spread

I've always wanted to make a trout spread and finally came up with this recipe, which is so simple and easy. My youngest sniffed it suspiciously the first time before trying it. After tasting it, she closed her eyes and smiled. "That's good," she said. Mission accomplished.

SERVES 4

8 ounces smoked trout, skin removed

8 ounces cream cheese, at room temperature

2 tablespoons fresh lemon juice

2 tablespoons finely chopped red onion

Salt and freshly ground pepper

Finely chopped chives or parsley, for garnish

Toasted bread or Homemade Crackers (page 168), for serving

1 Flake or chop the trout into little pieces and place in a bowl.

2 Add the cream cheese, lemon juice, onion, and salt and pepper to taste and mix until combined. (I find using my hands works best as it helps soften the cheese.)

3 Transfer to a serving bowl, garnish with the herbs, and serve with bread or crackers.

dates with goat cheese and walnuts

This is a supereasy and delicious appetizer. Something about the sweetness of the dates, the creaminess of the cheese, and the earthiness of the toasted walnuts just works in absolute harmony. Yum! **SERVES 4**

6 dates

6 tablespoons soft goat cheese

12 walnut halves, toasted (see page 339)

2 tablespoons extra virgin olive oil

1 Gently pull each date in half and remove the pit.

2 Top each date half with ½ tablespoon goat cheese followed by a walnut half. Drizzle each of the dates with a little oil.

kale chips

You can buy kale chips in the store, but they pale in comparison to homemade ones. How good are these? They are delicate and crunchy and delicious. Even my teenager routinely requests them. You can spice them up however you like, but, as usual, I love them just plain with some salt. **SERVES 4**

1 bunch kale, stems removed

1 tablespoon extra virgin olive oil

Salt

Crushed red pepper flakes, finely grated lemon zest, or grated Parmesan, for seasoning (optional)

1 Preheat the oven to 350°F. Line a baking sheet with parchment paper.

2 Tear the kale into large pieces. Transfer to a large bowl, add the oil, and toss to combine, massaging the oil into the kale.

3 Working in batches, if necessary, spread the leaves out in a single layer on the prepared sheet. Sprinkle with salt and roast for 10 to 15 minutes, until crisp and starting to darken. If desired, season with pepper flakes, lemon zest, or Parmesan. Let cool briefly before serving.

Use any type
of kale to
make chips.

panisse

A panisse is a fried chickpea cake famous in France. It's a savory, gluten-free piece of yumminess that's closely related to socca, a chickpea flour pancake that you can get cooked over a fire at the Nice flower market in France. Panisse is thicker and cut into fingers. I like to sprinkle mine with salt and pepper, but you can also use flavored or spiced salt. **SERVES 4 TO 6**

4 cups warm water

2 cups chickpea flour

1 teaspoon salt

Olive oil

Sea salt and freshly ground black pepper

1 In a saucepan, whisk together the water, chickpea flour, and salt for about 3 minutes. (It might look lumpy.) Place the saucepan over medium-low heat and cook, stirring, for 10 minutes, or until very thick.

2 Grease a 13 × 9-inch baking dish with plenty of oil. Spoon the chickpea mixture into the dish and flatten the surface. Allow to stand for 20 minutes to cool and set, then cut the mixture into 1 × 3-inch fingers.

3 In a large cast-iron skillet, heat ½ inch of the oil over high heat until shimmering. Working in batches, fry the fingers for 2 to 3 minutes per side, until golden brown. Drain on paper towels and season with salt and pepper to taste.

"gardooni"

This was Louie Cinquino's signature dish (he called wild cardoons—which is actually burdock—"gardooni"), a dish made with love and patience, and devoured within minutes of being served. It requires foraging the spring stems of the wild cardoon, which you will easily find at the edge of any woods, or even in your backyard. Harvest the stems of the plants before they sprout flower shoots and cut them close to the ground, trimming the bottom part and the leafy top. **SERVES 6 TO 8**

24 burdock stems

2 cups all-purpose flour

3 large eggs, lightly beaten

Olive oil, for shallow-frying

5 cloves garlic, chopped

Salt and freshly ground black pepper

Finely grated Romano cheese, for serving

1 Cut the stems into 4- to 5-inch lengths. Wash them and brush them down to remove the fuzz-like growth, scraping the edges with a knife to remove any stringy bits.

2 In a saucepan of boiling water, cook the stems for 7 to 10 minutes, until tender. Drain and cool under cold running water. Drain and pat dry with paper towels.

3 One at a time, roll the stems in the flour and dip into the beaten eggs, shaking to remove excess.

4 Pour 1 inch of olive oil into a large skillet and heat over medium-high heat. Add half the chopped garlic and, working in batches, add the stems and fry, turning, for 3 to 4 minutes, until golden. Transfer to a plate lined with paper towels. Season with salt and pepper and sprinkle with Romano.

5 Repeat with the remaining garlic and stems.

The Main Thing

Research has shown that nothing is more important when it comes to raising healthy, happy, smart, and well-adjusted kids than a family dinner. Whether it's a small meal or a big family get-together, there is something magical about sitting at a table and eating nourishing and yummy foods. In fact, I would go so far as to say that crankiness, meanness, short temper, and sadness could be greatly helped by a good, solid, organic meal cooked with love and eaten without drama.

What do I mean about drama? The dinner table is not the place for fights, shouting matches, or crying fits (even though we've all experienced these for sure!). But don't underestimate the power of food to heal, to bring people together, and create peace. A healthy and happy family is one that can eat together with joy, respect, and love—for each other and the food.

As a mom who works more than full time, I've always made dinner a priority. And if I can do it, you can do it. Many of these dishes can be made very quickly. Lots of them can be made in advance and frozen (or freeze the leftovers for another dinner). Some of them are more geared toward large family gatherings or weekend dinner parties. But all of them are brought to their simplest essence and greatly loved by all my family.

Some of these recipes call for expensive ingredients, but many don't. The most important thing is to choose birds, meats, and fish that are organic and humanely raised. Eating happy pigs and chickens is better for us. Eating a sustainably raised and properly caught fish makes the ocean healthier. At the very least, eating organic and humanely raised and harvested foods makes the planet healthier, and that benefits all of us.

Think of it as a form of charitable giving. You are spending money to prevent health problems, rather than having to give money to fix things later. So many problems are caused by conventionally grown foods that are full of environmental toxins, is that really worth a few dollars less at the supermarket? Each and every one of us has incredible power and impact to change the world for the better. Starting at the dinner table.

crispy roast chicken with gravy

Let's start at the very beginning. The most classic, easy, and delicious dinner you can make is roast chicken with gravy. You only really need three things: an oven, a whole chicken, and a roasting pan that can go from oven to stovetop for the gravy. You'll also need a bit of flour, water, salt, and pepper. But that's it. Nothing more! **SERVES 4**

1 whole chicken (about 4 pounds)

GRAVY

¾ cup water

¼ cup all-purpose flour

Salt and freshly ground black pepper

TIP: Don't throw out the chicken carcass—you can use it to make stock (page 111). If you're gluten-free, simply use the pan juices as a sauce.

1 Preheat the oven to 375°F.

2 Place the chicken, breast-side up, in a roasting pan and roast for 1 hour 20 minutes, or until the chicken is cooked through and golden. The chicken is cooked when the juices run clear (you can pierce it with a skewer or fork) and the legs feel loose.

3 Transfer the chicken from the pan to a serving plate, but first tilt the chicken slightly to drain the juices into the roasting pan. Set aside.

4 Place the pan on the stovetop over high heat and bring the juices to a boil.

5 To make the gravy: In a cup, whisk together the water and flour until smooth and combined. Add the flour mixture to the pan and stir with a spoon to scrape the bottom of the pan, releasing all the tasty roasted bits and flavor. Stir until thickened, about 1 minute. Add salt and pepper to taste.

6 Carve the chicken and serve with the gravy.

chicken cacciatore

This was my sister Heidi's favorite dish growing up and she taught me how to make it. Many chicken cacciatore recipes call for boneless chicken breasts, but I prefer to use the skin and bones for more flavor. Ultimately you can choose the cuts of chicken you and your family prefer. You can even cut up a whole chicken. **SERVES 4 TO 6**

1 cup all-purpose flour

½ teaspoon each salt and freshly ground black pepper

2 bone-in, skin-on chicken breasts

2 bone-in, skin-on chicken thighs

2 chicken drumsticks

¼ cup extra virgin olive oil

1 onion, chopped

1 green bell pepper, chopped

3 cloves garlic, chopped

6 cups tomato sauce, store-bought or homemade (page 111)

¼ cup chopped fresh basil leaves

¼ cup chopped fresh Italian parsley leaves

1 pound rotini pasta

1. In a shallow bowl, mix together the flour, salt, and pepper. Cut the chicken breasts in half crosswise. Dredge all the chicken evenly in the seasoned flour.

2. In a large Dutch oven, heat the oil over medium-high heat. Add the chicken, skin-side down, and cook for 7 minutes. Turn and cook about 7 minutes more, until golden and crispy. Remove the chicken from the skillet and drain on paper towels.

3. Reduce the heat to low, add the onion, bell pepper, and garlic and cook gently for 5 minutes, or until soft.

4. Add the tomato sauce, basil, and parsley and stir to combine. Return the chicken to the skillet and simmer for 30 minutes.

5. Meanwhile, cook the pasta according to package directions. Drain and divide among serving plates.

6. Top the pasta with a piece of chicken and spoon over the sauce.

chicken potpie

Chicken potpie was one of the very few things I ate growing up that came from a box in the freezer. You can still buy decent frozen, organic chicken potpie, but I never feel it's substantial enough for the whole family. So I make it myself. The Pennsylvania Dutch actually have a soup called chicken potpie, but it's made with noodles, not a crust. And really, chicken potpie is all about the crust. **SERVES 4 TO 6**

2 tablespoons butter

¼ cup all-purpose flour

1½ cups chicken stock, store-bought or homemade (page 111)

1 cup chopped raw or cooked chicken

2 carrots, chopped

2 ribs celery, chopped

2 potatoes, cut into small cubes

2 handfuls green beans, chopped

2 handfuls frozen peas

Salt and freshly ground black pepper

2 batches Incredibly Flaky Pie Dough (page 299), omitting the sugar

1 large egg, lightly beaten

1 Preheat the oven to 350°F.

2 In a skillet, melt the butter over high heat. Stir in the flour and cook until the mixture starts to foam. Add the stock and chicken, bring to a boil, and stir until the sauce is thickened.

3 Stir in the carrots, celery, potatoes, green beans, and peas. Season with salt and pepper. Remove from the heat and set aside.

4 On a lightly floured surface, roll each piece of pie dough to a ⅛-inch-thick round 12 inches in diameter.

5 Line a 9-inch pie dish with one round of the dough. Spoon in the filling, top with the second round of dough, and crimp the edges to seal. Brush the crust with the beaten egg and make a small incision in the top to allow the steam to escape as the pie is baking. Bake for 45 minutes to 1 hour, until the pastry is golden.

grilled lemon-garlic chicken

Nothing tastes quite as good as something cooked outdoors and infused with the flavor of wood smoke. Yes, I mean real grilling, with charcoal and wood. I always use natural wood charcoal, which I get at local high-end grocery stores, augmented by some real wood from our yard. This recipe is so quick and perfect for a night when you don't want to fuss too much. The secret to its quick cooking is to pound the chicken thin. **SERVES 4 TO 6**

4 to 6 boneless, skinless chicken breasts, trimmed of fat

½ cup extra virgin olive oil

1 lemon

2 cloves garlic, chopped

Salt

1 Using a meat mallet, pound the chicken breasts between 2 pieces of parchment paper to a ¼- to ½-inch thickness.

2 Transfer the chicken to a bowl with the oil and toss to combine. Finely grate the lemon zest over the chicken, juice the lemon, and add the juice to the bowl with the garlic and salt and toss to coat.

3 Prepare a grill or preheat a grill pan over high heat. Grill the chicken for 5 minutes per side, or until cooked through.

TIP: Serve with my Syrian Salad (page 44) and Roasted Cauliflower with Tahini Dressing (page 269).

ardie's garlic chicken

My mother was known for many recipes, but this is her most famous. It's a real crowd-pleaser and easy to make in either small or large batches. You can make it with any kind of chicken, skin on or skin off, boneless or bone-in. However, for the true Ardie taste, you have to make it with bones and skin. And you have to cook it until the skin is totally crispy and golden brown. **SERVES 4 TO 6**

6 tablespoons extra virgin olive oil

½ cup fine dried breadcrumbs (see page 338)

4 pounds bone-in, skin-on chicken parts of your choice

Salt

1 stick (4 ounces) unsalted butter

4 cloves garlic, crushed in a press

) Preheat the oven to 375°F. Place 3 tablespoons of the oil in a large roasting pan and set aside.

2 Place the breadcrumbs in a shallow bowl. Press each piece of chicken into the breadcrumbs and place, skin-side up, in the roasting pan. Sprinkle with salt and roast for 20 minutes.

3 Meanwhile, in a small saucepan, melt the butter over medium heat. Add the remaining 3 tablespoons oil and the garlic and cook, stirring, for 5 minutes, or until golden.

4 Brush each piece of chicken liberally with the garlic-butter mixture, return to the oven, and roast for 30 minutes longer, or until golden brown and cooked through.

cornell chicken

If you are in western New York State and you see a sign for barbecued chicken, the taste will not be anything remotely like what you would find in the South. I got this recipe from my former mother-in-law, and she got it from something she called "home-bureau," a ladies' get-together that taught them how to cook. **SERVES 4 TO 6**

1 large egg

½ cup extra virgin olive oil

1 cup apple cider vinegar

1 tablespoon salt

1½ teaspoons poultry seasoning

½ teaspoon freshly ground black pepper

1 whole chicken (about 4 pounds), cut into 8 pieces, or 4 pounds bone-in, skin-on chicken parts of your choice

TIP: For an authentic western New York experience, serve with No-Mayo Coleslaw (page 56).

1 Place the egg in a blender and pulse until beaten. Add the oil in a thin, steady stream and process until thickened. Add the vinegar, salt, poultry seasoning, and pepper and pulse to combine. Measure out 1 cup of the sauce and refrigerate.

2 Place the chicken in a shallow dish and pour over the remaining sauce. Cover and marinate in the fridge for 2 hours.

3 Prepare a grill to medium-high.

4 Brush the chicken with some of the reserved sauce and grill, turning, for 30 to 40 minutes, until the chicken is golden and cooked through. Baste the chicken with the sauce every 10 minutes or so.

FROM THE BLOG
"The recipe came from Robert Baker, a professor in the Ag School at Cornell University in 1950. It is still used all over upstate NY at firehouse and church fundraisers." —BARBARA

my country fried chicken

I love fried chicken (in moderation, of course). To me, the perfect fried chicken is organic, nice and batter-y, has its skin on, and is crispy. Buttermilk? Forget about it. I've tried cooking chicken with and without, and I don't think it makes enough of a difference to be worth searching it out. Brining? No way. Who's got the time and patience for that? This recipe is delicious, but it's easy and quick, too. Serve with my No-Mayo Coleslaw (page 56). **SERVES 4 TO 6**

1 large egg, lightly beaten

2 cups whole milk

4 cups all-purpose flour

1 tablespoon salt

2 teaspoons freshly ground black pepper

3 cups olive oil or lard

1 whole chicken (about 4 pounds), cut into 10 pieces (breasts halved)

1 In a shallow bowl, whisk together the egg and milk until combined. In a second shallow bowl, mix together the flour, salt, and pepper.

2 In a large cast-iron skillet, heat the oil over high heat to 350°F (use a deep-fry thermometer).

3 Dip each piece of chicken in the egg mixture, shaking to remove excess. Press into the flour mixture to coat well.

4 Once the oil is hot, working in batches, add the chicken and cook for 10 minutes, making sure the oil stays at about 325°F. Turn and cook about 10 minutes more, until golden and cooked through. Remove the chicken from the oil and drain on paper towels before serving.

TIP: For an extra crispy coating, you can double dip: Coat the chicken in a second round of egg and flour mixture before frying.

curry chicken

We never ate Indian food when I was a kid, except for this recipe. I am pretty sure my mother found it in The Joy of Cooking. *I've altered it a tiny bit (the original recipe calls for raisins or currants and I don't really care for those), plus I use brown basmati rice. I don't make it too spicy so my kids will eat it, but if I were making it for myself I would definitely spice it up.* **SERVES 4 TO 6**

1 cup brown or white basmati rice

1 cup all-purpose flour

Salt and freshly ground black pepper

4 to 6 bone-in, skin-on chicken parts: a combination of drumsticks, thighs, breasts

3 tablespoons unsalted butter

¼ cup extra virgin olive oil

1 tablespoon curry powder

1 green bell pepper, chopped

1 onion, chopped

1 clove garlic, finely chopped

2 cups chopped fresh or canned tomatoes

Slivered almonds, toasted, for serving

1 Preheat the oven to 375°F.

2 Cook the rice according to package directions.

3 Meanwhile, in a shallow bowl, mix together the flour with a little salt and pepper. Dust the chicken with the flour.

4 In a large heavy-bottomed ovenproof skillet or Dutch oven, melt the butter over medium-high heat. Add the chicken, skin-side down, and cook, turning, for 3 minutes per side, until well browned. Remove and set aside.

5 Add the oil and curry powder to the pan and cook until foamy. Add the bell pepper and onion and cook, stirring, for 8 minutes, until golden. Add the garlic and cook, stirring, for 1 minute. Add the tomatoes and stir to combine.

6 Return the chicken to the pan, transfer to the oven and bake, uncovered, for 40 minutes. Sprinkle with the slivered almonds and serve with the rice.

red beans and rice

This recipe is the result of getting totally lost in Harlem. I was on my way to a party in Fort Washington Park and my driver, a fellow named J. R. Crayton, and I missed a turn and spent an hour driving around lost. On our adventure he shared his recipe for beans and rice. The secret ingredient is coconut milk. J. R. says the coconut milk makes the rice tender, and it does. It also makes it creamy and rich, without tasting like coconut at all. **SERVES 8 TO 10**

2 smoked turkey wings (or one smoked turkey leg or one smoked ham hock)

8 cups water

3 cups white or brown rice

¼ cup plus 2 tablespoons coconut milk

1 can (14 to 19 ounces) red beans, drained and rinsed

Salt

Hot sauce (optional)

1 In a large soup pot, combine the turkey and water and bring to a boil over high heat. Reduce the heat to low and simmer, uncovered, for 2 hours, or until the meat comes away from the bones.

2 Strain the broth into a large pot. Shred the meat from the bones (discard the bones) and set the meat aside.

3 Add the rice and coconut milk to the broth and bring to a boil over high heat. Stir, reduce the heat to low, and simmer, covered, for about 20 minutes (or 40 minutes if using brown rice), stirring occasionally.

4 When the rice is almost tender, add the shredded meat, beans, and salt to taste and stir to combine. Remove from the heat and set aside for 5 minutes. Serve with hot sauce, if desired.

roast turkey

We raise turkeys every year on our family farm so I'm fortunate to have a local, organic source for Thanksgiving dinner. If you are looking for an organic bird, start with your local farmers' market. Then check your butcher or supermarket. Once you have the turkey, there are all sorts of fancy recipes calling for brining, stuffing, grilling, or deep-frying. I always lean toward simplicity—no stuffing, no trussing, no fussing. **SERVES 10 TO 12**

1 whole turkey (about 14 pounds)

Salt

GRAVY
¼ cup water

¼ cup all-purpose flour

Salt and freshly ground black pepper

1 Preheat the oven to 450°F.

2 Place the turkey, breast-side up, in a deep, high-sided roasting pan, sprinkle with salt, and roast for 1 hour. Reduce the oven temperature to 350°F and continue to roast for 2 hours, or until the turkey is golden and cooked through. (Allow 15 minutes per pound of turkey. The internal temperature should read 165°F on a meat thermometer when inserted into the thigh.)

3 Transfer the turkey from the pan to a serving platter, first making sure you tilt the bird slightly to drain the juices into the roasting pan. Set aside.

4 Place the pan over high heat on the stovetop and bring the juices to a boil.

5 To make the gravy: In a cup, whisk together the water and flour until smooth and combined. Add the flour mixture to the pan and stir with a spoon to scrape the bottom of the pan, releasing all the tasty roasted bits and flavor. Stir until thickened, about 1 minute. Add salt and pepper to taste.

6 Carve the turkey and serve with the gravy.

Talking Turkey

In a *New York Times* interview in 2015 with the former restaurant critic and best-selling author Ruth Reichl, I was totally vindicated when I read about her approach to turkey. "After decades as an editor who encouraged readers to apply elaborate cooking methods to the Thanksgiving turkey, Ms. Reichl breaks free from the tyranny of innovation and admits that simply shoving an unseasoned bird into a 450-degree oven is the best way to go." YES! I told you so!

roast goose

When I think of roast goose, I think of the Christmases of yore, of magical village streets covered in snow, of days when the only light was from fireplaces and candles, and people were living in tune with the rhythms of nature because there was no other way to live. Roasting a goose couldn't be easier, and what makes it so delicious is all the crispy skin and dark meat. Because goose is quite rich, serve it with simple steamed or sautéed greens and Mashed Potatoes (page 252).

SERVES 4 TO 6

1 whole goose (about 15 pounds)

Salt

2 apples, halved

TIPS: You can reserve the goose fat and pour it into a jar to keep in the fridge. It's lovely for frying or roasting vegetables. Make sure you save the goose carcass and bones to make stock later, so you can make my Goose, Barley, and White Bean Soup (page 124). If you can't start the soup that day or the next, freeze the carcass and make the stock later.

1 Preheat the oven to 400°F.

2 Place the goose, breast-side up, in a large high-sided roasting pan. Sprinkle the goose with salt and add the apples to the pan (they help absorb the fat). Roast for 30 minutes, then reduce the oven temperature to 350°F, and roast for 10 minutes more per pound. Geese are naturally fatty birds, so if there are a lot of drippings, carefully spoon or pour off some of the fat halfway through the cooking time (see Tips). Discard the apples.

3 Transfer the goose to a carving board and rest for 15 minutes before carving.

hamburger hash with mash

As a kid, I was a witness to the transformation of public school lunches from hot homemade food served on real dishes to prewrapped, premade food served on disposable paper trays. Funnily enough, one of my family's favorite recipes is something I used to eat in the early days of school lunches: hamburger hash. It's not a pretty dish, but it's so yummy that my kids ask for it all the time. Serve it with a green salad and you've got a meal. **SERVES 6**

MASHED POTATOES

3 pounds potatoes, peeled and chopped

5 tablespoons butter

½ cup whole milk

¼ teaspoon salt

HASH

3 tablespoons extra virgin olive oil

2 pounds ground beef

2½ cups beef stock or water

½ cup all-purpose flour

1 teaspoon salt

1 To make the mashed potatoes: In a saucepan, combine the potatoes with water to cover. Bring to a boil and cook for 12 to 15 minutes, until soft.

2 Drain the potatoes and return to the pan with the butter, milk, and salt and mash with a hand masher until smooth and combined. Set aside and keep warm.

3 To make the hash: In a large cast-iron skillet, heat the oil over high heat. Add the beef and cook, stirring to break it up, for 10 minutes, or until well browned and cooked through.

4 In a small bowl, whisk together the stock and flour. Pour into the skillet and cook, stirring, until thickened. Stir in the salt.

5 To serve, divide the mashed potatoes among plates and spoon the hamburger hash on top.

vietnamese rice paper rolls

Whoever said we have nothing to fear but fear itself could have been talking about rice paper rolls. I've wanted to make them for years, but dreaded the complexity, feared the differentness, and practically hyperventilated over finding the right moment to tackle the job. When I finally made them, I had to laugh to myself at how ridiculously easy it was. They're the perfect summer meal because they require almost no cooking, plus they're fresh and delicious. **SERVES 4**

DIPPING SAUCE

¼ cup fresh lime juice

1 tablespoon sugar

1 tablespoon fish sauce

1 tablespoon rice vinegar

1 tablespoon sesame oil

1 teaspoon chili oil, or freshly sliced chilis (optional)

1 large clove garlic, finely chopped

2 tablespoons chopped fresh cilantro

ROLLS

8 round rice paper wrappers (8-inch diameter)

16 fresh basil leaves, preferably Thai basil

16 fresh mint leaves

8 large wild-caught shrimp, cooked, peeled, and halved horizontally

1 large carrot, shredded

1½ cups finely shredded cabbage

2 ounces vermicelli rice noodles, soaked according to package directions

1 To make the dipping sauce: In a small bowl, whisk together the lime juice, sugar, fish sauce, rice vinegar, sesame oil, chili oil (if using), garlic, and cilantro. Set aside.

2 To make the rolls: Fill a wide shallow bowl with cold water. Dip a rice paper wrapper into the water for 10 to 20 seconds to soften slightly. Place on a clean surface and lightly pat dry. On the bottom half of the rice paper, layer 2 basil leaves, 2 mint leaves, 2 shrimp halves, and some carrot, cabbage, and noodles (don't overfill!).

3 Fold the bottom and side edges over the filling, and roll to form a cigar shape. Careful not to pull too tightly, as it can rip the paper. Repeat with the remaining wrappers and ingredients. Serve the rolls with the dipping sauce.

TIP: You can fill rice paper rolls with almost anything. Try shredded pork or chicken.

lamb meatballs

These lamb meatballs came from a craving for lamb kebabs (shish taouk at my local Middle Eastern restaurant), but I didn't have the right kind of lamb and it was too cold for grilling. The meatballs are quick, easy, and tasty, and great as part of a Middle Eastern spread including my Syrian Salad (page 44) and Rice Pilaf (page 261).

SERVES 4

1 pound ground lamb

¼ cup chopped fresh Italian parsley leaves

1 large egg

1 clove garlic, finely chopped

Salt

Extra virgin olive oil, for cooking

1 In a large bowl, combine the lamb, parsley, egg, garlic, and salt to taste and mix with your hands to combine. Pinch off small amounts of the lamb mixture and roll into small marble-size meatballs.

2 In a large cast-iron skillet, heat a little oil over high heat. Working in batches, cook the meatballs turning, for 3 minutes, or until well browned. Cover the skillet and cook until the meatballs are cooked through, about 3 minutes more.

mini meatballs

The whole point of this generous recipe is to make a big batch of meatballs you can freeze so that you can just pull them from the freezer at any time and make my Italian Wedding Soup (page 143) or spaghetti and meatballs. You can make them small or large; I prefer tiny, bite-size meatballs. **SERVES 6 TO 8**

2 pounds ground beef

1 pound ground pork

1 cup dried breadcrumbs (see page 338)

½ cup finely grated Romano cheese

2 large eggs

1 teaspoon salt

½ teaspoon freshly ground black pepper

3 tablespoons chopped fresh Italian parsley leaves

Extra virgin olive oil, for cooking

1 In a large bowl, combine the beef, pork, breadcrumbs, Romano, eggs, salt, pepper, and parsley and mix well with your hands to combine.

2 In a large cast-iron skillet, heat a little oil over high heat. Working in batches, pinch off small amounts of the mixture (the size of a marble), roll into mini balls, and add to the pan. Fry the meatballs for a few minutes on each side, or until well browned and cooked through. Drain on paper towels. Repeat until all the mixture has been cooked.

3 To freeze, place the cooled balls in a single layer on a baking sheet and freeze for 2 to 3 hours. Transfer to freezer bags and store in the freezer for up to 3 months.

FROM THE BLOG
"From one Maria to another, these were delicious! What's more, my picky eater ate five of them. More than I've ever seen her eat of any kind of protein. Thanks for a great recipe!" —**MARIA**

my tacos

I've never been particularly confident with Mexican food, especially tacos. While I crave and devour them and watch my family eat my tacos with gusto, there is always a little voice inside my head telling me they aren't Mexican enough or there must be better ones out there. But after eating my fair share of American tacos, I've come to believe that these are pretty damned tasty. **SERVES 6**

Extra virgin olive oil, for cooking

1¼ pounds flank steak

¼ teaspoon ground cumin

⅛ teaspoon chili powder

Salt

12 6-inch tortillas (see page 339)

Mexicali Beans (page 256)

1 cup shredded Monterey Jack cheese

½ head iceberg lettuce or green cabbage, shredded (about 3 cups)

Salsa, store-bought or homemade (page 172)

Guacamole, store-bought or homemade (page 173),

Sour cream, for serving (optional)

Hot sauce, for serving

1 Prepare the Mexicali Beans and keep warm.

2 While the beans are cooking, in a large cast-iron skillet or grill pan, heat a little oil over high heat. Season the steak with the cumin, chili powder, and salt to taste. Cook the steak for 3½ minutes per side for medium-rare. Rest for 5 minutes, then slice into strips against the grain and set aside.

3 Wipe out the skillet with paper towels, add a little more oil, and toast the tortillas on both sides until golden.

4 Set out the tortillas, steak, beans, cheddar, lettuce, salsa, guacamole, sour cream (if using), and hot sauce, for self-assembly.

TIP: You can also fill your tacos with sliced grilled chicken, pork tenderloin, or fish instead of steak. Also, finely sliced radishes make a nice topping.

italian sausage

Sausage is one of those things that most people would rather not know how it's made. Unless you're like me, and won't eat it unless you know exactly how it's made. Fortunately Rita was willing to share her father's recipe. I simply shape the mixture into patties. This is for a large quantity of meat, but the idea is you freeze the patties for future use; of course you could always halve the recipe. **MAKES ABOUT 30 PATTIES**

5 pounds ground pork

2 pounds ground beef

1 cup finely grated Romano cheese

½ cup chopped fresh Italian parsley leaves (or 2 tablespoons dried)

2 tablespoons fennel seeds

1 tablespoon salt

1 teaspoon freshly ground black pepper

1 teaspoon ground cayenne pepper (optional)

TIP: Serve the patties in a bun like a burger, or crumble them up and use in a pasta sauce, soup, or tomato sauce.

1 In a large bowl, combine the pork, beef, Romano, parsley, fennel, salt, black pepper, and cayenne (if using) and mix with your hands until well combined.

2 Shape the mixture into 2- to 3-inch patties. Cook them in batches in a large cast-iron skillet over high heat for 5 minutes per side, or until cooked through. Or, you can freeze the uncooked patties between sheets of parchment paper in an airtight container for up to 2 months. Thaw in the fridge overnight before cooking.

FROM THE BLOG

"This is delicious. I tried it with ground turkey instead of pork and all I can say is, Wow! I added some wine and slightly more fennel seed. I have been looking for a good Italian sausage recipe for years. Thank you."
—**MARYANN**

shepherd's pie

Sometimes we need the comfort of something hearty, warm, and yummy to ease the pain of winter. Shepherd's pie is just the thing. This is really easy and there's nothing fussy about it. **SERVES 4 TO 6**

3 tablespoons extra virgin olive oil

1 pound ground beef

1 cup mixed frozen vegetables (such as corn, carrots, and peas)

1 teaspoon salt

Freshly ground black pepper

¼ cup water

¼ cup all-purpose flour

POTATO TOPPING
6 medium potatoes, peeled and cut into quarters

½ cup whole milk

6 tablespoons butter

½ teaspoon salt

1 Preheat the oven to 375°F.

2 Pour the oil into a 2-quart baking dish, add the ground beef, vegetables, salt, and pepper to taste and mix to combine.

3 In a bowl, whisk together the water and flour until smooth and pour over the beef mixture. Bake for 30 minutes.

4 Meanwhile, to make the topping: In a saucepan, combine the potatoes with water to cover, bring to a boil and cook for 12 to 15 minutes, until soft. Drain and return the potatoes to the pan. Add the milk, 4 tablespoons of the butter, and the salt and mash with a hand masher until smooth and combined.

5 Remove the baking dish from the oven and turn the oven to broil. Spoon the mashed potatoes over the beef mixture and dot with the remaining 2 tablespoons butter.

6 Broil the pie for 5 to 10 minutes, until the topping is golden.

chicken-fried steak

This is a dish my oldest daughter once requested as a special birthday meal when she was really young and I had no idea what it was. Years later in Texas on business, I discovered that it's a real thing (the state claims to be the birthplace of chicken-fried steak). Since then, whenever either of us sees it on a menu, we order it and enjoy it sparingly. It's typically made with a cheap cut of beef, but I buy organic steak trimmed of the fat for a more "wholesome" version. Serve with steamed green beans and Mashed Potatoes (page 252) if desired. **SERVES 4 TO 6**

6 cube steaks
(8 ounces each)

Salt and freshly
ground black
pepper

2 cups whole milk

2 large eggs

2 cups all-purpose
flour

Olive oil, for
cooking

GRAVY
1 cup chicken
stock, store-bought
or homemade
(page 111)

½ cup all-purpose
flour

1 cup whole milk

Salt and freshly
ground black
pepper

1 Season the steaks with salt and pepper and set aside.

2 Place the milk and eggs in a shallow bowl and whisk with a fork to combine. Place the flour in a separate shallow bowl.

3 In a large cast-iron skillet, heat ½ inch of oil over high heat. Dip the steaks into the milk mixture, shaking to remove any excess, then press into the flour. Repeat for a second coating of each.

4 Working in batches, fry the steaks for 5 minutes per side, or until golden. Keep the steaks on a wire rack set over a baking sheet in a warm oven until ready to serve.

5 To make the gravy: Pour out most of the oil from the skillet, leaving the skillet lightly coated, and place over high heat. In a small bowl, whisk together the stock and flour until well combined. Pour into the skillet and stir with a wooden spoon until the mixture starts to thicken and turn brown.

6 Add the milk and stir constantly until thickened. Stir in salt and pepper to taste. Serve the steaks with the gravy.

ardie's pasties

This is one of my mother's most coveted recipes. While traditionally pasties were made as lunches for miners or other workers, in our family they were always served at a summer picnic. This recipe was one of the last things my mother asked me to make for her before she died. But she told me if I didn't use lard, she would refuse to eat them. I am grateful that she got me over my fear of lard! **MAKES 6 PASTIES**

FILLING
1 pound ground beef

4 potatoes, peeled and diced

1 onion, chopped

1½ teaspoons salt

½ teaspoon freshly ground black pepper

DOUGH
3 cups all-purpose flour

⅔ cup lard

1 teaspoon salt

⅔ cup ice water

6 tablespoons butter

Milk, for brushing

Ketchup, for serving

1 Preheat the oven to 425°F. Line a baking sheet with parchment paper.

2 To make the filling: In a bowl, combine the beef, potatoes, onion, salt, and pepper and mix with your hands to combine. Set aside.

3 To make the dough: In a large bowl, combine the flour, lard, and salt and mix with your fingertips until the mixture resembles coarse breadcrumbs. Add the ice water, a little at a time, and mix until a smooth dough forms.

4 Divide the dough into 6 even balls. Roll out one piece of dough on a lightly floured surface to an 8-inch round. Place 1 cup of the filling on one side of the round, top with 1 tablespoon butter, and fold the dough over to enclose, crimping the edges together to seal. Repeat to make 6 pasties.

5 Transfer the pasties to the prepared baking sheet, brush the tops with a little milk, and bake for 15 minutes. Reduce the oven temperature to 375°F and bake for 40 minutes longer, until golden and cooked through.

TIPS: This is my mother's basic version, but feel free to add spices, such as paprika or curry powder, and herbs, such as chopped fresh thyme or rosemary, to the filling mixture.

The last time I made pasties (with lard) for her, she taught me one of the most important cooking lessons. Recipes are great, but it's as much about *hand-feel.* If the dough feels too dry, add more lard or a bit of water. If it feels too wet, add more flour. Recipes change with the weather. Feel free to adapt.

FROM THE BLOG
"My mom always mixed carrots, onion, and potatoes with the meat, but rutabaga is a nice change, too." —JANIE

crispy-skin salmon with herb dressing

If I ask my kids what they want for dinner, given anything, they almost always ask for salmon. I love it when they do because it's so healthy, easy, and delicious. The key is to start with good salmon. I prefer to purchase wild-caught king salmon, which is a bit pricey but a rare and healthy treat, so I think it's worth it. The omega-3s alone are a powerful enough reason to devour it. Serve with Mashed Potatoes (page 252). **SERVES 4**

1½ pounds skin-on salmon fillet

Sea salt

Extra virgin olive oil, for cooking

HERB DRESSING

¼ cup extra virgin olive oil

3 tablespoons chopped fresh Italian parsley leaves

2 tablespoons chopped fresh dill leaves

1 small clove garlic, finely chopped

Sea salt

1 Cut the salmon fillet into 4 equal pieces and sprinkle with some salt.

2 In a large cast-iron skillet, heat a little oil over high heat. Add the salmon, skin-side down, and cook for about 5 minutes, or until the skin is crispy. Cover with a lid and cook for 1 minute more (or turn the fish and cook without the lid), or until cooked to your liking.

3 Meanwhile, to make the herb dressing: In a small bowl, stir together the oil, parsley, dill, garlic, and salt to taste.

4 To serve, drizzle the salmon with the herb dressing.

my glazed ham

This is a real crowd-pleaser and I often make it for parties using a whole bone-in ham. Whenever I make it, I get rave reviews. You bake it for a long time so the fat has a chance to form perfect crispiness. For a 15-pounder, double the glaze and bake the ham for 3 hours, glazing after 2. You can't go wrong, as long as the ham is heated through and the top is nice and dark and the fat is crispy. **SERVES 8 TO 10**

1 bone-in half ham (8 to 10 pounds)

Whole cloves, for decorating

¼ cup orange marmalade

¼ cup packed light brown sugar

3 tablespoons Dijon mustard

TIP: Keep the leftover ham bone for soup or stock. If not using right away, freeze it for later.

1 Preheat the oven to 350°F.

2 Place the ham in a large roasting pan. Score the ham fat in a diamond pattern and insert a clove into each diamond. Bake the ham for 1 hour, or until sizzling and fragrant.

3 Meanwhile, in a bowl, stir together the marmalade, brown sugar, and mustard.

4 Remove the ham from the oven, brush with one-third of the glaze, and bake for another hour, brushing twice more with the glaze during cooking time. Let the ham rest for 30 minutes before carving.

My Mother's Original

I posted my glazed ham recipe on my blog a few years ago, and imagine my surprise when I received an email from a blog reader and former Rodale Institute employee telling me she still makes my mother's ham glaze, and loves it. She got the recipe directly from my mother decades ago. Of course, I asked if I could have a copy of it and she very kindly sent it to me.

my mother's glazed ham

I believe this is the ham that plays a key role in one of my mother's most famous stories, which goes like this: My father called my mother one day and told her that someone was coming over for lunch. This was not unusual as my father was always bringing people home for meals, sometimes without any notice at all.

She decided to make her glazed ham. When the guest showed up for lunch, she discovered it was none other than James Beard! When my mother became angry at my father for not telling her in advance who it was, he said he didn't want her to worry and go overboard trying to impress. She always told the story about how awful my father was. My father told the story occasionally, with laughter. So here is her glazed ham recipe (although honestly, I still prefer mine!).

SERVES 10 TO 12

1 bone-in half ham (8 to 10 pounds)

Whole cloves, for decorating

1 cup packed light brown sugar

¼ cup yellow mustard

2 tablespoons all-purpose flour

Grated zest of 1 lemon

1 Preheat the oven to 350°F.

2 Place the ham in a large roasting pan. Score the ham fat in a diamond pattern and insert a clove into each diamond. Bake the ham for 1 hour.

3 Meanwhile, in a small bowl, combine the brown sugar, mustard, flour, and lemon zest and mix to a paste.

4 Remove the ham from the oven, cover with the paste, and bake for 1 hour more. Let the ham rest for 30 minutes before carving.

TIP: While most pork roasts are generally sold without skin, you can order pork loin with skin on from most butchers. The skin gets lovely and crunchy (just like fried pork rinds!). You can also roast it without the skin, but at the very least with a small layer of fat to keep it juicy.

roast pork with sauerkraut

Roast pork with mashed potatoes and sauerkraut is a traditional New Year's Day meal in Pennsylvania. But don't wait until January 1 to make it! It's a great and easy meal for weeknights or weekends and makes delicious leftovers for sandwiches, like my Roast Pork, Cabbage, and Garlic Butter Sandwich (page 144). This is my cheat's version of a pan sauerkraut. Serve with Mashed Potatoes (page 252).

SERVES 6 TO 8

1 boneless, skin-on (see tip opposite) pork loin roast (about 5 pounds)

2 tablespoons extra virgin olive oil, plus extra for roasting

1 tablespoon chopped fresh rosemary or 1½ teaspoons dried

Sea salt

1 small yellow onion, halved and thinly sliced

½ head cabbage, halved, cored, and thinly sliced

½ cup apple cider vinegar

½ cup water

⅓ cup apple cider

1. Preheat the oven to 400°F.

2. Place the pork loin, skin-side up, on a large rimmed baking sheet. Score the skin with a small, sharp knife at ½-inch intervals and rub with a little oil, the rosemary, and salt to taste.

3. Roast for about 1 hour, or until golden and crispy. (The internal temperature should read 145°F on a meat thermometer.) If the skin isn't crispy, turn the broiler on high and broil 3 to 5 minutes, until crispy. Let rest for 5 to 10 minutes.

4. While the pork is roasting, in a large cast-iron skillet, heat the 2 tablespoons oil over medium-high heat. Add the onion and a pinch of salt and cook for 3 minutes, until the onions are soft. Add the cabbage, vinegar, water, and cider and stir to combine. Bring to a boil, cover, reduce the heat, and simmer for 35 minutes, or until the cabbage is pale and tender.

5. Slice the pork and serve with the sauerkraut and mashed potatoes.

australian damper and dip

Every once in a while something magical happens because of my blogging, like being offered this recipe from an Aboriginal woman, Ningli, from Australia. Damper is a kind of quick campfire bread usually made in the hot coals of a campfire; and dip is a kangaroo curry that is totally delicious. Before you freak out about eating those cute kangaroos, Australians see kangaroo a bit the way Native Americans see deer and buffalo, an important part of a healthy diet and ecosystem. I've substituted the most easily purchased indigenous meat in my neck of the woods, and that is buffalo (or bison).

SERVES 4 TO 6

DAMPER

2 tablespoons unsalted butter, at room temperature, plus extra for the baking sheet

2½ cups all-purpose flour

2½ teaspoons baking powder

½ teaspoon salt

¼ cup whole milk

DIP

Extra virgin olive oil, for cooking

1 large white onion, chopped

2 cloves garlic, finely chopped

1 tablespoon curry powder, preferably Keen's*

1 To make the damper: Preheat the oven to 350°F. Grease a baking sheet with a little butter.

2 In a bowl, combine the flour, baking powder, and salt. Add the 2 tablespoons butter and rub it into the flour with your fingertips. Add the milk and mix with your hands until a sticky dough forms. (Add more milk if it feels dry.)

3 Place the dough onto the prepared baking sheet and shape into a 6-inch round loaf. Bake for 45 minutes, until golden and the damper sounds hollow when tapped.

4 Meanwhile, to make the dip: In a large heavy-bottomed saucepan, heat a little oil over medium-high heat. Add the onion and cook, stirring, 5 to 10 minutes, until golden and softened. Add the garlic and cook, stirring, for

1½ pounds buffalo tenderloin or steaks, cut into cubes

2 tomatoes, chopped

3 to 4 cups vegetable stock

2 tablespoons apple cider vinegar, or to taste

Salt and freshly ground black pepper

1 minute longer. Add the curry powder and stir until fragrant.

5 Add the meat and cook, stirring, until browned. Add the tomatoes and enough stock to cover the ingredients. Bring to a boil, reduce the heat to a simmer, and cook for 1 hour, or until thickened. Stir in the vinegar and salt and pepper to taste.

6 Serve the dip in the middle of the table with the damper, for dipping.

*Apparently, Keen's brand curry powder is a must in this recipe. I ordered some from Amazon. Keen's originated in England, but the Aussies have adopted it as their own. Keen's is pretty spicy for my little ones, so feel free to use your own curry powder.

aussie meat pies

It's not as easy as you might think to create the perfect Aussie meat pie recipe that would match the taste of the prize-winning pie I ate in Australia, from Mick's Bakehouse in Sydney. That pie was soft, crunchy, peppery, yummy goodness filled with meat and gravy. In trying to re-create it, I turned to Rodale's food director and a resident Aussie, Melanie Hansche (who also edited this book). She shared the recipe from her favorite bakery in Sydney, Bourke Street Bakery. I adapted the filling to suit my own taste, and with smaller quantities. I also consulted my Australian friend Marg Haymanson, who gave me the idea to use Worcestershire sauce in the filling. There are four parts to this recipe. Start the puff pastry the day before, then make the filling, followed by the short crust pastry, then finally assemble it all.

MAKES 6

2½ sticks (10 ounces) unsalted butter

2 cups cold all-purpose flour, plus extra for dusting

1½ teaspoons salt

¼ cup cold water

1½ teaspoons apple cider vinegar

PART 1
PUFF PASTRY

For years I've wanted to make puff pastry from scratch. Why? Because that's the only way I would know for sure it was organic. I started with the Bourke Street Bakery recipe, but halved it. Plus, their recipe calls for repeated 24-hour rests in the fridge. Look, let's get one thing straight—I'm not a pastry chef. I'm a hungry woman who is fundamentally lazy, even though I'm crazy enough to make puff pastry from scratch, so I went with just one resting period. So for that reason, this pastry may not be perfect, but I still found it delicious.

1 Cut 4 tablespoons (½ stick) of the butter into cubes and set at room temperature to soften slightly. Leave the remaining butter in the fridge to stay cold until you're ready to use it.

2 In a bowl, stir together the flour and salt. Add the cubed softened butter and rub it into the flour gently with your fingertips until it resembles coarse breadcrumbs.

3 In a cup, mix together the water and vinegar, then add it to the flour mixture and mix gently with your hands to combine. Transfer to a lightly floured surface and gently knead to make a smooth dough. Flatten the dough into a disk, cover with plastic wrap, and refrigerate for 30 minutes.

4 Take the remaining 2 sticks cold butter out of the fridge to soften a little, about 10 minutes. Roll the butter out between 2 sheets of parchment paper to a 4 × 4-inch square about ½ inch thick.

5 On a lightly floured surface, roll the chilled pastry out to a 4 × 8-inch rectangle. Place the butter on one side of the pastry and fold the rectangle over to cover it.

6 Now the fun begins. Roll the dough out into a long 6 × 18-inch rectangle. Then, pretending you are making a book, fold both short ends in toward the center, so the ends meet but do not overlap. (I found that a spatula or pastry cutter helps if it gets stuck.) Fold the pastry in

RECIPE CONTINUES

half again as if closing a thick book (the reason this process is formally called a "book turn"). Wrap in plastic wrap and refrigerate for 30 minutes.

7 Repeat step 6, rolling out the dough to a large rectangle and folding it as before. Always make sure that the closed side—the spine of your book—is on the right side so you work the dough evenly. Refrigerate for 24 hours.

8 The next day, remove the dough from the fridge and let it warm up slightly. Repeat the rolling and folding process two more times, refrigerating for 30 minutes in between. Chill the dough until ready to use.

PART 2

MEAT PIE FILLING

2 tablespoons extra virgin olive oil

1 onion, chopped

2 pounds cubed beef sirloin or ground beef

6 to 8 cups water

2 tablespoons apple cider vinegar

2 tablespoons Worcestershire sauce

2 teaspoons salt

2 teaspoons freshly ground black pepper

2 tablespoons cornstarch

1 In a large heavy-bottomed saucepan, heat the oil over medium-high heat. Add the onion and cook, stirring, for a few minutes to soften. Add the beef and cook, turning, for 8 minutes, until evenly browned.

2 Add enough water to cover the meat by an inch or so. Bring to a boil and skim any foam from the surface. Add the vinegar, Worcestershire sauce, salt, and pepper, reduce the heat to a simmer, and cook for 1 hour, or until the meat is tender. With a slotted spoon, transfer the meat to a bowl.

RECIPE CONTINUES

3 Bring the liquid in the pan back to a boil. Mix the cornstarch with a little water, add it to the pan, and stir to combine. Cook for 4 minutes, or until thickened. Return the meat to the pan and stir to combine. Set the filling aside to cool completely.

PART 3

SHORT CRUST PASTRY

2 cups cold all-purpose flour

½ teaspoon salt

10 tablespoons unsalted butter, cut into cubes and slightly softened

⅓ cup cold water

1 teaspoon apple cider vinegar

Short crust is a type of pastry that doesn't contain a leavening agent such as yeast, which is important so it doesn't puff up during baking. It's used for pies, tarts, and quiches. In America, we simply call it pie dough. This recipe has a little more water in it and is less crumbly than my usual piecrusts. You can use this for the bottom crust of any savory pie. Short crust has good integrity—it pops right out of the pan, and you can hold the pie in your hand to eat.

1 In a bowl, mix together the flour and salt. Add the butter and rub it into the flour gently with your fingertips until it resembles coarse breadcrumbs.

2 In a cup, combine the water and vinegar, add it to the flour mixture, and mix gently with your hands until the mixture just comes together. Transfer to a lightly floured surface and knead very gently to form a dough (it's okay if you can still see streaks of butter—this is what makes it flaky).

3 Divide the dough into 6 balls, flatten into disks, wrap in plastic wrap, and refrigerate for 30 minutes.

Short Crust Pastry (opposite)

Puff Pastry (page 230)

Meat Pie Filling (page 232)

1 large egg

TIP: The cooked pies freeze remarkably well. Wrap them in foil and plastic wrap and freeze. To reheat, pop them in a 375°F oven for 40 minutes.

PART 4
ASSEMBLY

1 Preheat the oven to 375°F.

2 Roll out each portion of the short crust pastry to a 6- to 7-inch round and use to line the bottom and sides of six 4½-inch pie tins. Trim any excess pastry.

3 Roll out the puff pastry dough to a ¼-inch thickness, being gentle so as to not crush all the lovely layers as you work. Cut out six 5-inch rounds from the dough to fit the tops of the pie tins (the lids are cut slightly larger than the pie tins to allow for some shrinkage during baking).

4 Divide the meat filling among the 6 tins.

5 Beat the egg with a little water to create an egg wash. Use the egg wash to glue the puff pastry lid to the top of the short crust and pinch together with your fingers. Brush the top with more of the egg wash and cut a slit in the pastry to allow steam to escape. Transfer to a baking sheet, and bake for 35 minutes or until golden.

TIP: You can substitute duck, chicken, or lamb. Anything goes!

nana's kugel

Nana's kugel is a tradition in our family. It's a savory, not sweet, kugel, with roots in her Lithuanian heritage. No matter who makes it or how, it never tastes the same or looks the same; but somehow, it has the essence of Nana's kitchen and our childhood in every bite. I prefer it thinner, rather than thicker, so that there's more crust on top and bottom than fluff in the middle. But the great thing about this recipe is that it's hard to screw it up and easy to personalize. You can eat this is a main with a simple green salad or as a side dish with roasted or braised meats. **SERVES 8 TO 10**

¼ cup extra virgin olive oil, plus extra for the baking dish

5 large potatoes, peeled

1 carrot

1 small onion

1 turnip (optional)

1 rib celery, finely chopped

1 cup chicken stock, store-bought or homemade (page 111)

2 large eggs, lightly beaten

½ teaspoon salt, or to taste

1 Preheat the oven to 400°F. Generously grease a 15 × 10-inch baking dish with olive oil.

2 Grate the potatoes, carrot, onion, and turnip (if using) on a large box grater or shred them in a food processor or blender. Place in a large bowl, add the celery and stock, and mix to combine.

3 Stir in the eggs, salt, and ¼ cup olive oil. Transfer to the prepared baking dish.

4 Flatten the mixture and bake for 1 hour, or until golden and crispy on top.

FROM THE BLOG

"Every woman on my husband's side of the family has a kugel recipe regardless if they're from Poland, Sweden, Switzerland, Germany, Czech Republic, Israel, or the US. You're correct in saying that you can't really mess it up! Everyone seems to want to make it their way." —DONNA

hoppin' john

Many hoppin' John recipes call for all sorts of things (spices, bell pepper, garlic). But after trying all the complicated variations, I went back, as usual, to the most basic of them all. So if you want to just call this black-eyed peas and rice, I'm totally fine with that. **SERVES 8 TO 10**

1 smoked turkey wing or smoked ham hock (about ¼ pound)

6 cups water

2 cups white rice

3 cans (14 to 19 ounces) black-eyed peas, drained and rinsed

2 tablespoons distilled white vinegar

Salt

Finely chopped scallions and hot sauce, for serving (optional)

1 Place the turkey or ham hock and water in a large soup pot and bring to a boil. Reduce the heat to low, partially cover, and simmer for 3 to 4 hours, until the meat starts to fall from the bones.

2 Meanwhile, cook the rice according to package directions.

3 Add the black-eyed peas to the meat and simmer for 30 minutes.

4 Remove the turkey or ham from the pot and shred the meat from the bones (discard the bones). Return the shredded meat to the pot. Stir in the vinegar and salt to taste.

5 Spoon the black-eyed peas over the rice. If desired, sprinkle with scallions and serve with hot sauce on the side.

paella

The best paella I ever had was on a sunny day at an outdoor café in Barcelona, Spain. Determined to make my own version, I've fortunately known a true Spaniard long enough that she was willing to share her mother's paella recipe. (Thanks, Fabiola Arredondo!) Of course, I've taken some liberties to simplify it, which, according to Fabiola, is a very Spanish thing to do: "Every good Spanish woman has her own version of paella." So here is my simplified version of authentic paella. **SERVES 6 TO 8**

6 cups chicken stock, store-bought or homemade (page 111)

1 small onion, peeled and left whole, plus 1 medium onion, chopped

½ teaspoon saffron threads

¼ teaspoon smoked paprika

½ cup extra virgin olive oil

4 bone-in, skin-on chicken thighs

1 pound chorizo sausage, sliced

4 scallions, chopped

4 cloves garlic, chopped

1 Preheat the oven to 325°F.

2 In a saucepan, bring the stock to a boil over high heat. Reduce the heat to a gentle simmer, add the whole onion, saffron, and smoked paprika and stir to combine. Simmer to infuse the flavors, cover, and set aside.

3 In a paella pan or large heavy-bottomed skillet, heat ¼ cup of the oil over high heat. Add the chicken and cook for about 3 minutes per side, until browned. Remove from the pan with a slotted spoon and set aside.

4 Add the chorizo to the pan and cook for a few minutes, turning, until browned. Remove from the pan with a slotted spoon and set aside.

RECIPE CONTINUES

1 pound wild-caught shrimp, peeled and deveined, with tails intact

1 pound squid, cleaned, bodies sliced into rings

3 cups paella or risotto rice (such as Bomba or Arborio)

1 large handful chopped fresh Italian parsley leaves

½ cup frozen peas

1 dozen littleneck clams, scrubbed and rinsed

Lemon wedges, for serving

5 Reduce the heat to medium, add the chopped onion, scallions, and garlic and cook for 5 minutes, stirring, until golden. Add the shrimp and squid and cook, stirring, for 1 to 2 minutes longer. Remove the shrimp and squid and set aside.

6 Add the remaining ¼ cup oil and the rice and cook, stirring, for 1 minute. Add the parsley and peas and stir to combine. Discard the whole onion from the stock and add the stock to the pan.

7 Arrange the chorizo, shrimp, squid, and chicken in the pan, making sure the chicken is on top so the skin can crisp. Add the clams to the pan and transfer to the oven. Bake, uncovered, for 20 minutes, until the stock has been absorbed. Remove from the oven, cover in foil, and let rest for 10 minutes.

8 Serve the paella with lemon wedges.

TIP: A paella pan is a really wide, shallow pan with a thin metal bottom designed specifically for this dish. The wide surface area means everything cooks consistently and the thinner base means the rice forms a nice crust on the bottom. You can also use a large skillet or wide saucepan, but the end result won't be quite as crisp (still delicious though!).

steamed clams
with brown butter

For our family, steamed clams with browned butter is ubiquitous. The recipe is so simple, it's only after one or two people asked me how to make it that I realized it's not second nature to everyone—how to cook clams—so here's the recipe. You kind of have to love it if you want to love us (with some exceptions, of course!). **SERVES 4**

4 pounds clams (littlenecks or cherrystones are perfect), scrubbed and rinsed

1 stick (4 ounces) butter

Crusty bread, for serving

1 Place the clams in a large pot with 1 or 2 inches of cold water in the bottom. (Clams should be tightly closed; discard any that do not close after a gentle tap.) Cover and bring to a boil over high heat, occasionally shaking the pan, for about 10 minutes, until the clams open.

2 Meanwhile, in a small skillet, melt the butter over medium heat and cook, swirling the pan occasionally, for 2 minutes, or until the butter starts to turn golden brown. Set aside.

3 To serve, place the pot in the middle of the table with tongs to pull out the clams and serve with the browned butter and crusty bread.

TIP: Clamshells are good for the compost pile. They provide much needed calcium to calcium-loving plants like tomatoes!

eggplant parmesan

I never liked eggplant Parmesan. My mother would cut thick slices, cover them in breadcrumbs, bake them, and add Hunt's tomato sauce from a can and not nearly enough cheese. But then I tasted it again at an Italian family reunion and was stunned that it could taste so good. I tracked down Mary Lynne Soto, the Cinquino cousin responsible for the recipe, and re-created it. To me the sign of a great recipe is when someone can describe it to you at a party, and you can make it successfully from that description. **Serves 4**

1 large eggplant

Salt

1 cup all-purpose flour

4 large eggs

Extra virgin olive oil, for cooking

1 clove garlic, sliced

½ cup grated Parmesan cheese (I prefer Romano)

8 ounces fresh mozzarella cheese, shredded

2 cups tomato sauce, store-bought or homemade (page 77)

1 Slice the eggplant crosswise as thinly as you can by hand (a mandoline makes them too thin). Place the slices in a colander, sprinkle with salt, and let stand for 20 minutes.

2 Preheat the oven to 350°F.

3 Place the flour in a shallow bowl. Place the eggs in a separate shallow bowl and lightly beat.

4 Rinse the eggplant slices and pat dry with paper towels. In batches, press each eggplant slice in the flour and then dip into the egg, shaking to remove excess.

5 In a large cast-iron skillet, heat the oil and garlic over medium heat. Working in batches, add the eggplant and fry 1 to 2 minutes per side, until golden. With a slotted spatula,

RECIPE CONTINUES

Eve and Lucia
not fighting
in the garden

transfer to a plate lined with paper towels. As you put the eggplant on the plate, sprinkle with the Parmesan.

6 Layer half the eggplant slices in a 13 × 9-inch baking dish and top with half the mozzarella. Pour over half the tomato sauce and layer with the remaining eggplant slices. Top with the remaining mozzarella, sauce, and sprinkle with any remaining Parmesan. Bake for 30 minutes, or until golden and bubbling.

TIP: For family reunions, double, triple, or quadruple this recipe!

pierogies

Pennsylvania is the land of pierogies, probably from all our Polish immigrants, and they are totally delicious. They aren't that hard to make from scratch, either. You can boil them, sauté them in butter or olive oil, bake them, or deep-fry them. When they are served at a traditional church supper, they are boiled and served with melted butter and sautéed onions. **MAKES ABOUT 32 PIEROGIES**

FILLING

1 large potato, peeled and cubed

3 tablespoons whole milk

1 tablespoon unsalted butter

½ cup shredded cheddar cheese

Salt and freshly ground black pepper

DOUGH

2 cups all-purpose flour

2 large egg yolks

½ teaspoon salt

½ cup lukewarm water or milk

1 To make the filling: In a saucepan, combine the potato with water to cover. Bring to a boil and cook for 12 to 15 minutes, until soft.

2 Drain the potatoes, return to the pan with the milk and butter and mash with a hand masher until smooth and combined. Add the cheddar and mix until melted and combined. Add salt and pepper. You should have about 1½ cups mashed potato. Set aside.

3 To make the dough: In a bowl, mix together the flour, egg yolks, and salt. Add only enough water or milk until the dough just comes together.

4 On a lightly floured surface, roll out the dough to a ⅛-inch thickness. Using a 3-inch round cutter, cut rounds from the dough. Gather the scraps, re-roll, and cut out more rounds.

5 Place a heaping teaspoon of the filling in the center of each round and fold it over into a half-moon, pressing the edges to seal. You may need to dab a little water on the edges to seal.

6 To cook, boil for 3 to 5 minutes, or sauté in butter in a cast-iron skillet over medium high heat for 3 to 5 minutes.

TIP: You can serve these with a tomato sauce, like ravioli. You can add spices or herbs to the mashed potato mixture. You can also fill with ground pork and sautéed onions instead of potato. The variations are endless.

Side
Shows

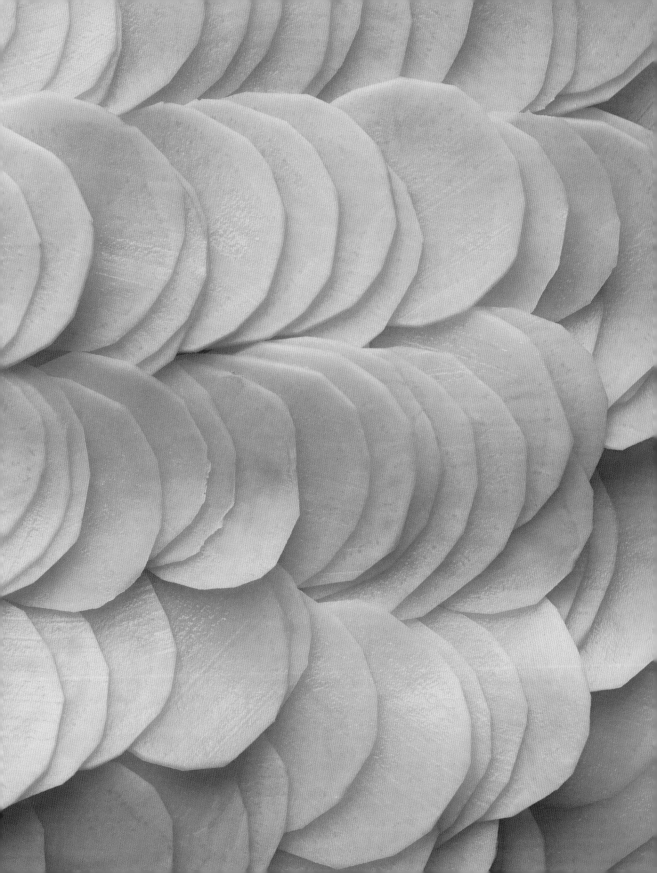

What makes a side a side? It's all relative. Most sides in our house are plain. Plain raw vegetables. Steamed green beans. Or even frozen peas. Gasp! You should never hesitate to use frozen organic vegetables as a side dish. But this is a cookbook, after all, so these sides span the spectrum of simple (mashed potatoes) to complex for special occasions (sausage stuffing). Some of them could be a meal in themselves (just add pasta to the crispy Brussels sprouts and you've got a main course) or a party appetizer (the marinated eggplant with mint, for example).

The important thing I've tried to do is capture the simple essence of something. And capture it organically. What that means is that I don't want to give up on my family's favorite foods just because we want to avoid "conventional" chemical ingredients and foods.

Take rice pilaf, for example. My kids and I used to love the classic packaged version, but it wasn't organic. It took me a while and some experimenting, but I finally figured out how to replicate the taste. And I made it taste better than the package. So now, it's the homemade version we all desire. And it's made from things I have around the house, so there is no extra packaging and the extra price that goes with all that "convenience."

Which I guess brings me to another point. Making things from scratch not only tastes better, but it can be cheaper, too. And if you are one of those people who says their kids won't eat vegetables? I have three recommendations. First, make sure that YOU eat vegetables. Kids will most often do what you do. Second, make sure you make the vegetables taste good. If that means adding some butter or cheese (or ranch dressing), so be it! Third, plant a garden with your kids. Kids who grow vegetables learn to love vegetables. It's a scientific fact.

mrs. cinquino's italian sausage stuffing

I grew up with my mother's favorite stuffing, but I never really liked it, and much preferred my grandmother's stuffing—even though she would put dried apricots in it. Then I met Lou (now my ex-husband) and tasted his mother's Italian sausage stuffing, and I knew I could never live without the recipe. Cooking the stuffing separately from the bird requires more liquid to keep it moist, but also results in a lovely crunchy top. This is best served with my Roast Turkey (page 206) and Pan Gravy (page 253). **SERVES 10**

12 cups cubed (1 inch) bread, white or wheat

1 onion, chopped

1 small head celery, trimmed and chopped

½ cup chopped fresh flat-leaf parsley leaves

2 to 3 tablespoons poultry seasoning (to taste)

Salt and freshly ground black pepper

1 pound hot Italian sausages, casings removed

4 tablespoons (½ stick) unsalted butter

1 cup whole milk, or more as needed

1 cup chicken stock, store-bought or homemade (page 111), or more as needed

1 Preheat the oven to 350°F.

2 In a bowl, mix together the bread cubes, onion, celery, parsley, poultry seasoning, and salt and pepper to taste. Break the sausage into small pieces and add to the bowl.

3 In a small saucepan, combine the butter, milk, and stock and heat over high heat until the butter has melted and the mixture is warmed through.

4 Pour the liquid gradually over the bread mixture until moist but not too wet. Transfer to a large baking dish and bake for 1 hour, or until golden and bubbling.

mashed potatoes

When I was much, much younger, I made instant (organic) mashed potatoes, thinking it was the most modern thing. But then I realized making mashed potatoes from scratch was just as easy and so much more delicious. So many people overcomplicate what is essentially already perfect. You can scale this recipe up easily to serve more people. Serve with my Crispy Roast Chicken with Gravy (page 195) or Crispy-Skinned Salmon with Herb Dressing (page 222). **SERVES 4**

4 large potatoes (such as russet or Yukon Gold), peeled and cubed

⅓ cup whole milk

4 tablespoons (½ stick) butter, melted

Salt

TIP: Try using blue potatoes in this recipe. They taste great and come out a lovely lavender color. I also love to add a bit of fresh chopped lovage if and when I can find it.

1 In a large saucepan, combine the potatoes with cold water to cover. Bring to a boil over high heat and cook for 10 to 12 minutes, until tender and soft.

2 Drain the potatoes, return to the pan, and mash with a hand masher.

3 Add the milk and melted butter and mash until smooth. Depending on the variety of potatoes you use, you may need less milk to achieve the right consistency. Start with less and add more if you need it.

4 Season with salt, stir to combine, and serve with your favorite main.

FROM THE BLOG

"Mashed potatoes have been a favorite since I was young. My grandmother taught me that warmed milk makes better mashed potatoes than cold from the fridge, better texture." **—BARBARA**

pan gravy

Gravy, real gravy, has to be one of the best foods on earth. It makes everything taste better (here's looking at you rice, potatoes, stuffing, and bread). Gourmet machinations just mess it up. I know some people make it in a saucepan with broth and giblets. I've never quite understood the appeal of that. I've only made gravy one way, and it's the way my mother made it before me, and the way my kids are already making it after me. Why mess with perfection? **SERVES 4 TO 6**

Pan drippings from roasting chicken or turkey

¼ to ½ cup all-purpose flour (depending on how many drippings you have)

1 cup water

Salt and freshly ground black pepper

1 After roasting a chicken or turkey (which I always do in a high-sided roasting pan), I transfer the bird to a platter, tilting the bird first so all its juices run into the roasting pan. Then place the roasting pan on the stovetop.

2 In a small bowl or glass, combine the flour and water and whisk with a fork until there are no lumps.

3 Heat the pan drippings over high heat until bubbling (spoon off some of the fat, if desired) and add the flour mixture, stirring continuously with a wooden spoon. Make sure you scrape all the browned bits from the bottom of the pan (that's where the flavor is!). Cook for a few minutes, stirring, until golden and thickened. Season with salt and pepper and stir to combine. Serve the pan gravy with the bird you just roasted.

oven fries

Sometimes a girl just needs some fries—definitely with a burger, and maybe with some fish. So, when I am cooking at home and in desperate need of fries, I make this recipe, which is exceedingly simple, easy, and delicious. There have never been leftovers. Ever. And if my son-in-law comes over, I have to quadruple the recipe.

SERVES 4

6 potatoes

¼ cup extra virgin olive oil

Salt

1 Preheat the oven to 425°F.

2 Wash the potatoes and peel them (or leave on if the skin is in good shape). Cut into fry shapes and place the potato pieces in cold water as you cut them to prevent browning.

3 Drain the potatoes in a single layer on paper towels or a clean kitchen towel and pat dry as much as possible.

4 Transfer to a rimmed baking sheet, add the oil, and toss until well coated (add more oil if you like). Spread the fries in a single layer, sprinkle with salt, and roast until golden and crisp, about 30 minutes (for thin fries) or 1 hour (for thick fries).

TIP: Feel free to add all sorts of spices and flavorings, although I have found plain to be the best and most deeply satisfying.

Purple potatoes are one of our favorites. Make them fried, boiled, mashed, or baked for a rich savory, colorful delight.

mexicali beans

For the most tasty and delicious tacos (page 215), huevos rancheros (page 8), or simply a side for any Mexican dish, these beans are packed with flavor and so quick and easy to make. I also spoon them on top of Nachos (page 174) for a quick snack or an easy meal. **SERVES 2**

Olive oil, for
the pan

1 teaspoon ground
cumin

1 teaspoon ground
chili powder

1 can (14 to
19 ounces) black
or pinto beans,
drained and rinsed

⅔ cup water

Salt and freshly
ground black
pepper

Hickory smoke
flavoring (optional)

1 In a saucepan, heat a little oil over medium-high heat. Add the cumin and chili powder and stir to combine. Cook, stirring, for 30 seconds, or until foamy.

2 Add the beans and stir to combine. Add water, salt and pepper to taste, and a drop or two of hickory flavoring (if using). Reduce the heat to low and simmer for 20 minutes.

bacon cornbread

I love real homemade cornbread. Not the dry, crumbly, and overly sweet kind that passes for cornbread these days. I like it moist, savory, warm, and comforting. And I like it with bacon. My youngest daughter thinks it needs a bit of sugar, but we just drizzle a little honey over her piece. Serve with soup, chili, or anything Southern. **SERVES 6 TO 8**

8 slices bacon

1½ cups whole-grain medium-grind cornmeal

¼ cup white whole wheat flour

1 teaspoon salt

1 tablespoon baking powder

4 tablespoons (½ stick) unsalted butter, cut into cubes

2 large eggs

2 cups whole milk

1 Preheat the oven to 425°F.

2 In a medium cast-iron skillet, cook the bacon over high heat until crisp. Drain on a plate lined with paper towels. Pour off all but 1 tablespoon of the bacon drippings.

3 In a bowl, mix together the cornmeal, flour, salt, and baking powder. Add the butter and rub it into the flour with your fingertips until it resembles coarse breadcrumbs.

4 In a separate bowl, whisk the eggs and milk together. Add to the flour mixture and stir to combine.

5 Break up the bacon into small pieces and stir into the batter.

6 Pour the batter into the skillet and transfer to the oven. Bake for 20 minutes, or until golden.

cheesy scalloped potatoes

I once had a brief but torrid affair with scalloped potatoes from a box. I first tasted them in my mid-30s at someone's house and became obsessed with their intense flavor. But after a while I realized that that flavor was salt, and probably some MSG. This recipe is my mother's original and the key thing is to cook the potatoes long enough so that they get truly soft. **SERVES 8**

2 pounds potatoes

Salt and freshly ground black pepper

1½ cups grated cheddar cheese

¾ cup whole milk

2 tablespoons extra virgin olive oil, plus extra for the baking dish

1 Preheat the oven to 350°F. Grease an 8-inch-square baking dish.

2 Thinly slice the potatoes using a mandoline. Soak the potato slices in a bowl of cold water for a few minutes to remove some of the starch. Drain on paper towels and pat dry.

3 Place a layer of potatoes in the bottom of the baking dish, slightly overlapping the slices. Season with salt and pepper, then sprinkle with ¼ cup of the cheddar. Repeat layers of potatoes, salt, pepper, and cheese, finishing with a layer of cheese. (You should have 5 or 6 layers.)

4 Pour the milk over the potato mixture and drizzle with the 2 tablespoons oil. Bake for 1 hour 15 minutes, or until the potatoes are tender and bubbling and the top is dark golden.

TIP: Feel free to experiment with different cheeses. My grandmother couldn't eat cheese, so she would make this with onions and olive oil.

sweet potato casserole

To me, the ubiquitous sweet potato casserole with marshmallows on top is not an essential part of a holiday meal. However, I made this for my daughter's in-laws from the U.K. for their first Thanksgiving experience and it's been a hit ever since. **SERVES 8 TO 10**

3 large sweet potatoes (about 1½ pounds total)

½ cup whole milk

4 tablespoons (½ stick) unsalted butter, melted

1 large egg

1 teaspoon vanilla extract

TOPPING
1 cup coarsely chopped pecans

¼ cup packed light brown sugar

¼ cup all-purpose flour

4 tablespoons (½ stick) unsalted butter, melted

Marshmallows (optional)

1 Preheat the oven to 350°F. Line a baking sheet with parchment paper.

2 Place the sweet potatoes on the prepared sheet and bake, in their skins, for about 1 hour. Set aside to cool slightly. Leave the oven on.

3 Peel the skins from the sweet potato and place the flesh in a large bowl with the milk, melted butter, egg, and vanilla and mash to combine. Transfer the mixture to a 9-inch greased baking dish.

4 To make the topping: In a bowl, mix together the pecans, brown sugar, flour, and melted butter. Sprinkle the mixture over the sweet potatoes and bake for 45 minutes, or until golden. If topping with marshmallows (as many as you like), add them for the last 5 to 10 minutes of baking time and bake until golden.

rice pilaf

We have always loved the boxed rice pilaf from the store that cooks up quickly and flavorfully. But I've stopped buying it, since it isn't organic. I experimented with making my own recipe and this is the tasty result. This goes really well with any sort of Middle Eastern food; serve with my Lamb Meatballs (page 212) and Eve's Hummus (page 167). **SERVES 4**

1 tablespoon extra virgin olive oil

1 tablespoon unsalted butter

1 teaspoon dried minced onion

½ teaspoon garlic powder

1 cup long-grain white or brown rice

½ cup slivered almonds

¼ teaspoon salt

2 cups chicken stock, store-bought or homemade (page 111)

1 In a large covered saucepan, heat the oil and butter over high heat. Add the dried onion and garlic powder and cook, stirring, until lightly toasted and fragrant.

2 Add the rice, almonds, and salt and stir to coat the rice.

3 Add the stock and bring to a boil. Reduce the heat to low and cook, covered, until the rice is tender and the liquid has been absorbed, about 20 minutes for white rice, 50 minutes for brown rice.

spicy savoy cabbage with anchovy crumbs

One of Louie Cinquino's traditional dishes at the Christmas Eve feast is what he called "Fooey." I have no idea where the term came from. It's one of those dishes that looks kind of weird and sounds like something I really wouldn't like to eat, but it has become one of my favorite things. It's hot, salty, and crispy all at once and it's so delicious. You need to use savoy cabbage, because the texture is softer and the taste is better for this dish. This is delicious with fish. **SERVES 6**

1 head savoy cabbage (about 2 pounds), cored and coarsely chopped

6 tablespoons extra virgin olive oil

2 cloves garlic, chopped

1 jar (3.5 to 4.5 ounces) anchovies in oil

¼ cup all-purpose flour

5 or 6 dried chiles (to taste), such as chile de árbol, Thai, or cayenne

1 Bring a large pot of water to a boil over high heat. Add the cabbage and cook for 5 minutes, or until wilted. Drain and set aside.

2 In a large cast-iron skillet, heat 3 tablespoons of the oil over medium-high heat. Add the garlic and cook, stirring, for 1 minute, until fragrant. Add the cabbage, reduce the heat to low, and cook for 15 minutes, or until very tender.

3 Meanwhile, in a small cast-iron skillet, combine the jar of anchovies with their oil and the flour and cook over medium-low heat, breaking up the mixture with a wooden spoon, for 7 to 8 minutes, until small, crunchy brown crumbs form. Transfer the anchovy crumbs to a small bowl, add 1 tablespoon of the olive oil, and stir to combine.

4 Wipe out the skillet. Heat the remaining 2 tablespoons oil over high heat. Add the chiles and fry, turning to make sure they cook on both sides, for 1 to 2 minutes, until they darken and crisp up. Transfer the chiles and oil to a bowl.

5 Serve the cabbage with the anchovy crumbs and chiles separately so people can add to taste.

Why does organic food sometimes cost more? Because you are buying happiness. Happy animals and happy nature makes happy people.

cheesy cowgirl cornbread

My daughter Lucia found the basis of this recipe in Highlights *magazine and asked if she could make it. The recipe was called Cowboy Cornbread and had sugar in it. We wanted our cornbread savory, not sweet, so we took the sugar out and renamed the recipe to suit the little cowgirl! Serve with my Venison Chili (page 123).*

SERVES 6 TO 8

2 cups grated cheese (such as cheddar or Colby)

1½ cups all-purpose flour

½ cup cornmeal

1 tablespoon baking powder

½ teaspoon salt

1¼ cups whole milk

2 large eggs, lightly beaten

½ cup vegetable oil

1 tablespoon unsalted butter

1 Preheat the oven to 350°F.

2 In a large bowl, mix together the cheese, flour, cornmeal, baking powder, and salt. Add the milk, eggs, and oil and using a wooden spoon or spatula, mix to combine.

3 In an 8-inch cast-iron or ovenproof skillet, melt the butter over high heat. Add the batter and transfer to the oven. Bake for 30 minutes, or until golden. For golden brown cornbread you can pop it under the broiler for 5 minutes to finish.

buttery biscuits

Did you ever make something good to eat and then realize that you were out of bread—or even worse, out of good bread—to serve with it? That's where biscuits come in. The best thing about these biscuits is they are super quick to make and, honestly, fairly foolproof. You can make them with white flour or whole wheat flour. You can add herbs or cheese. Serve them immediately with soup or ham, or just some jam. **MAKES ABOUT 12 BISCUITS**

2 cups all-purpose flour

1 tablespoon baking powder

½ teaspoon salt

1 stick (4 ounces) unsalted butter, cut into cubes

1 cup whole milk

1 Preheat the oven to 450°F. Line 2 baking sheets with parchment paper.

2 In a bowl, mix together the flour, baking powder, and salt. Add the butter and rub it into the flour with your fingertips until the mixture resembles coarse breadcrumbs.

3 Add the milk and stir gently to combine (do not overwork the dough). The consistency should be firm but not hard. If the batter seems too wet, add more flour. If the batter seems too dry, add more milk.

4 Drop big spoonfuls of the dough onto the lined baking sheets, allowing room for the biscuits to spread.

5 Bake until golden, about 15 minutes.

FROM THE BLOG
"We use this tried and true and super simple biscuit recipe on a regular basis. A yummy adjustment is substituting yogurt for the milk and stirring in some chopped chives." **—AMANDA**

yellow rice

Yellow rice gets its color from the spice turmeric, which is very good for you—it has anti-inflammatory and antioxidant qualities. The color makes me feel very tropical! To make this vegetarian, just use vegetable stock instead of chicken stock. Serve with my Crispy Roast Chicken with Gravy (page 195). **SERVES 4**

1 tablespoon butter

1 tablespoon extra virgin olive oil

1 tablespoon onion powder

1 teaspoon garlic powder

1 teaspoon ground turmeric

1 cup long-grain rice or basmati rice

½ teaspoon salt

2 cups chicken stock, store-bought or homemade (page 111)

1 In a saucepan, melt the butter in the oil over medium heat. Add the onion powder, garlic powder, and turmeric and cook briefly until foaming.

2 Add the rice and salt and stir to coat the rice with the spices.

3 Add the stock and bring to a boil. Cover, reduce the heat to low, and simmer for 15 to 20 minutes, until the liquid has been absorbed and the rice is tender. Fluff with a fork and serve.

cheesy grits

Grits are super easy and while they may start out as an acquired taste, they will quickly evolve into a regular craving. They are great for breakfast (add some cut-up ham or bacon) or for dinner with seafood, chicken, or just some cooked vegetables. **Serves 4**

1 cup grits

½ cup whole milk

2 tablespoons butter

1 cup shredded cheddar cheese

Salt and freshly ground black pepper

1 Cook the grits according to the package directions.

2 Add the milk, butter, cheddar, and salt and pepper to taste and stir until the cheese has melted and is combined.

roasted cauliflower with tahini dressing

I think my favorite cuisine of all time is Middle Eastern, and I've been learning to make it myself so that I don't have to order every single thing on the menu when I go to my favorite local Middle Eastern restaurant, Aladdin. (And invariably end up too full!) One of my favorite appetizers is arnabit, *which is roasted cauliflower with a garlicky tahini dressing. Serve with my Lamb Meatballs (page 212) and Rice Pilaf (page 261), or even without the dressing—plain roasted cauliflower is delicious.* **SERVES 4 TO 6**

1 head cauliflower, leaves removed

2 tablespoons extra virgin olive oil

Salt

Chopped fresh flat-leaf parsley or cilantro leaves, for garnish

TAHINI DRESSING
⅓ cup tahini

⅓ cup warm water

¼ cup fresh lemon juice

3 cloves garlic, crushed in a press

Salt

1 Preheat the oven to 425°F.

2 Cut the cauliflower into small florets, discarding the large stems, and arrange on a large rimmed baking sheet. Drizzle with the oil, season with salt, and toss to combine.

3 Spread the cauliflower out in a single layer and roast for 35 minutes, or until deep golden brown.

4 Meanwhile, make the tahini dressing: In a bowl, stir together the tahini, water, lemon juice, garlic, and salt to taste until smooth. Add a little more water if the mixture is too thick.

5 To serve, transfer the cauliflower to a serving dish, drizzle with the tahini dressing, and garnish with the parsley or cilantro.

kousa

This is also a regular appetizer at my local Middle Eastern restaurant, Aladdin. It's fried zucchini with lemon and garlic. Generally, if I ask my kids if they want zucchini, they say no. But if I make this dish, it's gone in 2 minutes. Serve with my Grilled Lemon-Garlic Chicken (page 199) and Rice Pilaf (page 261). **SERVES 4**

2 zucchini (about 1 pound)

¼ cup extra virgin olive oil

Salt

3 tablespoons fresh lemon juice

1 clove garlic, crushed in a press

1 Slice the zucchini into thin rounds (but not too thin, about ¼ inch thick).

2 In a large skillet, heat the oil over medium-high heat. Working in batches, cook the zucchini for 2 to 3 minutes per side, until golden brown. Transfer to a plate and lightly season with salt.

3 To serve, combine the lemon juice and garlic and pour over the zucchini.

maya's spiced roasted squash

My daughter Maya fell in love with a simple appetizer of roasted squash at New York's ABC Kitchen (which showcases many local and organic offerings on its menu). This is her version of that dish. It goes great with my Crispy Roast Chicken with Gravy (page 195). **SERVES 4**

1 butternut or other winter squash (2 to 3 pounds)

2 tablespoons plus 1 teaspoon extra virgin olive oil

½ teaspoon plus ⅛ teaspoon ground cumin

½ teaspoon plus ⅛ teaspoon ground cinnamon

½ teaspoon plus ⅛ teaspoon sea salt

Pinch of cayenne pepper (optional)

Lemon wedges, for serving

1 Preheat the oven to 400°F. Line a rimmed baking sheet with parchment paper.

2 Peel the squash, halve it, and scoop out the seeds, reserving the seeds. Cut the squash into 1-inch pieces and transfer to a bowl. Drizzle the squash with 2 tablespoons oil, sprinkle with ½ teaspoon each of the cumin, cinnamon, and salt. Add the cayenne (if using) and toss to combine.

3 Spread the squash on the prepared baking sheet and roast for 40 minutes, or until the squash is golden and very tender.

4 Meanwhile, separate the squash seeds from the strings but do not wash them. Place the seeds in a bowl, drizzle with 1 teaspoon oil and sprinkle with the remaining ⅛ teaspoon each cumin, cinnamon, and salt. Toss to combine.

5 Remove the baking sheet from the oven and make room at one edge. Spread the seeds on the sheet. Return the squash and seeds to the oven and roast for 10 minutes, or until the seeds are browned and crisp and the squash is golden.

6 Transfer the squash to a serving dish, sprinkle with the seeds, and serve with lemon.

crispy brussels sprouts

I used to hate Brussels sprouts. In fact, as a child I once went to bed without any dinner because I tried to hide them in my water glass, and then I tried to feed them to the dog. I've adapted this recipe from a book once recommended by an old friend. By John Thorne, it's called Simple Cooking, *and it's the kind of cookbook that you read like a novel. This recipe has since become a family favorite.* **SERVES 4**

1½ pounds Brussels sprouts

3 tablespoons unsalted butter

3 tablespoons extra virgin olive oil

2 cloves garlic, chopped

¾ cup coarse dried breadcrumbs (see page 338)

½ cup finely grated Romano cheese

Salt and freshly ground black pepper

1 Trim the bases of the sprouts with a small knife and discard any brown outer leaves. Halve lengthwise.

2 In a large pot of boiling water, blanch the Brussels sprouts for 3 minutes, or until they turn bright green. Drain and rinse under cold running water. Pat dry.

3 In a large cast-iron skillet, melt the butter in the oil over medium-high heat. Add the sprouts and cook, turning, for 2 minutes, or until dark golden and starting to crisp. Add the garlic and cook, stirring, for 1 minute, or until golden.

4 Add the breadcrumbs and cook until the breadcrumbs are golden and crispy, about 2 minutes. Add the Romano and stir until melted. Season with salt and pepper to taste.

TIP: These go really well with a holiday ham or turkey, or with my Roast Pork with Sauerkraut (page 227). You can also toss it with hot pasta to make a tasty main.

celery with brown butter and toasted almonds

The first time my mother made this, I thought it was a weird combination. She used to toast almonds and put them on top of almost everything. Now my whole family loves it. It goes really well with fish or chicken. **SERVES 4**

2 cups chopped celery

3 tablespoons butter

¼ cup slivered or chopped almonds, toasted (see page 339)

1 Place the celery in a saucepan with a little water and cook over medium heat for 3 minutes, until slightly softened.

2 In a small skillet, melt the butter over medium-high heat and cook until browned.

3 Drain the celery and transfer to a serving dish. Pour the browned butter over the celery and sprinkle with the almonds.

broiled tomatoes with cheese

Whenever we had steak on the grill growing up, we always had broiled tomatoes with cheese on the side. They are super easy to make and great in summer when you have an abundance of tomatoes. Use any fresh-from-the-garden tomatoes, or beefsteaks from the store or market. **SERVES 4 TO 6**

3 tomatoes, halved crosswise

¼ cup finely chopped white onion

½ cup shredded cheddar or Monterey Jack cheese

¼ cup dried breadcrumbs (see page 338)

3 tablespoons butter

Salt and freshly ground black pepper

) Preheat the broiler to high. Place the tomatoes, cut-side up, in a broiling pan or baking dish.

2 Divide the onion, cheese, and breadcrumbs among the tomatoes and top each with a dab of the butter.

3 Broil for 3 to 5 minutes, until the cheese is melted and the breadcrumbs are golden.

marinated grilled eggplant with mint

Many years ago I saw a recipe in Gourmet *magazine for marinated eggplant and ripped it out. I've added my own twist to it (a little less fuss, a little less sugar, and so forth) and it's totally delicious. Perfect for a party because you can make it in advance, it also makes a great appetizer or side with my Grilled Lemon-Garlic Chicken (page 199). It would be divine on an antipasto platter, too.* **SERVES 4**

1 large eggplant

Salt

5 tablespoons red wine vinegar

⅔ cup extra virgin olive oil, plus extra for brushing

1 clove garlic, crushed in a press

½ cup chopped fresh mint (I prefer apple mint)

1 Cut the eggplant crosswise into ¼-inch-thick rounds. Sprinkle with salt and set aside in a colander for 30 minutes. Rinse the eggplant and pat dry with paper towels.

2 Prepare a grill or preheat a large grill pan over high heat. Brush both sides of the eggplant with oil. Brush the grill grates or pan with more oil and grill the eggplant for a few minutes per side, until tender and charred. Transfer to a 13 × 9-inch baking dish.

3 In a bowl, mix together the vinegar, ⅔ cup oil, garlic, and mint. Drizzle the mixture over the eggplant and marinate at room temperature for 2 to 3 hours or overnight in the fridge. Bring to room temperature before serving.

applesauce

My daughter Eve and I once found an old apple tree on our property from which we collected a giant basket of the ugliest apples you ever saw—but they made the best sauce! It's really easy to make and freeze, and my kids love it. The best apples for sauce are the ones that are tart (like Granny Smiths) and too mangled for regular eating. Serve immediately as a side to my Roast Pork with Sauerkraut (page 227). It's also perfect with potato latkes or in my breakfast parfait (page 19).

MAKES 12 CUPS

24 tart apples

2 tablespoons
fresh lemon juice

6 whole cloves

2 sticks cinnamon

Granulated sugar
(optional)

1 Peel, core, and chop the apples.

2 Fill a large saucepan with 2 inches of water (around 4 cups) and place on the stovetop over low heat. Add the apples, lemon juice, cloves, and cinnamon and stir to combine. Cook, uncovered, for 45 minutes, or until completely softened and the apples have broken down.

3 Try the sauce. If it is too tart, add sugar to taste (up to ½ cup).

fresh cranberry sauce

Generally, there are three types of people: those who won't eat cranberry sauce at all; those who like it cooked and gelatinous; and those who prefer their sauce raw. I fall firmly into the raw camp. It is simply not a Thanksgiving meal without that tart, sweet, palate-cleansing, gorgeously magenta blob of cranberry sauce on my plate. The recipe I use is easy, but it needs to be made a day or two in advance for the sauce to reach its peak flavor. **MAKES 3 CUPS**

2 cups fresh cranberries, rinsed and drained

2 oranges or tangerines

½ cup sugar (or to taste)

1 Place the cranberries in a food processor or blender. Squeeze the juice from the oranges and add it to the cranberries.

2 Trim the ends from the oranges and then coarsely chop, skin and all. Add to the processor and blend until roughly chopped (not smooth).

3 Transfer to a bowl, add half the sugar, and stir to combine. If it is too tart, add a little more sugar to taste (up to ½ cup). Refrigerate for at least 24 hours to allow the flavors to develop.

TIP: It's especially important to use organic citrus in this recipe since you are using the skins.

I'm more of a cook than a baker. My freewheeling, improvisational style doesn't lend itself well to the exact science of baking, nor to the finicky fripperies of decorating and icing cakes. However, a few times a year on birthdays and holidays, I do like to bake. Or sometimes, I'll bake when my family is craving something sweet and good. However, they know what to expect by now—it will taste absolutely fabulous and be organic, but probably look like something the dog dragged in.

Let me explain. By the time I was old enough to pay attention, both my grandmothers were too old to bake with me, and my mother was a very utilitarian baker, although a few of her classics are in this chapter. Plus, my father demonized sugar, and my grandfather wrote a book called *Natural Health, Sugar and the Criminal Mind,* so there wasn't much of an opportunity to learn how to ice a cake in our household!

And so for the sake of this cookbook, I decided to overcome my baking demons and learn how to go all the way with baking. I learned a lot. But I also learned I don't have the patience to spend so much time on something that's going to end up being eaten very quickly. So this chapter isn't too fancy, but it is as delicious and nourishing as dessert can be. And as a busy person dedicated to simplicity, I have found the simplest and easiest methods for baking from scratch.

I'm really driven to bake because I want the immediate gratification and deliciousness of a good piece of cake or pie, but I want it organic and homemade. You can make most of these recipes as quickly as it would take you to drive to the supermarket and back—and they will taste a lot better. As I've said before, I don't believe in demonizing anything, whether it's sugar or dessert, as long as it's organic and in moderation.

Ultimately, baking is about community and connecting with others, whether it's at a birthday, a bake sale, or a funeral. It's one of those things that unites us, and that's what I love about it.

old-fashioned chocolate layer cake

Rita Cinquino saved this recipe from a 1940's McCall's *magazine. She made it for my daughter Eve's eighth birthday and it instantly became a family classic. It's absolutely delicious and not too sweet, with that fluffy chocolate-cake goodness that everybody loves. What's cool about this recipe is that it doesn't use any "power tools," and the resulting cake is so light that it almost seems impossible.* **SERVES 8**

Butter and flour, for the pans

1 stick (4 ounces) unsalted butter, at room temperature

2½ cups packed light brown sugar

3 large eggs

3 ounces unsweetened chocolate, melted (see page 339) and cooled to room temperature

2¼ cups cake flour

2 teaspoons baking soda

½ teaspoon salt

½ cup buttermilk (see Basic Baking Tips, page 286)

2 teaspoons pure vanilla extract

1 cup boiling water

2 batches Whipped Cream Frosting (page 326)

1 Preheat the oven to 350°F. Grease and flour two 9-inch round cake pans.

2 In a large bowl, cream the butter, or work with your hands, until it's soft. Add the brown sugar, a little at a time, and continue creaming until it's all incorporated. (Use a spoon or a whisk. The mixture should be light and fluffy.)

3 Add the eggs, one at a time, beating the batter well with a fork or a spoon after each addition.

4 Stir in the melted chocolate.

5 Sift the flour, baking soda, and salt into a large bowl. Sift one-third of the flour mixture into the batter and stir to combine. Add half the buttermilk and stir gently. Repeat with the flour mixture and buttermilk and finish with the remaining flour mixture.

RECIPE CONTINUES

TIPS: When icing the cake, regularly dip the knife in hot water and wipe with a kitchen towel for a smooth finish. For a mocha-flavored cake, substitute hot coffee for the boiling water in the recipe.

6 Add the vanilla to the boiling water. Add the water to the batter and stir to combine. (Don't be alarmed by the thin consistency of the batter!)

7 Divide the batter between the prepared pans and bake for 25 to 30 minutes, until a skewer inserted in the center comes out clean. Let cool slightly in the pan, then turn the cakes out onto a wire rack to cool completely.

8 Spread one cake layer with frosting. Place the second layer on top and spread the sides and top of the cake with the remaining frosting.

FROM THE BLOG
"My husband is not a big chocolate fan, but I pleaded with him to try this cake. He didn't want to, but eventually he did and loved it! He almost ate the whole thing and then asked me to bake another one." —CINDY

Basic Baking Tips I Had to Learn the Hard Way

BAKING

1. To keep a cake from sticking to the pan, coat the pan with cooking spray or butter, and then cut a round of parchment paper to fit the bottom of the pan. (Place the pan on parchment paper, trace around the bottom with a pencil and cut the round out, making sure you cut inside the pencil marks. Use the parchment paper to line the base of the pan.) This tip saved me years of disasters.

2. Let the cakes cool—I mean really, *really* cool—before you frost them.

3. I used to scoff at buttermilk, until I found organic buttermilk at the farmers' market. The real stuff is thick and creamy and works really well. The acid in buttermilk results in more airy and tender baked goods. The best substitute for buttermilk I've seen is as follows: Combine 1 cup whole milk with 1 tablespoon lemon juice or distilled white vinegar, stir, and let stand for 10 minutes before using it in your recipe. It won't be as thick as the real thing, but it will do the trick.

4. To keep cupcakes from spilling over the sides of the muffin cups, only fill the cups two-thirds of the way up. Doh! Why don't they tell you that in college?

5. To keep cupcakes from sinking in the middle, make sure they are fully cooked before removing from the oven.

FROSTING

1. Have you ever heard of a crumb coat? I hadn't until I asked for some professional baking help. It enabled me to make my first-ever frosted cake that didn't look horrible. The basic idea is that first you do a thin coat of frosting that catches the crumbs (and holds them in place); refrigerate the cake for half an hour to set a little. Then you frost the cake with the remaining frosting.

2. There is a reason cakes often have a lot of frosting on them—it hides the crumbs and cracks.

3. Frosting can be very temperature-sensitive, which is why it melts easily in the heat and goes very hard in the fridge. If it's going to be a hot day, don't use coconut oil because it will liquefy and melt. But in the winter, coconut oil is perfectly fine to use.

my mother's chocolate cake

From my mother, I learned how to serve an army. She was constantly pulling a cake out of the freezer when my father unexpectedly brought business guests home for dinner. This cake was a regular at those dinners, which she had frozen, already spread with buttercream frosting, in a square disposable aluminum pan. You can easily double the recipe to pop a second cake in the freezer, just like my mom did. **SERVES 18**

Coconut oil and flour, for the pan

1¾ cups all-purpose flour

¾ cup unsweetened cocoa powder

1½ teaspoons baking soda

1 teaspoon salt

2¼ cups packed dark brown sugar

1¼ cups shortening (I use coconut oil)

2 large eggs

2 teaspoons pure vanilla extract

1½ cups buttermilk (see Basic Baking Tips, opposite page)

½ batch Buttercream Frosting (page 327)

1 Preheat the oven to 375°F. Grease and flour a 15 × 10-inch rimmed baking sheet.

2 Sift the flour, cocoa, baking soda, and salt into a small bowl and set aside.

3 In a large bowl, combine the brown sugar and shortening and mix very well with a spoon, making sure all the brown sugar is evenly distributed. Add the eggs and vanilla and mix well to combine.

4 Alternately add the flour mixture and buttermilk to the batter, mixing between additions, until everything is well combined.

5 Pour the batter into the prepared baking sheet and bake for 25 minutes, or until a skewer inserted in the center comes out clean. Remove from the oven and allow to cool completely in the pan on a wire rack.

6 Frost the top of the cake with the Buttercream Frosting (though I prefer the Almost-Vegan Frosting on page 331). Cut into 18 squares.

grandma harter's crumb cake

This cake was a regular cake in my mother's repertoire, although it was always known as Grandma's Crumb Cake. More of a traditional coffee cake than a dessert cake, it only takes about 10 minutes to mix together and about an hour to bake. It has the feel of something you could bake quickly to take to a friend or neighbor who needs cheering up. As for the taste, it's the taste of my childhood. **SERVES 8**

Butter, for the pan

2 cups all-purpose flour

2 teaspoons baking powder

1½ cups sugar

1 stick (4 ounces) cold unsalted butter, chopped

¼ cup coconut oil

1 teaspoon ground cinnamon

Pinch of salt

2 large eggs

¾ cup whole milk

1 Preheat the oven to 375°F. Grease a 9-inch round cake pan.

2 Sift the flour and baking powder into a large bowl. Stir in the sugar.

3 Add the butter and coconut oil and use your fingertips to gently work them into the flour until the mixture resembles coarse breadcrumbs. Measure out ¾ cup of the mixture and stir in the cinnamon and salt. Set aside for the crumb topping.

4 Add the eggs and milk to the remaining mixture and beat with a spoon until smooth.

5 Pour the batter into the prepared pan, sprinkle with the crumb topping, and bake for 1 hour, or until a skewer inserted in the center comes out clean. Transfer the pan to a wire rack to cool completely.

TIP: Grandma Harter used all butter or lard. I use half butter and half coconut oil, but you can do whatever you want.

heirloom molasses cake

I was cleaning out one of my mother's closets after she passed away and found some recipes written in either my grandmother's hand or some distant female relative's. This cake caught my eye. Its measurements were a little imprecise, but after trial and error, I produced this dark, moist, and rich cake. We made it for Alice Waters when she came to dinner and she had seconds. **SERVES 10 TO 12**

Butter, for the pan

1½ sticks (6 ounces) unsalted butter

3½ cups white or whole wheat flour

1 cup packed dark brown sugar

½ teaspoon salt

1 cup molasses

2 large eggs, lightly beaten

1 teaspoon baking soda

1 cup hot water

1 Preheat the oven to 350°F. Grease a 13 × 9-inch baking pan.

2 Melt 4 tablespoons (½ stick) of the butter and set aside. Chop the remaining 1 stick butter and keep cold.

3 Sift the flour into a large bowl. Add the brown sugar and salt and mix to combine. Measure out 1½ cups of the dry mixture and set aside.

4 Add the melted butter, molasses, eggs, baking soda, and hot water to the remaining mixture and mix well to combine. Pour the batter into the prepared pan.

5 Add the cold chopped butter to the reserved flour mixture and use your fingertips to gently work the butter into the flour until it resembles coarse breadcrumbs.

6 Sprinkle the crumb mixture over the batter, gently pressing into the batter. Bake 30 to 40 minutes, until a skewer inserted in the center comes out clean. Transfer the pan to a wire rack to cool completely.

banana cake

I've been making banana muffins for years, but don't often crave that ubiquitous style of banana cake with cream cheese frosting. (I think it's a bit overdone.) But I had a craving one birthday, and given that I knew my oldest daughter, who has never eaten or touched a banana in her life, wasn't likely to bake me one, I baked it myself. **SERVES 6 TO 8**

Butter and flour, for the pans

2 cups all-purpose flour

1 teaspoon baking powder

½ teaspoon baking soda

1 cup sugar

½ teaspoon salt

1 stick (4 ounces) unsalted butter, at room temperature

2 large eggs, lightly beaten

⅓ cup buttermilk (see Basic Baking Tips, page 286)

1 teaspoon pure vanilla extract

2 very ripe bananas, mashed

1½ batches Banana Buttercream Frosting (page 327)

1 Preheat the oven to 350°F. Grease and flour two 9-inch round cake pans.

2 Sift the flour, baking powder, and baking soda into a large bowl. Add the sugar and salt and mix to combine.

3 Add the butter, eggs, buttermilk, vanilla, and bananas and beat with a hand mixer until well combined, about 6 minutes. The mixture may seem a little dry. This is normal.

4 Spread the batter into the prepared pans and bake for 15 to 20 minutes, until a skewer inserted in the center comes out clean. Let cool for 5 minutes in the pans, then turn out onto a wire rack to cool completely.

5 Place one of the layers on a cake plate. Spread with one-third of the frosting. Top with the second layer and frost the top and sides of the cake with the remaining frosting.

FROM THE BLOG
"Delicious! Made it last night with the sad old bananas that were just about ready to give up and drop off their perch in exhaustion. Cheers all around from the crowd!" —RENEE

my mother's hickory nut cake

This cake is a family classic my mother made often, and this wouldn't be a family cookbook without it. **SERVES 8 TO 10**

Butter, for the pans

1 stick (4 ounces) unsalted butter, at room temperature, plus extra for the pans

1½ cups sugar

1 teaspoon pure vanilla extract

2 cups cake flour

2 teaspoons baking powder

¼ teaspoon salt

¾ cup whole milk

4 large egg whites, beaten to stiff peaks (see page 337)

1 cup finely chopped hickory nuts

Buttercream Frosting (page 327)

1 Preheat the oven to 375°F. Grease two 9-inch round cake pans and line the bottoms with rounds of parchment paper.

2 In a large bowl, using a hand mixer, beat the butter, sugar, and vanilla on medium speed until light and fluffy, about 2 minutes.

3 Sift the flour, baking powder, and salt into a separate bowl.

4 Alternately add the flour mixture and milk to the butter mixture, mixing well after each addition until combined.

5 Gently fold in the egg whites and nuts with a spatula.

6 Divide the batter between the prepared pans and bake for 30 minutes, or until a skewer inserted in the center comes out clean. Let cool completely in the pans on a wire rack.

7 Remove the cakes from their pans and place one layer on a cake plate. Spread with one-third of the frosting. Place the second layer on top and frost the top and sides of the cake with the remaining frosting.

lemon bundt cake

I'd never made a Bundt cake before, but felt it would be a nice addition to this book. Plus, I love lemon in baking. Making a Bundt is nowhere near as scary as I thought. Let's put it this way, if I can make this cake, you can make this cake! The secret is greasing the Bundt pan really well so the cake pops right out. **SERVES 8 TO 10**

Butter and flour, for the pan

3 cups all-purpose flour

1½ cups sugar

2 teaspoons baking powder

½ teaspoon salt

2 sticks (8 ounces) unsalted butter, melted

1 cup whole milk

4 large eggs

2 tablespoons finely grated lemon zest

1½ teaspoons pure vanilla extract

1 teaspoon pure lemon extract

Lemon Glaze (page 328)

1 Preheat the oven to 375°F. Grease and flour a 10-inch Bundt pan.

2 Place all of the ingredients (except the glaze) in a large bowl and mix well to combine. Pour the batter into the prepared pan.

3 Tap the pan on the kitchen counter a few times to help the batter settle and make sure there are no bubbles in the mixture.

4 Bake for 50 minutes, or until a skewer inserted in the cake comes out clean. Let cool in the pan for 10 minutes, then carefully invert onto a wire rack to cool completely.

5 Transfer the cake to a serving plate and drizzle with the glaze.

moravian sugar cake

The area in Pennsylvania I am from was settled by Moravians in the early 1700s. They're known for celebrating in church with a "Lovefeast," which is about strengthening the bonds of harmony and goodwill by sharing sugar cake and coffee in the pews. What's not to love about that? With its distinctive brown sugar topping, this delicious loaf is perfect for brunch or afternoon tea. **SERVES 10 TO 12**

⅓ cup lukewarm water

2 teaspoons active dry yeast

½ teaspoon plus ½ cup granulated sugar

1¼ sticks (5 ounces) unsalted butter, melted

1 large egg

½ teaspoon salt

1 cup milk, scalded (see page 339)

½ cup mashed potatoes (page 252)

3 cups all-purpose flour, plus extra for dusting

Butter, for the pan

1 In a small bowl, combine the yeast, water, and ½ teaspoon of the granulated sugar and set aside in a warm place for 10 minutes or until bubbles have appeared on the surface and the yeast has activated.

2 Using a hand mixer (or in a stand mixer with the paddle attachment), beat ⅓ cup of the melted butter, the egg, salt, and remaining ½ cup granulated sugar until light and fluffy. It will be quite thick.

3 Add the scalded milk and mashed potatoes and stir to combine. Add the yeast mixture and stir to combine.

4 Gradually add the flour until the dough starts to come together. Transfer to a floured surface and knead, adding more flour if necessary, until combined but still sticky, about 13 minutes. Place in a lightly greased bowl, cover with a clean, damp kitchen towel, and let rest in a warm place until the dough has doubled in size, about 2½ hours.

**1 cup packed light
brown sugar**

**½ cup all-purpose
flour**

**4 tablespoons
(½ stick) unsalted
butter**

**Pinch of ground
cinnamon**

5 Grease a 13 × 9-inch baking pan. Press the
dough into the pan, cover, and rest until
puffed up, about 1½ hours.

6 Preheat the oven to 350°F.

7 Brush the remaining melted butter evenly over
the dough and poke holes in the dough every
2 inches or so with your finger, being careful
not to touch the bottom.

8 To make the topping: In a bowl, combine the
brown sugar, flour, butter, and cinnamon and
use your fingertips to form a crumbly mixture.
Sprinkle over the dough, making sure to fill
the holes.

9 Bake for 20 to 25 minutes, until golden and
cooked through. Cut into squares to serve.

simple yogurt cake

Do you remember the first time you asked someone for a recipe? This was mine. I was in fifth grade taking a special painting class with my art teacher, Mr. Allen, and his wife brought out a cake at break time. I must have eaten five pieces. I couldn't believe it when she said it was yogurt cake. When I was in fifth grade, it was really weird to eat yogurt! The consistency is very light, like a tea bread. **SERVES 8**

Butter, for the pan

1 stick (4 ounces) unsalted butter, at room temperature

1 cup packed light brown sugar

1 large egg

1 teaspoon pure vanilla extract

2 cups white whole wheat or all-purpose flour

1 teaspoon baking soda

½ teaspoon baking powder

¼ teaspoon salt

1½ cups plain or flavored regular or Greek yogurt

¼ cup turbinado sugar

1 Preheat the oven to 350°F. Grease a 9-inch round cake pan.

2 In a large bowl, using a hand mixer, beat the butter and sugar until light and fluffy, about 3 minutes. Beat in the egg and vanilla.

3 Sift the flour, baking soda, baking powder, and salt into the bowl and mix gently to combine. Fold in the yogurt until very well combined.

4 Spread the batter into the prepared pan and sprinkle with the turbinado sugar. Bake for 45 minutes, or until a skewer inserted in the center comes out clean. Let cool in the pan for 10 minutes, then turn out onto a wire rack to cool completely.

FROM THE BLOG
"I made this and it was wonderful! I used lemon yogurt and will be using a different flavor next time. I see endless possibilities. And my homemade tangy yogurt will be fabulous in it as well!"
—BARBARA

cardamom-coconut cake

I tasted this cake at the Esalen Institute in Big Sur, California, which is about as authentically hippie as you can get in America these days. The food there is amazing, especially this cake. The institute was kind enough to share the recipe with me. It's a vegan cake, which is why there's so much cornstarch in it, and it had a superfluffy vegan icing that I've tried to replicate. **SERVES 8 TO 10**

Coconut oil, for the pan

1½ cups all-purpose flour

¾ cup cornstarch

2 teaspoons baking soda

1 teaspoon baking powder

1 teaspoon ground cardamom

1 cup unsweetened shredded coconut

¾ cup sugar

1½ cups coconut milk

½ cup coconut oil, melted

Vegan Frosting (page 329)

Shredded coconut, for decorating (optional)

1 Preheat the oven to 350°F. Grease a 13 × 9-inch baking pan.

2 Sift the flour, cornstarch, baking soda, baking powder, and cardamom into a large bowl. Add the shredded coconut and sugar and mix to combine.

3 Add the coconut milk and coconut oil and mix well to combine. Pour the batter into the prepared pan and bake for 25 to 30 minutes, until golden. Cool completely in the pan on a wire rack.

4 Spread the frosting over the cake and, if desired, sprinkle with shredded coconut. Cut into squares to serve.

vanilla cupcakes

When my youngest daughter, Lucia, once requested vanilla cupcakes for her birthday, of course I had to figure out how to make them. My family was shocked at how good these turned out, especially given I used half the sugar of a comparable recipe! I made them in mini muffin tins and the tops round up nicely with no shrinkage.

MAKES 24 MINIS OR 12 REGULAR CUPCAKES

Coconut or olive oil cooking spray

1½ cups all-purpose flour

2 teaspoons baking powder

¾ cup granulated sugar

¼ teaspoon salt

1 stick (4 ounces) unsalted butter, melted

½ cup whole milk

2 large eggs

2 teaspoons pure vanilla extract

Creamy Vanilla Frosting (page 328)

1 Preheat the oven to 350°F. Coat 24 cups of a mini muffin tin or 12 cups of a regular muffin tin with a little cooking spray or line with paper liners.

2 In a large bowl, stir together the flour, baking powder, sugar, salt, melted butter, milk, eggs, and vanilla.

3 Divide the batter evenly among the muffin cups.

4 Bake until puffed and golden and a skewer inserted comes out clean, 12 to 15 minutes for minis, 15 to 20 minutes for regular cupcakes. Transfer to a wire rack to cool completely. Spread the cupcakes with the frosting to serve.

incredibly flaky pie dough

Haika is one of my favorite bakers; she started the first organic bakery in the region where I live. Her secret for flaky piecrust will astound you. She mixes the butter into the flour at room temperature, and then puts it into the fridge to cool. Her theory is that when you use cold butter you overwork the dough. Every "professional" recipe I've seen calls for chilled butter and water—but none produces a crust as flaky as Haika's! I have to say it's quicker and easier to mix and the end result is divine. **MAKES ENOUGH FOR ONE 9-INCH PIECRUST**

1½ cups all-purpose flour

½ teaspoon salt

1 tablespoon sugar (see Tip)

5 tablespoons unsalted butter, at room temperature

5 tablespoons lard, at room temperature

4 to 6 tablespoons water, as needed

TIP: If making a savory pie, simply omit the sugar.

1 In a large bowl, mix together the flour, salt, and sugar.

2 Add the butter and lard and mix as gently and quickly as possible with your fingertips until the mixture resembles coarse breadcrumbs. At this point, place the mixture in the fridge until chilled, about 30 minutes.

3 Add water, 1 tablespoon at a time, and mix quickly to form a smooth dough. Flatten into a disk, wrap in parchment or wax paper, and refrigerate for at least 30 minutes or until you are ready to roll it out.

FROM THE BLOG

"Yes! At last, a simple recipe for making dough that comes out well. All of the recipes that I have also recommend that the butter be as cold as possible before blending it into the flour, which as you know, is very hard to do, and keeps you working the mixture until you end up with tough dough." **—DONNA**

pumpkin pie

Do you have a recipe for something that everyone loves but you? It's not that I dislike pumpkin pie, I just don't love pumpkin pie. And yet, every year my family begs me to make my pumpkin pie. I don't mind making it. I don't mind eating it, either. But I definitely won't eat it without vanilla ice cream and whipped cream. **SERVES 8**

Incredibly Flaky Pie Dough (page 299)

2 cups Pumpkin Puree (page 325) or canned organic puree

¼ cup granulated sugar

¼ cup packed light brown sugar

¼ cup maple syrup

2 tablespoons molasses

2 large eggs, lightly beaten

1 teaspoon ground cinnamon

¼ teaspoon ground cloves

¼ teaspoon ground ginger

¼ teaspoon ground nutmeg

½ teaspoon salt

1 cup heavy (whipping) cream

1 Make the dough and refrigerate as instructed.

2 To make the filling: In a large bowl, mix together the pumpkin puree, both the sugars, the maple syrup, molasses, eggs, cinnamon, cloves, ginger, nutmeg, salt, and cream until well combined. Set aside.

3 Preheat the oven to 425°F.

4 On a lightly floured surface, roll out the pie dough to a round ¼ inch thick. Line a 9-inch pie dish with the dough, trim any overhanging dough, and crimp or decorate the edge.

5 Pour the pumpkin mixture into the pie shell and transfer to the oven. Bake for 15 minutes, reduce the temperature to 350°F, and bake for 45 minutes longer, until set in the center. Let cool before serving.

TIP: For a lovely patterned edge, simply press the edge of a dinner spoon evenly around the rim of the pie. Press a teaspoon inside the larger spoon indents.

the easiest summer fruit pie

This pie was born out of frustration, deception, and laziness. I was in the process of baking a glazed strawberry pie when my eldest daughter declared she didn't like cooked fruit in the glaze. So while she wasn't looking, I filled the bottom half of the pie with berries and baked it, and then covered it with fresh berries once it was out of the oven. Topped with some fresh whipped cream, the pie was gone by the morning. **SERVES 8**

Incredibly Flaky Pie Dough (page 299)

6 cups chopped fresh fruit (such as berries, cherries, or peaches)

½ cup sugar

1 tablespoon fresh lemon juice

1 tablespoon tapioca starch

3 tablespoons unsalted butter, cut into pieces

Pinch of salt

Whipped cream or ice cream, for serving

1 Preheat the oven to 375°F.

2 On a lightly floured surface, roll out the pie dough to a round ¼ inch thick. Line a 9-inch pie dish with the dough, trim any overhanging dough, and crimp or decorate the edge (see Tip).

3 Place the fruit in a bowl, sprinkle with the sugar and lemon juice, and mix to combine. Halve the mixture and divide between 2 bowls.

4 Add the tapioca starch to one bowl and stir to combine. Pour this mixture into the pie shell, dot with the butter, sprinkle with the salt. Bake for 35 to 40 minutes, until the filling is bubbling and the pastry is golden. Set aside to cool.

5 When the pie has cooled, top with the reserved fresh fruit (leaving excess liquid behind in the bowl) and serve immediately with whipped cream or ice cream.

glazed strawberry pie

This is the real recipe I wanted to make before my daughter declared her distaste for a cooked fruit glaze (see The Easiest Summer Fruit Pie, page 303). It's based on a bit of a local legend where I live, and the original, from Hess's Patio Restaurant, was about 8 inches high and glorious. My glaze is all natural, organic, and without food coloring.

SERVES 8

GLAZE

1 cup strawberries, hulled

¾ cup water

¼ cup sugar

1 teaspoon fresh lemon juice

1½ tablespoons cornstarch dissolved in 1½ tablespoons water

PIE

Incredibly Flaky Pie Dough (page 299)

5 cups whole strawberries, hulled

Whipped cream, for serving

TIP: You can also make this with blueberries or stone fruits such as peaches, cherries, or nectarines.

1 To make the glaze: In a blender, puree the strawberries and transfer to a small saucepan. Stir in the water, sugar, and lemon juice and bring to a boil over medium-high heat. Add the cornstarch mixture and cook, stirring, for 3 to 5 minutes, or until thickened. Strain through a fine-mesh sieve into a bowl and set aside to cool.

2 To make the pie: Preheat the oven to 350°F.

3 On a lightly floured surface, roll out the pie dough to a round ¼ inch thick. Line a 9-inch pie dish with the dough, trim any overhanging dough and crimp the edge. Line the bottom of the pie shell with foil and fill with pie weights or dried beans. Bake for 12 to 15 minutes. Remove the pie weights or beans and bake for 10 to 12 minutes longer, until golden. Set aside to cool.

4 Arrange the fresh berries tightly in the baked pie shell, drizzle with the glaze, and refrigerate for 1 hour. Serve with whipped cream.

chocolate chip molasses cookies

I'm not a frequent baker, but something about an impending hurricane (Irene) made me want to have some cookies on hand. A long time ago, I combined molasses and chocolate chips to create a really good cookie, so my goal was to replicate that taste memory. I prefer them with walnuts, though nobody else in my household does. Just as well because I would have to eat them all myself. **MAKES 4 DOZEN COOKIES**

2 sticks (8 ounces) unsalted butter, at room temperature

¾ cup sugar

½ cup molasses

¼ cup whole milk

1 large egg

1 teaspoon pure vanilla extract

2¼ cups white or whole wheat flour

½ teaspoon baking soda

½ teaspoon salt

9 ounces semisweet chocolate chips

1 cup chopped walnuts (optional)

1 Preheat the oven to 375°F. Line 2 large baking sheets with parchment paper.

2 In a large bowl, using a hand mixer, beat the butter and sugar until pale and creamy. Beat in the molasses.

3 Add the milk and egg, beating well. Beat in the vanilla.

4 Add the flour, baking soda, and salt and beat to form a smooth dough. Fold in the chocolate chips and walnuts (if using).

5 Drop the dough by tablespoons onto the lined baking sheets, allowing room to spread. Bake, in batches if necessary, for 10 minutes, until golden. Transfer to a wire rack to cool.

aussie anzac biscuits

The Anzac biscuit (biscuit is what they call a cookie Down Under) is a love letter in baked form. Anzac stands for Australia New Zealand Army Corps, and it was the official biscuit that women sent to their menfolk who went off to war. The recipe is made without eggs so that it would last a long time without spoiling. As I tasted my first home-baked Anzac, I thought of all the women who had made these, not knowing what might happen to their loved ones. **MAKES 3 DOZEN COOKIES**

1½ cups rolled oats

1 cup coconut sugar (or granulated sugar)

1 cup unsweetened shredded coconut

½ cup all-purpose flour

½ cup whole wheat flour

¾ teaspoon baking soda

¼ cup boiling water

1 stick (4 ounces) unsalted butter, melted

¼ cup golden syrup or honey (see Tip)

TIP: These are traditionally made with golden syrup instead of honey.

1 Preheat the oven to 350°F. Lightly grease 2 baking sheets or line with parchment paper.

2 In a large bowl, mix together the oats, sugar, coconut, and flours.

3 In a small bowl, dissolve the baking soda in the boiling water. Stir in the melted butter and honey.

4 Add the butter mixture to the dry ingredients and mix well to combine.

5 Drop the dough by tablespoons onto the prepared baking sheets and press to flatten into 2½-inch rounds (allowing room to spread). Bake, in batches if necessary, for 15 minutes, or until golden. Transfer to a wire rack to cool.

FROM THE BLOG
"Oh, yes! I love these . . . butter and coconut . . . could anything be more wonderful. I also love the story. Years ago I cut an article out of the LA Times food section about traditional cookies (biscuits) from Down Under. I think I'll dig it out!" —JUDI

chocolate chip and brown butter oat cookies

Born out of my obsession with coconut, these cookies took an even better turn when I decided to add oats. They are absolutely delicious. And they're completely nourishing since they're organic and made with whole wheat flour. And now that we know that even butter is healthy—which I have known all along—they feel positively virtuous.

MAKES 4 DOZEN COOKIES

2 sticks (8 ounces) unsalted butter

¾ cup packed light or dark brown sugar

½ cup coconut sugar

1¼ cups whole wheat flour

1 teaspoon baking soda

Pinch of salt

1 cup steel-cut oats or rolled oats

1 cup unsweetened shredded coconut

9 ounces semisweet chocolate chips

2 large eggs, lightly beaten

1 teaspoon pure vanilla extract

1 Preheat the oven to 350°F. Line 2 baking sheets with parchment paper.

2 In a medium skillet, melt the butter over high heat and cook for 5 minutes, or until browned. Set aside to cool.

3 In a large bowl, stir together the sugars, flour, baking soda, and salt. Stir in the oats, shredded coconut, and chocolate chips and mix well to combine. Add the browned butter, eggs, and vanilla and mix to combine.

4 Drop the dough by tablespoons onto the lined baking sheets, leaving room for the cookies to spread. Bake, in batches if necessary, for 10 to 15 minutes, until golden and crisp on the edges. Transfer to a wire rack to cool.

snickerdoodle cookies

These cookies are my youngest daughter Lucia's special cookies—not because of the cookie, but because of what snickerdoodle *stands for. It's code for: "Mom, please pay attention to me!" It's a long story, but a sweet one. Sweet enough to have a snickerdoodle to go with it.*

MAKES 4 DOZEN COOKIES

2¾ cups all-purpose or whole wheat flour

1¼ cups sugar

2 sticks (8 ounces) unsalted butter, at room temperature

2 large eggs

3 teaspoons ground cinnamon

2 teaspoons cream of tartar

1 teaspoon baking soda

¼ teaspoon salt

1 Preheat the oven to 375°F. Line 2 baking sheets with parchment paper.

2 In a large bowl, mix together the flour, 1 cup of the sugar, the butter, eggs, 1 teaspoon of the cinnamon, the cream of tartar, baking soda, and salt.

3 In a small bowl, combine the remaining ¼ cup sugar and 2 teaspoons cinnamon.

4 Roll tablespoons of the dough into balls, roll in the cinnamon sugar, and place on the lined baking sheets, allowing room to spread.

5 Bake, in batches if necessary, for 10 to 12 minutes, until golden and crisp around the edges. Transfer to a wire rack to cool.

flourless peanut butter cookies

For us old timers, the Nutter Butter jingle is sure hard to get out of your head if you remember it. This cookie is the cure. And it's gluten free. (Too bad my gluten-free family members don't like peanut butter.) You can make these as plain peanut butter cookies, or fill them with frosting so they taste just like a fluffernutter sandwich.

MAKES 44 COOKIES

2 cups chunky or smooth peanut butter

2 cups packed light brown sugar

1 cup coarsely chopped salted roasted peanuts

2 large eggs

1 teaspoon baking soda

½ batch Vegan Frosting (optional; page 329)

1 Preheat the oven to 350°F. Line 2 baking sheets with parchment paper.

2 Place the peanut butter, sugar, peanuts, eggs, and baking soda in a bowl and mix to combine.

3 Roll tablespoons of the dough into balls and place on the lined baking sheet. Flatten by creating a crosshatch pattern on each cookie with a fork. Bake, in batches if necessary, for 9 to 12 minutes, until golden. Let the cookies cool on the baking sheet for a few minutes before transferring to a wire rack to cool completely.

4 If desired, sandwich the cookies with frosting.

gingerbread person cookies

This recipe comes from a former employee, Roger Amerman, who used to make the cookies for all of his coworkers at Christmas, each one custom-decorated for each person. My family and I love making them, but only learned recently that baking them on parchment paper–lined cookie sheets prevents mass decapitation! Decorate these as you see fit. **MAKES 2 DOZEN COOKIES**

2¼ cups all-purpose flour

½ cup sugar

1 stick (4 ounces) unsalted butter, at room temperature

½ cup molasses

1 large egg

1½ teaspoons ground cinnamon

1 teaspoon baking powder

1 teaspoon ground cloves

1 teaspoon ground ginger

½ teaspoon baking soda

½ teaspoon ground nutmeg

½ teaspoon salt

1 In a large bowl, mix together all the ingredients until they just come together to form a smooth dough. Cover and refrigerate for 1 hour.

2 Preheat the oven to 350°F. Line 2 baking sheets with parchment paper.

3 On a lightly floured surface, roll the dough to a ⅛ inch thickness. Using person-shaped cookie cutters, cut shapes from the dough. Re-roll the scraps and cut out more cookies.

4 Place the cookies on the lined baking sheets. Bake, in batches if necessary, for 10 minutes, or until the edges are a bit darker and slightly firm to the touch. Let cool on the baking sheet for a few minutes before transferring to a wire rack to cool completely.

sober mini fruitcakes

A really long time ago, someone I loved dearly didn't do the right thing by me. And when he came to ask for forgiveness, he brought along a fruitcake he had made himself. I had never really tried fruitcake before, and when I did, not only did I love it, but I could also taste his sorrow and regret. It was sweet and spicy and fruity and rich. So now, whenever I taste fruitcake, I taste forgiveness. This is my sober version, made without the traditional brandy, in mini muffin tins (far less intimidating than a loaf). **MAKES 36 MINI MUFFINS**

1 cup chopped candied cherries

1 cup chopped candied pineapple

1 cup chopped candied citrus peel

1 cup chopped pecans or walnuts

3 tablespoons golden raisins

1 stick (4 ounces) unsalted butter, at room temperature

½ cup sugar

2 large eggs

½ teaspoon pure lemon extract

¼ teaspoon salt

1 cup all-purpose flour

1 Preheat the oven to 350°F. Grease the cups of mini muffin pans.

2 In a large bowl, mix together the cherries, pineapple, citrus peel, nuts, and raisins. Set aside.

3 In a large bowl, using a hand mixer, beat the butter and sugar until pale and creamy.

4 Add the eggs, one at a time, beating well after each addition. Beat in the lemon extract and salt. Beat in the flour. Stir in the fruit and nut mixture and mix well to combine.

5 Divide the batter evenly among the muffin cups and bake for 20 minutes, or until a skewer inserted in the center comes out clean.

FROM THE BLOG
"I'm a fruitcake fan, too. I use combinations of just about any dried organic fruit I can find at the natural food store instead of commercial candied fruits. Dried and sweetened cranberries make good substitutes for candied cherries." —JEAN

cinnamon buns

It was a snow day when I finally had time to make my first-ever batch of cinnamon buns the way I wanted them—with some whole wheat flour. And even then they were light, fluffy, and delightful. I wouldn't call this recipe easy, but it's not hard either. A kitchen timer is useful. In the end, they're not that time-consuming—I started these after breakfast, and they were ready before lunch. **MAKES 12 BUNS**

DOUGH

1⅓ cups whole milk

⅓ cup vegetable oil

⅓ cup granulated sugar

1 envelope (¼ ounce) active dry yeast

1½ cups whole wheat flour

1⅓ cups all-purpose flour

1 teaspoon salt

½ teaspoon baking powder

½ teaspoon baking soda

1 | To make the dough: In a large heavy-bottomed pan, combine the milk, oil, and granulated sugar. Heat over medium-low heat until the mixture just comes to a boil. Remove from the heat, cover, and let stand for 45 minutes.

2 | Add the yeast, stir to combine, and set aside for 5 minutes or until bubbles have appeared on the surface and the yeast has activated.

3 | Stir in the whole wheat flour and 1 cup of the all-purpose flour. Cover with a kitchen towel and set aside until the dough has risen and doubled in size, about 1 hour.

4 | Add the remaining ⅓ cup all-purpose flour, the salt, baking powder, and baking soda and mix to combine with a spoon or your hands.

5 | Transfer the dough to a well-floured surface and, using your hands, press into an 11 × 15-inch rectangle about ½ inch thick.

RECIPE CONTINUES

CINNAMON BUTTER

4 tablespoons (½ stick) unsalted butter, melted

2 tablespoons granulated sugar

1 tablespoon ground cinnamon

GLAZE

1 cup powdered sugar, sifted

2 tablespoons whole milk or heavy cream

1½ tablespoons unsalted butter, at room temperature

Pinch of salt

TIP: If the glaze is too thick, add a little cream or milk for a runnier consistency. The heat of the buns will also melt the glaze a little before it sets.

6 To make the cinnamon butter: In a bowl, combine the melted butter, granulated sugar, and cinnamon. Brush the mixture evenly over the top of the dough.

7 Starting at one long end, gently roll the dough into a log shape. (I use a bench scraper to help me along.) Slice the log into twelve 1- to 1½-inch-thick slices and place them, cut-side down, into 2 greased pie dishes. Cover with a kitchen towel and let stand for 30 minutes as they rise some more.

8 Preheat the oven to 400°F.

9 To make the glaze: In a bowl, vigorously whisk the powdered sugar, milk or cream, butter, and salt until smooth (see Tip). Set aside.

10 Bake the buns for 15 minutes, or until golden. Let stand for 5 minutes, then drizzle the glaze over the buns and allow to set (or eat straight away!).

FROM THE BLOG

"These are top-notch. I was always a tad hesitant to work with yeast, but I decided to try this and it was so easy! These are by far the best tasting cinnamon rolls I have ever had. This recipe is a keeper and will definitely be passed down to my daughters; thanks so much for sharing!"
—TERRI

banana, coconut, and pineapple bread

This is based on my mom's banana bread recipe, which I've tweaked because I'm a little obsessed with coconut. Plus, the addition of pineapple makes it extra moist. A great way to get rid of overripe bananas, it's made with no fuss and no muss, and usually devoured minutes later. **SERVES 8**

Coconut oil, for the pan

1 cup whole wheat flour

1 cup all-purpose flour

1 tablespoon baking powder

½ teaspoon salt

1 cup mashed overripe bananas (about 3)

1 cup coarsely chopped fresh or canned pineapple

⅔ cup sugar

½ cup unsweetened shredded coconut

⅓ cup coconut oil, melted

2 large eggs

1 Preheat the oven to 350°F. Grease a 9 × 5-inch loaf pan with coconut oil and line the bottom and sides with parchment paper.

2 Sift the flours, baking powder, and salt into a medium bowl. In a separate large bowl, mix the bananas, pineapple, sugar, shredded coconut, coconut oil, and eggs until combined. Add the dry ingredients to the wet and mix until just combined.

3 Pour the batter into the prepared pan and bake for 1 hour, or until a skewer inserted in the center comes out clean. Let cool for 10 minutes in the pan, then turn out onto a wire rack to cool completely.

TIP: You can skip the pineapple or the coconut for a more classic loaf.

banana and walnut muffins

My youngest daughter calls these Happy Cakes (because they make her happy when I make them). I like to make them in mini muffin tins for ease of eating. One of my daughters doesn't like walnuts, so I spoon half the batter into the pans, mix the rest with walnuts and then spoon in the rest. I would happily eat these instead of cake on my birthday, but with frosting. **MAKES 24 MINI MUFFINS**

Butter, for the muffin tin

2 overripe bananas, mashed

2 large eggs

½ cup plain yogurt

2 cups white whole wheat flour

¾ cup granulated sugar

½ cup walnuts, coarsely chopped

1 teaspoon baking soda

1 teaspoon salt

Demerara sugar, for sprinkling (optional)

1 Preheat the oven to 350°F. Grease 24 cups of a mini muffin tin.

2 In a large bowl, mix together the bananas, eggs, and yogurt. Add the flour, granulated sugar, walnuts, baking soda, and salt and mix to combine.

3 Spoon the batter into the muffin cups. If desired, sprinkle the tops with demerara sugar. Bake for 15 minutes, or until a skewer inserted in the center comes out clean. Let cool in the pan for 5 minutes, then transfer to a wire rack to cool completely.

TIP: To make regular-size muffins, use a 12-cup muffin tin and bake for 18 minutes.

orange-cranberry muffins

I love this flavor combination, especially in fall when the cranberries are fresh. I prefer the unsweetened juicy tartness of fresh cranberries here. You can make mini muffins or even a loaf with the batter—just make sure you adjust the baking times, baking until a skewer inserted comes out clean. **MAKES 12 MUFFINS**

Butter, for the pan

1 cup all-purpose flour

1 cup whole wheat flour

½ cup granulated sugar

1 teaspoon baking soda

1 teaspoon salt

¼ teaspoon baking powder

1 tablespoon finely grated orange zest

½ cup fresh orange juice

⅓ cup unsalted butter, melted

1 large egg

2 cups fresh cranberries or 1 cup unsweetened dried cranberries

Turbinado sugar (optional), for sprinkling

1 Preheat the oven to 350°F. Grease 12 cups of a muffin tin or line with paper liners.

2 In a bowl, mix together the flours, granulated sugar, baking soda, salt, and baking powder. Add the orange zest, orange juice, melted butter, and egg and mix well to combine. Fold in the cranberries.

3 Divide the batter among the muffin cups. If desired, sprinkle the tops with turbinado sugar. Bake for 15 to 20 minutes, until a skewer inserted in the center comes out clean. Transfer to a wire rack to cool.

spiced pumpkin muffins

If I'm going to bake something, I want it fast. That's why I use my mini muffin pans for most quick breads and muffins. (Who has time to wait for a whole loaf to bake?) I like my pumpkin a little gingery and filled with spices; these little things taste like fall.

MAKES 24 MINI MUFFINS

Butter, for the pan

1 cup all-purpose flour

1 cup whole wheat flour

1 cup granulated sugar

1 teaspoon baking soda

1 teaspoon salt

¼ teaspoon baking powder

½ teaspoon ground cinnamon

¼ teaspoon ground cloves

¼ teaspoon ground ginger

¼ teaspoon ground nutmeg

1 cup Pumpkin Puree (page 325) or canned organic puree

⅓ cup unsalted butter, melted

⅓ cup maple syrup

1 large egg, lightly beaten

1 tablespoon molasses

Turbinado sugar, for sprinkling

1 Preheat the oven to 350°F. Grease 24 cups of a mini muffin tin.

2 In a large bowl, mix together the flours, granulated sugar, baking soda, salt, baking powder, and spices. Add the pumpkin puree, melted butter, maple syrup, egg, and molasses and mix well to combine.

3 Divide the batter evenly among the muffin cups. Sprinkle the tops with turbinado sugar. Bake for 15 to 18 minutes, until a skewer inserted in the center comes out clean. Transfer to a wire rack to cool.

TIP: You can make standard muffins or even a loaf with this mixture—just make sure you adjust the baking time, baking them until a skewer inserted comes out clean.

fluffy scones

There are two kinds of scones in the world, the dense kind that is more like Irish soda bread, and the fluffy kind that is served for morning or afternoon tea in Britain and other countries in the Commonwealth. In Australia, they bake scones using lemonade (or what we call lemon soda), which apparently makes the dough extra light. This is my version with whole wheat flour and without the soda, but some other sparkle instead. **MAKES ABOUT 12 SCONES**

2½ cups all-purpose flour

1 cup whole wheat flour

⅓ cup sugar

2 tablespoons baking powder

1½ teaspoons salt

⅔ cup sparkling water, at room temperature

1 cup heavy (whipping) cream

Milk, for brushing

Strawberry jam and whipped cream, for serving

TIPS: The key to a fluffy scone is to not overwork the dough—use a light touch! And press the cutter or glass down without twisting. You can add raisins or other dried fruit.

1 Preheat the oven to 425°F. Line a baking sheet with parchment paper.

2 In a large bowl, mix together the flours, sugar, baking powder, and salt. Make a well in the center, add the sparkling water and cream, and mix very gently until the mixture just starts to come together.

3 Transfer the mixture to a lightly floured surface and knead gently and quickly to form a dough. Press out the dough to 1 inch thick. Using a 2-inch round floured cookie cutter or water glass, cut rounds from the dough and place close together on the baking sheet (this will help them rise upward). Gather the scraps, gently push together, and repeat to cut out more scones.

4 Brush the tops with milk and bake for 15 minutes, or until golden and risen. Serve warm with jam and whipped cream.

basic fruit crisp

Every once in a while I find myself with too much ripe fruit—more than can be eaten before it goes bad. The solution? A fruit crisp. I've experimented a lot with toppings and found that a good topping has to be crunchy. This one is perfect. I have visions of adding nuts, seeds, ginger, or spices to the mixture, but as with a good pair of jeans or a perfect black dress, why mess with the basics? **SERVES 6 TO 8**

6 cups chopped fruit (such as peaches)

1 tablespoon fresh lemon juice

CRUNCHY TOPPING
1¼ cups all-purpose flour

¾ cup packed light or dark brown sugar

¾ cup rolled oats

1 or 2 pinches of salt

1 stick (4 ounces) unsalted butter, melted

Vanilla ice cream, for serving

1 Preheat the oven to 375°F.

2 Place the fruit in the bottom of a 13 × 9-inch baking dish (or smaller individual dishes if you want to impress dinner party guests), sprinkle with the lemon juice, and toss to combine.

3 To make the topping: In a bowl, mix together the flour, brown sugar, oats, and salt. Stir in the melted butter until well combined.

4 Sprinkle the topping evenly over the fruit mixture and bake for 35 minutes, or until golden and bubbling. Serve with vanilla ice cream.

chocolate brownies
with salted caramel frosting

Personally, I prefer a cakey brownie to a fudgy one, but this errs on the fudgy side. It is inspired by the Fat Witch Brownies *cookbook, by Patricia Helding, but with half the sugar, because you are going to want to frost them with my salted caramel frosting.* **MAKES 16 BROWNIES**

Butter and flour, for the pan

9 tablespoons unsalted butter, chopped

6 ounces unsweetened chocolate, chopped

¾ cup sugar

¾ cup whole milk or buttermilk

3 large eggs

2 teaspoons pure vanilla extract

1½ cups all-purpose flour

¾ teaspoon baking powder

¼ teaspoon salt

Salted Caramel Frosting (page 326)

1 Preheat the oven to 350°F. Grease and flour an 8 × 8-inch baking pan.

2 In a heatproof bowl, combine the butter and chocolate and set over a small saucepan of gently simmering water. Stir until melted and smooth. Set aside to cool to room temperature.

3 In a large bowl, beat together the sugar, milk, eggs, and vanilla. Stir in the melted chocolate mixture. Add the flour, baking powder, and salt and mix just until combined.

4 Pour the batter into the prepared pan and smooth the top. Bake for 15 minutes, or until crisp around the edges but still soft in the middle.

5 Let cool completely in the pan before frosting. Cut into 16 squares to serve.

betty's pumpkin roll

Betty is a wonderful Pennsylvania Dutch woman who did my laundry for over 20 years (she retired at age 87). Every Christmas she would bring me a pumpkin roll. This is her recipe. **SERVES 10 TO 16**

Butter and flour, for the pan

1 cup granulated sugar, plus extra for sprinkling

¾ cup all-purpose flour

⅔ cup Pumpkin Puree (opposite) or canned organic canned puree

3 large eggs

2 teaspoons ground cinnamon

1 teaspoon baking soda

CREAM CHEESE FILLING
8 ounces cream cheese, at room temperature

4 tablespoons (½ stick) unsalted butter, at room temperature

½ teaspoon pure vanilla extract

1 cup powdered sugar, sifted

1 Preheat the oven to 350°F. Grease and flour a jelly roll pan.

2 In a large bowl, using a hand mixer or whisk, whisk together the granulated sugar, flour, pumpkin puree, eggs, cinnamon, and baking soda until well combined.

3 Pour the batter into the prepared pan and spread to the edges. Bake for 15 minutes, or until the cake feels springy to the touch.

4 Let the cake cool for 5 minutes in the pan. Meanwhile, sprinkle a clean kitchen towel with granulated sugar. Run a butter knife around the edges of the cake to help it release. Carefully flip the cake onto the towel. Using the towel to help, gently roll the cake from a long side of the cake to form a tube. Allow to cool completely on a rack, about 1 hour.

5 To make the filling: In a bowl, using a hand mixer, beat the cream cheese, butter, vanilla, and sugar on medium speed until smooth, about 1 minute.

6 Gently unroll the cake, spread with the filling, and re-roll. Wrap in foil and refrigerate for 2 to 3 hours. Slice the roll to serve.

pumpkin puree

For all recipes that call for pumpkin, this is the quick and easy way to cook it up so you can really say it's from scratch. **MAKES ABOUT 2 CUPS**

1 medium sugar pumpkin (about 2 pounds), halved and seeded

1 Preheat the oven to 350°F.

2 Place the pumpkin, cut-side down, on a baking sheet and roast for 1 hour, or until softened.

3 Let cool slightly and scoop out the seeds. Spoon the pumpkin flesh into a food processor or blender (discard the skin) and process until smooth.

whipped cream frosting

This frosting is super light and fresh tasting and is great on a fluffy cake. **MAKES ENOUGH FOR A 9-INCH LAYER CAKE**

3 cups heavy (whipping) cream

½ cup powdered sugar, sifted

¼ cup unsweetened cocoa powder (optional)

1 teaspoon pure vanilla extract

1 In a bowl, stir together the cream, sugar, cocoa (if using), and vanilla. Chill in the refrigerator for 2 hours.

2 When you are ready to frost a cake, remove from the fridge and whisk for 1 to 2 minutes with a hand mixer until stiff peaks form. Make sure the cake is well cooled before frosting.

salted caramel frosting

Great for brownies, cupcakes, or cakes. It's super quick, easy, and delicious. **MAKES ENOUGH FOR A 9-INCH CAKE**

2 tablespoons unsalted butter

¼ cup packed dark brown sugar

3 tablespoons whole milk or heavy cream

2 teaspoons pure vanilla extract

¼ teaspoon sea salt

2 cups powdered sugar, sifted

1 In a small saucepan, melt the butter over medium-low heat. Add the brown sugar and milk and cook for 1 minute, or until the sugar melts. Remove from the heat and set aside to cool a little.

2 Transfer the butter mixture to a bowl. Using a hand mixer on high speed, beat in the vanilla and salt. Reduce the speed to low, gradually add the powdered sugar, and beat until light and fluffy, about 5 minutes. For a creamier frosting, add a little more milk or cream.

buttercream frosting

This is the traditional quick and easy buttercream. It can be a bit heavy and buttery. If you need to make it softer to spread, use a little more milk. **Makes enough for a 9-inch cake**

4 cups powdered sugar, sifted

2 sticks (8 ounces) unsalted butter, at room temperature

2 tablespoons whole milk

1 teaspoon pure vanilla extract

Using a whisk or hand mixer (or in stand mixer with the paddle attachment) on medium speed, beat together the sugar, butter, milk, and vanilla until light and fluffy, about 3 minutes, stopping once to scrape down the sides and along the bottom of the bowl.

banana buttercream frosting

If you like bananas, you will like this recipe. The banana really adds a punchy flavor. **Makes enough for a 9-inch cake**

2 cups powdered sugar, sifted

1 stick (4 ounces) unsalted butter, at room temperature

½ small very ripe banana

1 tablespoon whole milk

½ teaspoon pure vanilla extract

Using a whisk or hand mixer (or in stand mixer with the paddle attachment) on medium speed, beat together the sugar, butter, banana, milk, and vanilla until light and fluffy, about 3 minutes, stopping once to scrape down the sides and along the bottom of the bowl.

creamy vanilla frosting

This frosting was developed by Pennsylvania-based professional baker Haika, and I adapted it because I have an aversion to frostings that are too buttery. **MAKES ENOUGH FOR A 9-INCH CAKE**

1¼ cups powdered sugar, sifted

1 stick (4 ounces) unsalted butter, at room temperature

¾ cup chilled heavy (whipping) cream

¼ teaspoon pure vanilla extract

¼ teaspoon salt

1 Using a whisk or hand mixer (or a stand mixer with the paddle attachment), beat the sugar and butter on medium speed until pale and fluffy, about 2 minutes.

2 Gradually add the cream and increase the speed to high. Beat until smooth, 3 to 5 minutes.

3 Beat in the vanilla and salt.

TIP: The addition of cream means there is less butter in this version, for a lighter touch. This frosting is softer and best for cakes and cupcakes.

lemon glaze

Use to glaze Bundt cakes, pound cakes, muffins, or cupcakes. The addition of cream means it won't harden; it stays soft and creamy.
MAKES ENOUGH FOR A 9-INCH CAKE OR BUNDT CAKE

1 cup powdered sugar, sifted

1½ tablespoons fresh lemon juice

1½ tablespoons heavy cream

1 tablespoon finely grated lemon zest

In a bowl, whisk together all the ingredients until smooth.

vegan frosting

If you are vegan or dairy-free, this is the right frosting for you.

MAKES ENOUGH FOR A 9-INCH CAKE

½ cup vegan shortening, at room temperature

½ cup butter-flavored vegan shortening

3½ cups powdered sugar, sifted

¼ cup soy, almond, or coconut milk

2 teaspoons pure vanilla extract

Pinch of salt

1 Using a whisk or hand mixer, beat the shortenings on medium speed to combine, about 2 minutes.

2 Add the sugar and beat until creamy, about 3 minutes.

3 Scrape down the sides of the bowl and add the milk, vanilla, and salt. Beat on high speed to incorporate and until the frosting is fluffy, about 6 minutes longer.

vegan coconut frosting

I love coconut, so this is a twist on the vegan frosting.

MAKES ENOUGH FOR A 9-INCH CAKE

½ cup vegan shortening, at room temperature

¼ cup butter-flavored vegan shortening

¼ cup coconut cream*

3½ cups powdered sugar, sifted

¼ cup soy, almond, or coconut milk

2 teaspoons pure vanilla extract

Pinch of salt

1 Using a whisk or hand mixer, beat the shortenings and coconut cream on medium speed to combine, about 2 minutes.

2 Add the sugar and beat until creamy, about 3 minutes.

3 Scrape down the sides of the bowl and add the milk, vanilla, and salt. Beat on high speed to incorporate and until the frosting is fluffy, about 6 minutes longer.

* This is the hardened layer of cream from the top of a refrigerated can of coconut milk.

almost-vegan frosting

For this frosting, I turned to food personality David Joachim, who posts pictures of incredible cakes on Facebook (in between his cycling injuries and escapades). Of all the frostings I've made and tried, I like this one the best. **MAKES ENOUGH FOR A 9-INCH CAKE**

½ cup vegan shortening, at room temperature

4 tablespoons (½ stick) unsalted butter

¼ cup coconut cream*

3½ cups powdered sugar, sifted

¼ cup whole milk

2 teaspoons pure vanilla extract

Pinch of salt

1 Using a whisk or hand mixer (or in a stand mixer with the paddle attachment), beat the shortening, butter, and coconut cream on medium speed to combine, about 2 minutes.

2 Add the sugar and beat until creamy, about 3 minutes.

3 Scrape down the sides of the bowl and add the milk, vanilla, and salt. Beat on high speed to incorporate and until the frosting is fluffy, about 6 minutes longer.

* This is the hardened layer of cream from the top of a refrigerated can of coconut milk.

the last word

Don't worry about being a member of the "clean plate club." Many of us grew up hearing the message that we should eat everything on our plate because of all the starving children in the world. A lot of us also grew up with struggles around weight, not learning to recognize when we are full and feeling guilty about food. So here are some final thoughts to leave you with:

- According to the Nobel Prize–winning economist, Amartya Sen, most famines have absolutely nothing to do with food production and everything to do with political instability and persecution. If you want to end hunger, you have to end war.

- Don't believe it when people say we need to increase production and need to farm more land or we will never "feed the world." According to all the best science and research, the only way to feed the world for a long, long, long time is through organic farming and a diverse and local food system. That's true for America and it's true for Africa, too.

- Listen to your body. Listen to your heart. Use food to nourish, not to anesthetize. And as Michael Pollan says, "Eat food. Mostly plants. Not too much."

- And I'll add: Eat organic. It will make you happier.

appendix

Here's a roundup of handy tools, cooking terms, and techniques explained, which relate to some of the recipes in this book. They helped me become a better cook and hopefully will help you, too!

Essential Tools

FOR SOUP: Soup pot + spoon + a good chef's knife + blender + cutting board + sieve + colander

FOR BAKING: Parchment paper + cake pans and baking sheets + mixing bowls + whisk + measuring cups + measuring spoons + rubber spatula + timer + stand or hand mixer

FOR PASTA: Large pot + colander + manual pasta maker + wooden spoon + cheese grater

FOR SALAD: Salad spinner + cutting board + mandoline + chef's knife + vegetable peeler + serving utensils + serving bowl + box grater

FOR MAINS: Large cast-iron skillet + large cutting board + large mixing bowl + grill pan + deep roasting pan + baking dish + heavy-bottomed saucepan with lid

FOR SIDES AND SNACKS: Mortar and pestle + rimmed baking sheets + masher + large box grater + small serving bowls

POTS AND PANS: The materials I have found are the safest to cook with are cast iron skillets, enamel-coated pots, glass and ceramic casserole dishes, and stainless steel. I avoid using non-stick cookware and aluminum, as they have been associated with health concerns.

FOOD STORAGE: For both environmental and health reasons, I always try to use glass, stainless steel or paper for all food storage. Plastic should never be put in the microwave (or metal, for that matter). Glass jars make excellent storage vessels.

What Does Organic Really Mean?

There can be a lot of confusion or debate about what organic really means and what the true definition or the spirit of the definition is. Fortunately, after decades of debate and even more decades of negotiation, the USDA has created a living, breathing definition that people can trust because in order to qualify to use the USDA Organic seal, a farmer or food processor must pass a yearly inspection and document compliance. The essence of the meaning of organic, as defined by the USDA is this:

✓ No synthetic fertilizers, pesticides, fungicides, and herbicides

✓ No sewage sludge

✓ No irradiation

✓ No genetic engineering (GMOs)

✓ Organic livestock must have access to the outdoors and grass in humane conditions and must be fed certified organic feed

✓ No antibiotic or growth hormones used on animals

My grandfather, JI Rodale, was the founder of the organic movement in America, and his philosophy was that **HEALTHY SOIL EQUALS HEALTHY FOOD EQUALS HEALTHY PEOPLE.** And today, that is still the philosophy behind the research we do at the Rodale Institute in Maxatawny, Pennsylvania, which is home to the longest running study comparing organic farming to conventional farming. Not only have we proven that organic farming is more productive (especially in droughts and floods), more profitable, and more efficient than conventional farming, but in fact if we want to feed the world, organic farming is the only way to do it for the long term. All of our research has been replicated and validated around the world, including by the USDA.

So . . . play this game with your kids in the store: Look for the little green label! When Lucia was little and she would ask me for every sugary chemical thing in the store, I told her that if she found the USDA organic label on it, I would buy it for her. Not only did she find the game super fun, but she stopped bugging me for the other stuff. And know she can taste the difference (organic tastes better!).

Beets are beautiful,
healthy, and delicious.
And you can eat the
root, the stems, and
the leaves.

Some Terms Explained

BARLEY: Barley is a grain that comes in two types: hulled barley and pearl barley. The former has had the hull removed, but is still wrapped in its bran layer, which makes it dark, chewy, and nutty. It's technically a whole grain. Pearl barley on the other hand has been polished to remove the bran, making it softer and more subtly flavored. You can use in grain salads, stews, and soups (such as my Lamb and Barley Soup, page 133). Just be aware that pearl barley cooks faster.

BEATING EGG WHITES: If you're a novice baker and ever wondered what a recipe means when it calls for beating egg whites to stiff peaks, here's an easy guide. Egg whites are whipped to trap air and are then incorporated into a recipe to yield a light and fluffy result. You need air for meringues, mousses, soufflés, and some cakes. Start with eggs at room temperature (take them out of the fridge 30 minutes before you need them) and make sure your metal or ceramic bowl and whisk or beaters are completely clean and dry. Any oily residue can affect the result, which is why you shouldn't use a plastic bowl. Start beating on low to medium speed. At first the egg whites will get foamy, and then as you continue to beat, peaks will begin to form. At this stage, when you pull the whisk or beaters out, the peaks will collapse. These are "soft peaks." Usually at this stage of the recipe you would add sugar and keep beating until the mixture is thick, white, and glossy and the peaks stay upright when you remove the beaters. These are "stiff peaks." A good test to see if the mixture is stiff enough is to tip the bowl upside down—the mixture should stay in the bowl!

BLANCHING VEGETABLES: Blanching veggies is common practice if you're planning to freeze some yourself, but I mainly use this technique to partially cook or soften vegetables I'm going to use in salads or as a side dish where I still want a little crunch. Blanching involves plunging vegetables quickly in boiling water for a minute or two and then refreshing them in a bowl of iced water to stop the cooking process. This is great for green beans and asparagus, and not only makes them more vibrant but also helps lock in all the nutrients.

DRIED BEANS AND CHICKPEAS: While I tend to use organic canned beans and chickpeas in my recipes because they're convenient, it's actually pretty easy and economical to cook with dried beans. You just need to factor in the time the beans need to soak—usually 8 hours or overnight. Why do you soak beans? So they cook more quickly and so some of the, er, gas-inducing compounds are reduced! Cover your beans with plenty of water—by at least 2 inches—and soak overnight. Rinse, transfer to a large pot, and cover with 2 inches water. Simmer for 30 minutes to 2 hours depending on the bean, until tender. Drain the beans and proceed with your recipe.

HARD-BOILED EGGS: Anyone who has ever tried to make hard-boiled eggs from fresh organic eggs knows they're almost impossible to peel without significantly damaging the shape. After decades of struggling, seeking advice of all sorts, and testing, I think someone finally figured it out! Local Pennsylvania chef Allan Schanbacher suggested I try steaming them and it works! Place the eggs in a steaming basket set over boiling water in a pot, cover, and steam for 12 minutes for hard-boiled eggs. If not serving right away, put them in the fridge to store until ready to use and peel. They will keep fresh in the fridge for a few days. See page 175 for my deviled egg recipe, and page 177 for my pickled red beet eggs.

HOMEMADE DRIED BREADCRUMBS: It's so easy to make dried breadcrumbs from old bread that there's really no need to buy the store-bought ones. I prefer to use leftover bread that isn't too dense (a light farmhouse wheat bread). Cut the bread into cubes and bake in a 200°F oven for 1 to 2 hours, until completely dried out. For chunky crumbs ideal for stuffing, leave them as is. For finer crumbs, simply crush them to the desired consistency. They will keep in an airtight container or jar for up to 2 weeks.

MELTING CHOCOLATE: Here's a thing I learned about melting chocolate—it's temperamental and you need to do it slowly because it can actually burn! The easiest way to melt chocolate is on the stove in a glass or metal bowl set snugly over a small saucepan of simmering water. Fill a small saucepan about one-third full with water and bring to a boil. Reduce to a simmer and fit the bowl over the top (so the bowl is not touching the water). Chop the chocolate, place it in the bowl, and stir occasionally until it's melted and smooth. Remove from the heat and proceed with your recipe.

SCALDING MILK: Sometimes baking recipes call for scalded milk (as in the Moravian Sugar Cake on page 294). Scalding the milk improves the cake's rise. The whey protein in milk can prevent the dough from rising properly; scalding the milk denatures the protein, making the milk a better food for yeast and resulting in a fluffier product.

TOASTING NUTS: Heat a skillet over medium heat. Add the nuts and toast, stirring or shaking the skillet often to avoid burning, for about 6 minutes, or until fragrant and browned in spots. Alternatively, preheat the oven to 350°F. Spread the nuts on a rimmed baking sheet and toast for 10 minutes, or until fragrant and browned.

TORTILLAS: You only need two ingredients to make your own corn tortillas from scratch: masa harina (a type of corn flour) and water. How easy is that? You can find masa harina in the baking aisle of some large grocery stores or at Latin American stores or online. Simply combine 2 cups masa harina, 1½ cups hot water, and ½ teaspoon salt in a bowl and mix to combine. Knead it for 1 to 2 minutes to form a springy dough. Pinch off a few tablespoons of dough and roll it into a ball. Using a rolling pin, roll it into a 6-inch-wide and ⅛-inch-thick round. Cook in batches in a cast-iron skillet over medium-high heat for 1 to 2 minutes each side, until golden. Wrap in a clean kitchen towel to keep warm.

acknowledgments

There are many people to thank for this book, starting with everyone at Rodale, past, present, and future, who contributes to what we do and enables me to do what I do. We are an awesome team that is devoted to accomplishing our mission of inspiring health, healing, happiness, and love in the world. Starting with you.

I'm especially grateful to my blog coordinators who have helped me post and manage these recipes over the years: Maria Luci, Dana Burland, and Heather Hurlock. Plus, Katie Hunsburger who reads all my blog posts and is always relieved when a recipe comes through rather than some of my other more challenging topics. And Kathleen Oswalt, my assistant, who guards my writing time and schedule with a flaming sword.

I'd like to thank my co-conspirator and editor of this book, Melanie Hansche, for answering my prayer to the universe for a "minister of food" and moving all the way from Australia and leaving the employ of food celebrity Donna Hay to join Rodale. I'm also grateful she assembled a crack Aussie team to photograph and style my recipes (here's looking at you, Con Poulos and Simon Andrews). I tell you, these recipes photograph a lot better than when I make them, but they *are* my recipes!

I'd like to thank the book team at Rodale: Gail Gonzales, Jennifer Levesque, Jeff Batzli, Dervla Kelly, and Rae Ann Spitzenberger who helped guide, advise, design, refine, and shepherd this project over many months. Nancy Bailey deserves a special shout-out since she has copyedited almost all of my books and blogs and is retiring after this one.

Deep gratitude to all my blog readers and commenters, especially Donna in Delaware and Alice Green. If it weren't for you, I would have stopped, because the only compensation I receive for doing this is feeling *heard*.

Thanks to the bakers who taught me the secrets of baking: Haika Powell, Allan Schanbacher, David Joachim, and especially Renae Rzonca,

for letting me into the back baking room at the Emmaus Bakery—a dream come true!

A loving thank you to all the Cinquinos—especially Mike and Michelle, Anthony and Susan, Nicholas and Rebecca, and Liz, and including the extended Cinquino and Argana clan, who have inspired me with their love of food and passion for growing and eating and coming together with food. And of course, to Lou Cinquino, for introducing me to all of them and putting up with my experimenting, critiquing, and crabbiness in the kitchen for so many years.

Special thanks to my daughters, who have watched me progress from an inexperienced cook who often started fires and burned a lot of things, to a mom who is now actually cheerful and happy in the kitchen (although I still burn things). And I'd especially like to thank them for putting up with my crazy schedule and complicated life and being patient while I'm writing at the computer at home and on weekends, which is more often than not. And to Tony Haile, my hungry son-in-law who loves my stuffing and fries. And to Alex Maloney, who feels like family. Thanks for loving my cooking.

To my sisters, Heather and Heidi, who have shared the weight, the joy, and the responsibility of cooking over the years. What I find fascinating is that each of us makes Nana's Kugel (see recipe, page 236) in a completely different way, and yet it always tastes like kugel. And thanks to my brother Anthony and his wife, Florence (and Florence's family), who have brought a love for French cooking to our lives.

And while there are many famous chefs and writers who have inspired me over the years, I find myself thinking more of friends who have inspired me. Friends like Ian Jackson, who has shared his love for Australia with me and made me want to learn to make Aussie meat pies and Anzac "bikkies." Friends like Holly Walck Kostura, my amazing yoga teacher, who sometimes comes to my house and makes things to eat that become our favorites. (Two of her soups are in this book.) And friends like Kimbal Musk, whom I've bonded with over how to roast a chicken, but we'll never agree on how to make gravy. Despite our differences on the topic of gravy, we share an intense passion for changing the world through #realfood. (And having fun while doing it.) And David Totah, who once climbed over a table set for 202 people in order to sit next to me. Thanks for sharing my belief that art, spirit, and love are as important as food. I love you all dearly!

And then there is Gigi. Gigi is my Miss Jeannie, always cleaning up after me and making sure I come home to a clean kitchen. We've been a team for more than 34 years. First as a babysitter and then in my home for 18 years as so much more than that. THAT's how I do what I do. And with gratitude to Elvin Laracuente and Patti Rutman, as well.

Thanks to everyone at the Rodale Institute who has worked hard over the years to show that organic is the only way to feed the world. You have all made the world a much better place!

To every person, chef, restaurant and market that made me taste something for the first time that would wake me up and make me NEED to make it for myself, I thank you. To all the food magazines I've ripped pages out of and saved for decades. To all the food leaders who have inspired me: Alice Waters, Michel Nischan, Michael Pollan, as well as John Seymour and Angela who were with me at that amazing meal in a German farmhouse where a woman with pink cheeks served a full head of cauliflower cooked and covered with a cheese and ham sauce. I still haven't gotten that recipe right, but one day I will!

To all the companies that have grown the organic industry and made organic food so much more accessible for everyone—but especially for me in Pennsylvania. You've made my life so much easier and delicious.

And this may seem weird, but thanks also to all the people who have made my life really difficult. What you have succeeded in doing is actually making me stronger and certainly making the sanctuary of my loving home, family, and kitchen even more sacred.

And lastly, to all the people who grow our food, and especially to the farmers who grow it organically.

index

Underscored page references indicate sidebars. **Boldface** references indicate photographs and illustrations.